OLVES

SHE WOLVES

THE *NOTORIOUS* *QUEENS* OF ENGLAND

ELIZABETH NORTON

Cover illustration: Queen Matilda, courtesy of the British Museum

First published 2008
This edition published 2009

The History Press
The Mill, Brimscombe Port,
Stroud, Gloucestershire, GL5 2QG
www.thehistorypress.co.uk

British Library Cataloguing in Publication Data.
A catalogue record for this book is available from the British Library.

ISBN 978 0 7509 4736 7

Typesetting and origination by The History Press
Printed in Great Britain

Contents

Accused Queens – Innocent Women?

Medieval England saw many queens. Some are remembered as saintly, or at least very nearly saintly, some are barely remembered at all and others are remembered as being truly notorious. Every century from the eighth to the sixteenth boasted at least one notorious queen who would provide scandal for chroniclers' works for centuries to come. Their reputation and the salacious details of their lives that survive make these women some of the most vivid and interesting personalities of the medieval period. However, their lives were not always recorded truthfully. Chroniclers and other writers had their own motivations for writing about the women which were distinct from simply recording events as they happened. Some accused queens were guilty of their crimes, others were innocent – such matters were not important to those writing, who were more interested in the subject of female power than making a detailed analysis of the facts. Medieval women did not conventionally wield power and the very existence of queens was something of a contradiction when women sought to redefine the queenly role as more than just the traditional king's wife.

The question, therefore, is: were these queens really as bad as their reputations suggest? Undoubtedly, some queens, such as the unfaithful Catherine Howard, were entirely unsuitable for the role in which they found themselves and can clearly be shown to be bad queens. But can they also be said to be bad women? Isabella, the She-Wolf of France, for example, is probably one of the most notorious of all the women discussed in this book, but was she truly wicked? Isabella invaded England and was a leader in the coup which led to her husband's deposition and murder, allowing her to rule England with her lover. This was clearly a scandalous course of action to take. However, Isabella, as a woman, had been sorely tried. She was married as a child to the homosexual Edward II and endured humiliation throughout her early marriage. Later she suffered undisguised hostility from her husband and his favourites. For Isabella, this was too much to bear, directly impacting on her later behaviour. Certainly to her contemporaries she was notorious but to modern observers and to Isabella herself, her actions were understandable.

Isabella of France's actions can be understood in a study of her as a woman and who can say that the saintly Matilda of Scotland, queen to Henry I, for example, would not have acted similarly if she had been married to Edward II? As a woman, Isabella of France's actions can be understood, but as a queen she is remembered as notorious and has been systematically vilified for centuries.

Why then, are some queens classed as notorious and others not? By the late eighth century, queenship had been developing in England for centuries and people already had a strong idea of just what a good queen should be. The Anglo-Saxons believed that a good queen was a passive one, fertile and religious but of no political consequence during her husband's reign, with only the potentially powerful role of queen mother to look forward to. First and foremost, Anglo-Saxon queens were not expected to take action for their own benefit, instead acting through the medium of their male kinsmen. This was the model that the Anglo-Saxons queens Eadburh, Judith of France, Aelfgifu of the House of Wessex, Aelfthryth, Emma of Normandy, Aelfgifu of Northampton and Edith Godwine were expected to fulfil and each of them, in their own ways, failed in the eyes of their contemporaries and later observers. Some of this failure can be attributed to their characters and some to their circumstances, nonetheless they all failed to live up to the model of the good queen.

In 1066, William the Conqueror portrayed himself as heir to Edward the Confessor and an Anglo-Saxon king. His wife, Matilda of Flanders, consequently also portrayed herself as an Anglo-Saxon queen, consciously emulating her predecessors in the role. By using ideas of Anglo-Saxon queenship, Matilda and her immediate successors took Anglo-Saxon ideas of what a good queen should be into the post-conquest period. This role was enthusiastically taken up by the early Norman queens: Matilda of Flanders, Matilda of Scotland, Adeliza of Louvain and Matilda of Boulogne, and they were each, in their own ways, remembered as good queens.

In this period, however, the queens did not just slavishly follow the model of their predecessors and the Norman and Angevin queens also added to the model of what makes a good queen. The Norman conquest meant that, for the first time in English history, England was not the centre of the king's domains. For several centuries, the English kings ruled much of France and clearly these extensive lands meant that they could not be everywhere at once. The existence of continental lands meant that queens were quickly expected to play their part in ruling the empire. In the post-conquest period, queens were regularly expected to rule as regents for their husbands and sons whilst the king was absent, carrying out a wide range of political and administrative tasks. This naturally increased the political power that queens could wield although, again, they were expected to rule in the name, and in the interests of, their male kinsmen. The policy did however serve to increase the profile of the queen and it witnessed a number of very political queens. Empress Matilda, Eleanor of Aquitaine, Isabella of Angouleme, Eleanor of Provence, Eleanor of Castile and Isabella of France, for example, were all important European-wide political figures but, in appearing to be acting for their own good on a number of occasions, they are also remembered as notorious. Women were simply not expected to have political ambitions of their own. Furthermore it seems that to their male contemporaries, political women appeared almost threatening and unnatural, which made them easy targets for censure.

In the fifteenth and sixteenth centuries, queenship remained similar to what it had been in earlier periods and the definition of a good queen remained remarkably stable. However, with the loss of the empire, the scope for political action also waned and the queens once again found themselves in a more Anglo-Saxon constricted role than they had previously enjoyed. With only limited lands, the fifteenth- and sixteenth-century kings spent most of their time in England, supervising their own affairs.

They therefore had little need of a regent and so had no need to promote their wives and mothers as their predecessors had done. Fifteenth- and sixteenth-century queens were expected to revert to a more passive role than they had done earlier. This does not seem to have been a problem for many of the mild queens of the period, such as Catherine of Valois and Elizabeth of York. However, Joan of Navarre, Margaret of Anjou, Elizabeth Woodville, Anne Boleyn, Catherine Howard, Lady Jane Grey and Mary I all looked for, or had forced upon them, something more in their queen-ship and all, ultimately, failed to be remembered as good queens due to the outrage of their contemporaries.

The idea of what a good queen should be therefore remained remark-ably stable during the medieval period and it was a concept that was understood throughout society. The queens themselves also certainly understood it and some, like Isabella of France, tried to be good queens for much of their lives, as their stories show. The women studied here all, for one reason or another, failed to live up to the model of a good queen and often went so far beyond what was expected of them that they were quickly considered notorious. The boundaries defined by the model were restrictive and if a royal woman failed to act in this way, regardless of the reason, she left herself open to attack.

The lives of these women make for interesting reading and today they appear fascinating compared to the colourless good queens. However, even today they are still viewed as somewhat unsavoury and have been labelled by their contemporaries and afterwards as 'She-Wolves'.

PART I

PRE-CONQUEST QUEENS:

MURDER, ADULTERY & INCEST

Pre-Conquest Queens

It is sometimes claimed that the Anglo-Saxons did not have queens and most studies of English queenship begin in 1067, with the arrival in England of Matilda of Flanders, the wife of William the Conqueror. This is a great over-simplification, however, and it was during the Anglo-Saxon period that the office of queen was actively developing. The pre-conquest period also saw some of medieval England's most colourful and notorious queens and, as the kings' wives sought to extend their political status and create their own role as queen, they met with active opposition from their male-dominated society. This also brought them to the detailed interest of the chroniclers for the first time. During the medieval period the vast majority of chroniclers were male churchmen, cut off from women in general and conditioned to be suspicious of their motives. The interest of the chroniclers serves to highlight in detail the lives of women for the first time but these men were also writing for a reason – usually to hold their female subjects up as a notorious example of how a woman should not behave.

The claim that the pre-conquest period was without queens can be explained by the fact that many of the early kings' wives were deliberately not accorded the title of queen. This is attributed to the actions of Eadburh, a particularly notorious queen, who allegedly murdered her husband before disgracing herself on the continent. The truth of this claim is now impossible to verify but she is certainly not the most plausible candidate for her husband's murderer, if indeed he was murdered at all. It is certain, however, that there was a deliberate policy during and after the ninth century of de-emphasising the role of queen, a role that could lead to such great female power. [1] By vilifying Eadburh, the chroniclers and the male elite were able to argue that it was the women themselves who had forfeited their right to a political role and that women were fundamentally unfit to be public figures. Throughout the Anglo-Saxon period queens tended to only attract the attention of chroniclers and other contemporaries when they were alleged to have acted notoriously. Although many were denied the actual title of queen, kings' wives can still be identified as queens and the title 'lady', which was commonly used to describe a king's wife, became an important status term in its own right. [2] The popular wife of Alfred the Great is the first queen to be certainly associated with the title 'lady' and it was to be an acceptable title even to powerful queens like Emma of Normandy. Clearly, therefore, the Anglo-Saxons had queens, even if some went by another, less controversial title.

Although Anglo-Saxon queens existed, they are often shadowy figures in contemporary or later sources and many exist only as a name on a page or as the mother of a particular son. The identity of the first wife of Aethelred II the Unready, for example, is an enigma and, although she was apparently called Aelfgifu, whether she was the daughter of Ealdorman Ordmaer or Ealdorman Thored of York is a mystery. [3] It is even possible that this confusion hides the fact that this king was married twice before he took his more famous last wife and, in any event, this early wife (or wives) appears to have done little to merit any remark by contemporaries. Other early queens also survive only as a name. The wife of Aethelred I, for example, was probably the '*Wulfthryth Regina*' who witnessed a charter of this king during his reign. [4] Nothing else is known of this woman, however, bar the fact that she apparently bore her husband two sons. The simple fact behind this obscurity was that most women did conform to recognised female spheres of influence and so escaped the attention of the male writers who were uninterested in such feminine pursuits.

Anglo-Saxon queens therefore have been frequently forgotten and, where stories of their lives survive at all, they generally highlight some conspicuous act of goodness or wickedness. The first wife of King Aethelwulf, Osburh, for example, is remembered for her piety and goodness.[5] She was, apparently, a major influence on the education of her son, Alfred the Great, offering him a fine book of English poetry if he could learn to read it for himself.[6] This was an acceptable face of queenship and one that was promoted by medieval chroniclers. In reality, however, it is Alfred who is the centre of this story and his mother's behaviour merely helps to highlight his brilliance. Asser, the chronicler who first recorded this story and later writers were not interested in promoting the queen. She was merely present in the story to act as a vehicle for her son's cleverness and ingenuity.

This is a similar position to the stories surrounding the Anglo-Saxon period's two saintly queens. Edmund I's first wife, St Aelfgifu was, according to William of Malmesbury 'a woman always intent on good works. She was so pious and loving that she would even secretly release criminals who had been openly condemned by the gloomy verdict of a jury'.[7] St Aelfgifu would apparently give her fine clothes away to poor women and, following her death, her grave was the scene of a number of miracles, testifying to her sanctity.[8] The second wife of St Aelfgifu's son, Edgar, was also venerated as a saint and according to William of Malmesbury, this Wulfthryth 'did not develop a taste for repetitions of sexual pleasure, but rather shunned them in disgust, so truly is she named and celebrated as a saint'.[9] These two women survive as examples of what a male-dominated society and male chroniclers thought an Anglo-Saxon queen should be: saintly, passive and essentially an extension of her male kinsmen, her goodness reflecting favourably upon them. This was the ideal in both the Anglo-Saxon and later medieval period and, even by the ninth century, society had very clear ideas of how a queen should behave if she was to be judged a good queen by the Church and her peers.

The examples of Osburh, St Aelfgifu and St Wulfthryth show that Anglo-Saxon queens were expected to be pious to the point of saintliness. However, there were also other qualities expected of queens and all of the pre-conquest queens would have been aware of this. Queens were expected to be of noble birth and the importance of their birth family could have important consequences for their sons. Osburh, for example, is described in a contemporary source as 'noble in character and noble by birth' and it was clearly important for her son's biographer to stress this fact.[10] Alfred the Great's wife, Eahlswith was also described by Florence of

Worcester as being of noble descent, as was her daughter-in-law, Ecwyna, the first wife of Edward the Elder.[11] Clearly, therefore, queens were expected to be of a good family and provide a good lineage for their sons. This also featured highly in a description of an ideal pre-conquest queen, provided by Emma of Normandy of the eleventh century. According to Emma, an ideal queen could be described as 'a lady of the greatest nobility and wealth, but yet the most distinguished of the women of her time for delightful beauty and wisdom, inasmuch as she was a famous queen'.[12] Clearly, therefore, Anglo-Saxon queens had a lot to live up to.

Queens were not just supposed to be of noble birth, however. They were also expected to fulfil a defined role at court. Their first duty was, of course, to bear sons. However, they were also expected to actively protect the Church. For example, the tenth-century queen, Aelfthryth, was appointed to be the head of the nunneries in England by her husband.[13] Her husband's grandmother, Eadgifu, also played a major role in the Church and was instrumental in persuading her son, King Eadred, to retain the services of the important churchman, St Aethelwold, in England.[14] As well as religion, queens also played an important role in the way in which the king was presented to the world. Edith Godwine, for example, apparently personally selected the clothes that her husband, Edward the Confessor wore.[15] According to an account commissioned by her, Edward 'would not have cared at all if it had been provided at far less cost. He was, however, grateful of the queen's solicitude in these matters, and with a certain kindness of feeling used to remark on her zeal most appreciatively to his intimates'.[16] This account makes it clear that, without the queen, the king would not have been displayed at his best and his majesty would, therefore, have been diminished.

Anglo-Saxon queens needed to ensure that they filled the role of queen successfully as these women were in a uniquely vulnerable position. Divorces were easy to obtain in pre-conquest England and many of the Anglo-Saxon kings enjoyed a succession of wives, simply repudiating them when they had tired of them. At least one king did not even bother to repudiate his first wife when he married his second, simply maintaining both as his queens in different areas of his empire.[17] Queens were often pitted against each other and regularly had to fight for survival. The tenth-century kings Edward the Elder and Edgar, for example, each had three wives in quick succession and following the death of a king the actions of these rival wives and their sons often caused chaos in England. Since the position of wife was so precarious, queens often strove to gain power through their sons and, in the pre-conquest period, the position of queen mother was much more powerful than that of king's wife. This was often a role for which women fought and some queens resorted to murder in order to achieve it.

Pre-conquest queens therefore had a defined role that they were expected to fulfil and failure to do so could be costly. However, in spite of the general insignificance of Anglo-Saxon queens, there were some who came to prominence for negative reasons. Rivalry between queens was common; on occasion both political murder and adultery were used in order to secure a political role at court. Some women were also remembered for indulging in incest in order to secure their position at court. The Anglo-Saxon period ended 1,000 years ago in 1066 and it is difficult to know if there is truth in these allegations. Some of the charges were undoubtedly trumped up as a useful way of neutralising a political woman. On the other hand, some of the allegations are likely to have been true and there is no doubt that some Anglo-Saxon queens did commit, or were at least complicit in, political murders and political rivalry. What is forgotten in the lurid stories surrounding them however is that kings also indulged in political murder and the history of the Anglo-Saxon monarchy is littered with suspiciously early deaths and succession disputes. The real difference is that these actions do not damn the kings as they damn the queens. A king can be called a murderer and still be considered a great king. Such was King Aethelstan who was responsible for the murder of his brother Edwin. All the Anglo-Saxon queens associated with murder are considered to have been nefarious queens and their reputations were damned by association. The difference is, of course, that queens are women and kings are men. Society was patriarchal and men were supposed to lead political and sometimes morally dubious lives. Women on the other hand were not. With the exception of the accounts commissioned for Emma of Normandy and Edith Godwine all the sources from the period were written by men who were conditioned to view political women with suspicion anyway. Their accounts destroyed the reputations of the queens.

The Anglo-Saxon period saw over twenty women who could claim the position of king's wife and thus queen. It is the notorious queens, such as Judith of France, Aelfgifu of the House of Wessex, Eadburh, Edith Godwine, Aelfthryth, Emma of Normandy and Aelfgifu of Northampton who are truly remembered and details of their lives were used as cautionary tales for later queens for many centuries to come. Each of these women is remembered for some act, or acts, of wickedness and each made a conscious choice to abandon the traditional ideal of queenship in favour of something more powerful and lasting, to varying success. It is therefore these women who can be described as the pre-conquest 'She-Wolves', the notorious queens of England.

Incestuous Queens

Judith of France & Aelfgifu of the House of Wessex

Many Anglo-Saxon queens survive in sources only as brief mentions – the mother of a particular son, the giver of some gift to the Church. Little else remains to even indicate that these women existed. This obscurity does not extend to all the early queens and some queens were not content to merely remain in the shadows, instead attempting to take a more political role. However for Anglo-Saxon and later writers a queen's place was in the background and any attempt made to escape from this was generally met with fierce criticism. Queens who attracted notoriety throughout their lifetimes often continued to attract criticism over the centuries and, throughout the medieval period, the idea of a political and autonomous woman was generally frowned upon by the male chroniclers. Two early queens whose reputations have suffered in this way are Judith of France and Aelfgifu of the House of Wessex, both of whose names are associated with the unsavoury practice of incest. Their reputations and the attacks on their characters can be directly linked to their attempts to take control of their own lives in a way previously unheard of for early medieval women.

The life of Judith of France is much better documented than that of the the later Aelfgifu. Judith was born into political importance as a daughter of the greatest royal house in Europe, that of Charles the Bald, king of the Franks, and his wife, Ermentrude.[1] She was the couple's eldest child and would have been born in Francia around a year after their marriage in December 842. Judith was named after her grandmother, the Empress Judith, a woman who had been a particularly powerful and dominant political figure. As a young widow, the Empress Judith had almost single-handedly secured the throne of Francia for her son Charles and it was as a compliment to her that Charles called his eldest daughter Judith.[2] Judith would have been raised on stories of the Empress's activities and these stories probably caught the young Judith's imagination as she was growing up. She may also have been aware of her grandmother's difficult reputation as a powerful and dominant woman, but also as an example of what was not really acceptable for a woman.

For all the stories about her famous grandmother, Judith would have been aware from an early age that her future was unlikely to be anywhere near so eventful. The Carolingian dynasty that ruled Francia jealously guarded its royal blood and princesses were seldom allowed to marry and allow this inheritance to pass out of the immediate family of the king. Instead, the vast majority of Carolingian princesses were consecrated as nuns and this would have been the fate that Judith expected. Judith herself would show that she had no predisposition for the religious life and later in life she fought passionately against attempts to ordain her as a nun. It was probably with relief, as well as some apprehension, that Judith received the news, when she was twelve years old, that a very different future had been arranged for her by her father. She resolved to take the opportunity offered to her, whatever the consequences.

Judith was probably not aware, from her place in the royal nursery, of changes that were occurring in her father's kingdom. The mid-ninth century saw the appearance of the Vikings across Europe and, in the summer of 856, a Viking attack on the Seine heralded six years of fierce attacks on the kingdom of Charles the Bald. Charles probably looked around to neighbouring kingdoms for support and his interest fell on the kingdom of Wessex, ruled by the elderly King Aethelwulf. Aethelwulf also appears to have sought out Charles as an ally and in 855, he passed through Francia on a pilgrimage to Rome.[3] He remained at Rome a year before returning to Francia for an extended visit.

King Aethelwulf had become King of Wessex in 839 and by 855 he would have been around fifty years old, several years older than Judith's own father, Charles the Bald. King Aethelwulf had also been married before, to Osburh, daughter of Oslac, the king's butler.[4] Osburh appears to have been a dutiful wife and bore Aethelwulf several children. However by 856 she was either dead or had been repudiated by her husband, and Aethelwulf was ready to marry again. It seems likely that his choice quickly fell on Judith as the only daughter of Charles the Bald who was of marriageable age and Charles, desperate for allies against the Vikings, was forced to agree to the match.

Judith would have had no involvement in the arrangements for her marriage to Aethelwulf and the first she knew of the match may well have been when she was summoned to attend her own wedding in September 856. Aethelwulf would have been eager to form an alliance with the prestigious Carolingian dynasty and it is unlikely that he sought a meeting with his bride before he agreed to the match. Judith also would probably have only met her future husband for the first time a few days before the wedding and as a twelve year old girl, Aethelwulf must have seemed impossibly elderly to her. Judith may also have been excited by the prospect of becoming a queen and escaping a nunnery and she appears to have made no protest against marrying a man nearly forty years her senior.

If Judith was excited about becoming a queen, her father, Charles the Bald, was determined that she should become one. Queens of Wessex were typically given only a very low status and denied the title of queen, instead being known as 'king's wife'.[5] Charles the Bald, perhaps remembering his own mother's difficulties as a young second wife faced with adult stepsons, apparently insisted that Judith be accorded the full rights of a queen. Judith would have approved of this and probably took an interest in the ceremonies as they were prepared for her wedding. She would have been raised to be familiar with the idea of her all-powerful father and it probably would not have occurred to her that he could be wrong. To her contemporaries in Wessex, however, the prospect of crowning a queen was unappealing.

Aethelwulf and Judith were married on 1 October 856.[6] Judith probably felt proud adorned in all her finery to reflect her status as a Carolingian princess, although she must also have felt anxious about marrying the elderly Aethelwulf. She would also have known that she was to be the centre of attention at the lavish marriage ceremony and, once the marriage itself had taken place, the ceremonies changed in order to provide a coronation for Judith in her new role as Queen of

Wessex. The rite for the coronation had been devised especially for Judith at her father's command and a crown was placed on her head by the Bishop of Reims.[7] Judith was also anointed with holy oil and prayers were said over her womb, suggesting that any children that she produced would have an enhanced claim to Aethelwulf's throne.[8] It seems possible, from this, that Charles had negotiated with Aethelwulf that any son borne by Judith would succeed in preference to Aethelwulf's elder sons and Judith would have been aware that her primary duty was to bear Aethelwulf a son. It may also have been reasoned, given the ages of the bride and groom, that divine help was necessary if the couple were going to be capable of producing a child together.[9]

Judith's coronation was a clear indication of Charles the Bald's hopes for the succession to the throne in England and the first known instance of such an event in relation to an English queen. The very fact of her coronation greatly enhanced her status relative to earlier English queens, particularly her predecessor, Aethelwulf's first wife. This fact would have been apparent to everyone gathered for the wedding as well as Aethelwulf's elder sons in England. Soon after the wedding, Aethelwulf attempted to return home to England with Judith and discovered just how clear his actions had been to his eldest son, Aethelbald. Aethelbald at first refused to receive his father back in the kingdom, rising in rebellion against him.[10] This rebellion caught Aethelwulf by surprise and it must also have been worrying for Judith who had been led to believe that she would be well received in her new home. After much negotiation it was agreed between Aethelwulf and Aethelbald that the kingdom would be divided with Aethelbald taking the richer western part of the kingdom and Aethelwulf the eastern part.[11] It was probably a chastened Aethelwulf who finally escorted Judith home to his much diminished kingdom.

Aethelbald's rebellion had a great effect on the remaining years of Aethelwulf's reign but it also had an effect on Judith herself, along with her reputation. Up until Aethelbald's rebellion, Judith appears to have had a good, if bland, reputation and to have been accepted as yet another passive 'king's wife'. However, the circumstances of the rebellion and the fact that it was clearly connected with her marriage caused Judith's reputation to take a turn for the worst. For example according to William of Malmesbury, Aethelbald's rebellion:

Arose on account of his [Aethelwulf's] foreign wife, yet he held her in the highest estimation, and used to place her on the throne near himself, contrary to the West Saxon custom, for the people never suffered the king's consort either to be seated by the king, or to be honoured with the appellation of queen, on account of the depravity of Edburga [Eadburh], daughter of Offa, King of the Mercians.[12]

Judith appears to have been allotted much of the blame for the rebellion, an unfair position given the fact that she had not yet set foot in her husband's kingdom or, indeed, had any say in the marriage that had been arranged for her. To William of Malmesbury however, who was writing several centuries after Judith died, and other chroniclers, Judith as a potentially powerful woman would always be suspect. Most of the chroniclers at that time and afterwards were monks who were already cut off from women and suspicious of their motives. In her early career, it was Charles the Bald and Aethelwulf who shaped Judith's life, but it is always Judith, as a prominent woman and thus under suspicion, who received the lion's share of the blame. The example of an earlier queen, Eadburh, appears to have been uppermost in the minds of the people of Wessex when Judith arrived as a consecrated queen and Judith attained something of this queen's sullied reputation. Eadburh survives as a stereotype of a wicked queen against which other women could be compared, as Judith apparently was.

Much of the suspicion and unpopularity that surrounded Judith both during her lifetime and later was due to her position as an anointed queen. Judith, as a foreigner, was unlikely to have understood the hostility directed towards her but Aethelwulf must have been fully aware of the situation. However he made no attempt to make this situation any easier for his young bride and appears to have kept to the terms of his agreement with Charles until the end of his life, insisting that Judith be given a throne beside him as his queen.[13] Judith, raised to be fully aware of her status as a descendant of Charlemagne, would probably not have expected anything different and may not have been aware of how damaging her adoption of the trappings of queenship was to her reputation. Certainly, she seems to have enjoyed her position as a queen and sought to extend her role even after Aethelwulf's death.

Aethelwulf's spirit was probably greatly affected by his son's rebellion and his health may have begun to decline. In spite of Charles the Bald's and probably Aethelwulf's hopes, no child was forthcoming from the marriage and it is possible that Aethelwulf unfairly came to view Judith as the cause of his misfortune. He had little time to dwell on his demotion to the eastern part of his kingdom, however, and he died only two years after the wedding in 858.[14] The death appears to have been expected. Aethelwulf made a will several months before his death, although no mention was made of Judith.[15] Aethelwulf probably assumed that his young widow would simply return to her father in Francia – but Judith herself had other ideas.

Until the death of Aethelwulf, sources mentioning Judith tended to be lukewarm and sometimes critical in their attitude to her, but following Aethelwulf's death they became overtly hostile. Judith would not have been shocked at Aethelwulf's death and his will suggests that he endured a long illness. During that time, she had probably taken stock of her own position regarding the death of her husband and may well have made plans for her own future. Judith would have been well aware that her father expected her to enter a nunnery and the prospect of returning to Francia with its life of seclusion may not have been appealing, especially since she had gained a taste for politics from her time as queen. In 858, Judith apparently decided to take action on her own behalf and either approached, or was approached by, her stepson, Aethelbald, with a view to making a second marriage and retaining her position as queen.

No details survive of the arrangements for Judith's second marriage but it seems likely that Judith took the initiative and her family in Francia were in no way involved. She would have realised that, like everyone in England, her family would be shocked at the news that she had married her own stepson and, although there was no blood relationship between the couple, it was well understood in England at the time that such a match was incestuous. Today also it is difficult to escape the view that such a marriage was distinctly unsavoury and it was something that would not have been sanctioned by the Church or the people of England or Francia. Both Judith and Aethelbald would have been well aware of this view before their marriage and must have made a conscious decision to defy conventional viewpoints.

The Anglo-Saxons clearly viewed a marriage between a stepmother and her stepson as immoral and irreligious, as can be seen in the reference to an earlier marriage in Kent that was recorded by the Venerable Bede:

> The death of Ethelbert and the accession of his son Eadbald proved to be a severe setback to the growth of the young Church; for not only did he refuse to accept the Faith of Christ, but he was also guilty of such fornication as the Apostle Paul mentions as being unheard of even among the heathen, in that he took his father's [second] wife as his own. His immorality was an incentive to those who, either out of fear or favour of the king his father, had submitted to the discipline of faith and chastity, to revert to their former uncleanness.[16]

According to Bede, a marriage between a stepmother and her stepson ushered in a wave of immorality and damaged the very fabric of the Church in England. He clearly considered such a marriage to be disgusting beyond words and something that even non-Christians would not deign to indulge in – harsh criticism indeed from the pious Bede. That such a view was still current is clear from the words of Judith's own contemporary, Asser, in his description of her second marriage:

> Once King Aethelwulf was dead, Aethelbald, his son, against God's prohibition and Christian dignity, and also contrary to the practice of all pagans, took over his father's marriage-bed and married Judith, daughter of Charles, king of the Franks, incurring great disgrace from all who heard of it; and he controlled the government of the kingdom of the West Saxons for two and a half lawless years after his father.[17]

Asser was clearly deliberately attempting to draw parallels with the much earlier reign of Eadbald of Kent in his description of the marriage and it once again shows the hostility with which this incestuous marriage was viewed. By carrying out incest, both Aethelbald and Judith were seen as ushering in a period of lawlessness and anarchy in England that was a direct result of their own immorality. Later chroniclers saw the marriage in the same light, with the twelfth-century historian, William of Malmesbury, for example, writing that 'Ethelbald, base and perfidious, defiled the bed of his father by marrying, after his [Aethelwulf's] decease, Judith his step-mother'.[18] Clearly, Judith's second marriage was not one that improved her already shady reputation in England.

Before their marriage Judith and Aethelbald would both have been aware that they would be heavily criticised for their actions. Both would have been raised to view such a marriage as incestuous and it seems likely that only higher political considerations enabled them to so subvert the morals of society. Both would have been uncomfortably aware that, according to the rules of the Church and society, Judith was every bit Aethelbald's mother as if she had given birth to him herself, despite the fact that she must have been several years his junior. However they would also have been aware, from the earlier example of Eadbald of Kent, that such a marriage could yield great political benefits and it is possible that the Church viewed the marriage more severely than secular members of their court. Once again, for Judith, the chroniclers both of her time and later were mostly celibate churchmen and Judith, as a woman drawn into sexual immorality by political considerations, would always be considered notorious.

Aethelbald was described by his contemporary, Asser, as 'grasping'[19]. This suggests that he was highly ambitious and, on his father's death, wanted to ensure that he gained possession of the kingdom of Wessex without sharing it with his brothers. He appears to have become quickly established as Aethelwulf's successor but, given that there was no established law of inheritance in England at that time, he would have been eager to ensure that the throne was also secured for his sons on the event of his own death. Aethelbald's rebellion demonstrates that he keenly appreciated the additional eligibility that Judith's coronation would confer on her sons and it seems likely that it was Judith's additional status as an anointed queen that made her a desirable bride, in spite of the obvious difficulties incurred in the match. Aethelbald almost certainly hoped that his own sons, as children of a consecrated mother, would have a more legitimate claim to the throne than the children of his younger brothers.[20] He may also have hoped to secure an alliance with Charles the Bald through the marriage although this was probably a secondary consideration.

For Aethelbald, therefore, the marriage had sound political advantages that outweighed the disadvantages of its incestuous nature. For

Judith too there were advantages in a marriage to her stepson. Judith had already spent two years as the anointed Queen of Wessex and she is unlikely to have relished any return to Francia and removal to a nunnery. She appears to have gained a taste for political power and she would have been only too aware that a marriage to Aethelbald, her husband's successor, was her only hope of retaining her status as queen in England. Little evidence survives from Aethelbald's brief reign but Judith certainly appears to have been politically prominent. For example one charter specifies Judith as Queen, second only to her husband, Aethelbald, and his brother, Aethelberht, Underking of Kent.[21] In this document, Judith was given a prominence unusual even to later Anglo-Saxon queens and she witnessed above all the attendant bishops and noblemen. In spite of its incestuous nature, Judith's second marriage brought her tangible benefits, allowing her to maintain her status and prominence as a queen and a political figure.

In spite of the advantages conferred on both parties by the marriage, Judith's second marriage proved to be no more lasting than her first and, in 860, Aethelbald died, leaving Judith once again as a childless widow.[22] This second marriage had been, like her first, a political match and it is unlikely that Judith was unduly affected personally by the death. However, it may have been sudden and Judith does not appear to have had time to make plans for herself as she had done on Aethelwulf's death. Aethelbald's successor, Aethelberht, does not appear to have considered making a marriage with his stepmother and Judith must have known that she had no further role to play in England. Soon after Aethelbald's death she returned home to her father, bowing to the inevitable at last.

Interest in Judith by English chroniclers ended with her return to Francia as a childless, and still teenaged, widow. Her reputation in England had been irretrievably blackened by her incestuous second marriage and her conduct after her return to Francia would only have served to further enhance this opinion of her. Upon her return to Francia, Judith was sent to Senlis nunnery by her father.[23] Once again, however, Judith showed an independent spirit that shocked her contemporaries. After only a short time in her convent she made contact with Count Baldwin of Flanders and the pair eloped, marrying quickly without the consent of her father. The couple then fled to the court of

Pope Nicholas I and enlisted his support, in spite of the fact that the Church expressly censured the remarriage of widows.[24] The couple's quick thinking presented Charles the Bald with a *fait accompli* and, in spite of his objections, he was forced eventually to accept the marriage.[25] Judith of France disappears from history after her third marriage but she appears to have created a life for herself that brought her happiness and, at the very least, allowed her to escape from the unwelcome nunnery. Certainly, this marriage proved more lasting than her English marriages and she bore Baldwin children.

Judith of France is remembered for her notorious marriage to Aethelbald and appears in the chronicles only as a source of scandalous behaviour. There is no doubt that the behaviour of Judith, as an independent woman, was considered shocking to the church chroniclers of her era and later and also a dangerous example of female autonomy to male patriarchs for centuries to come. Not many people, men or women, defied Charles the Bald, the most powerful ruler in Europe, but Judith did, as a teenaged and powerless widow and her actions would inevitably provoke outrage. In spite of the disapproval she received throughout her lifetime, she was able to shape her own life in a way which was unusual for early medieval women and she appears to have been able to secure happiness for herself. Judith was probably aware of her unfavourable reputation but chose to ignore it, seeking personal satisfaction over the good opinion of her contemporaries. This was also a path taken by her much later queenly successor, Aelfgifu of the House of Wessex. Despite the similarities in the stories of the two women, Aelfgifu's life turned out very differently to that of Judith.

Aelfgifu of the House of Wessex is also remembered as a queen who was involved in incest, and like Judith of France, it is on this that her reputation rests. The story of Aelfgifu of the House of Wessex leaves her open to two charges of incest and, although neither would have been considered as horrifying to contemporaries as Judith of France's conduct, both proved to be useful tools with which Aelfgifu could be criticised and, finally, politically neutralised. Unlike Judith, for Aelfgifu these charges are unlikely to be true but, for medieval women, accusations were not easily forgotten and nothing destroyed a woman's reputation so well as allegations of sexual impropriety.

Aelfgifu of the House of Wessex was the wife of Eadwig, who rose to the throne in 955 at the young age of fifteen. According to the *Chronicle of Aethelweard*, Eadwig 'for his great beauty got the nick-name "All-Fair" from the common people. He held the kingdom continuously for four years and deserved to be loved'.[26] This implies a positive view of Eadwig's reign but it is the only favourable source and Eadwig was almost universally derided by contemporaries, as was Aelfgifu. Eadwig had succeeded to the throne in a contested succession and many of the leading churchmen of the day, including Oda, Archbishop of Canterbury, and Dunstan, Abbot of Glastonbury, favoured the accession of Eadwig's younger brother, Edgar. This led to a hostile portrayal in the sources of both Eadwig and his wife.

Aelfgifu of the House of Wessex never appears to have attained the prominence in England of Judith of France and she was certainly never crowned. Hostile portrayals of her in sources such as the *Life of St Dunstan* also deny that she was Eadwig's wife and in the most famous incident surrounding her, Aelfgifu appears in the guise of an immoral courtesan. According to the *Life of St Dunstan*, Eadwig slipped away from his coronation feast. When his absence was noticed, Abbot Dunstan and his kinsman, Bishop Cynesige, were sent to fetch the king back.[27] Everyone in attendance at the feast suspected that the king had left in order to enjoy the company of a mother and her daughter, both of whom hoped to entice him into marriage. According to the *Life*:

When in accordance with their superior's orders they had entered, they found the royal crown, which was bound with wondrous metal, gold and silver and gems, and shone with many-coloured lustre, carelessly thrown on the floor, far from his [Eadwig's] head, and he himself repeatedly wallowing between the two of them [the mother and daughter] in evil fashion, as if in a vile sty. They said: "Our nobles sent us to ask you to come as quickly as possible to your proper seat, and not to scorn to be present at the joyful banquet of your chief men". But when he did not wish to rise, Dunstan, after first rebuking the folly of the women, replaced the crown, and brought him with him to the royal assembly, though dragged from the women by force.[28]

The *Life of St Dunstan* gives the lurid details of this encounter and, through its depiction of what can only be described as a 'threesome' between the king and the two women, it effectively damned the reputations of the three people involved for all later historians. There is also something distinctly unsavoury about the participation of Aelfgifu and her mother, Aethelgifu, in the seduction of the king and it is hard to resist the implications of incest that the participation of a mother and daughter implies. The *Life of St Dunstan* portrays Aethelgifu as a ruthless procuress, determined to win the king at all costs, and Aelfgifu as a willing participant.

That the *Life of St Dunstan* does not tell the whole truth about Aelfgifu is clear from other scattered sources. Aelfgifu is known to have been from a wealthy noble family and both she and her mother were also of royal descent – clearly not the common whores that the *Life* suggests.[29] She was also the king's wife, rather than a concubine and it is likely that the marriage helped provide Eadwig with a power base in southern England.[30] Although Aethelgifu, as Aelfgifu's mother, may well have helped arrange her daughter's marriage to the king, in reality it seems impossible that she would have gone quite as far as the *Life* suggests in order to ensure the king's compliance. It is also worth looking at the *Life* itself, the earliest source for the coronation incident. St Dunstan, who always strove to be the current king's chief counsellor, was not well disposed towards queens. One of Aelfgifu's successors as queen, Aelfthryth, would also have difficulty with the powerful Dunstan. He recognised the potential influence a queen could have over a king and, always uneasy with powerful women, he sought to keep them in the background by any means possible. In Aelfgifu's case he denied that she was even the king's wife, depicting her as a concubine and, in the process, he utterly destroyed her reputation. Aelfgifu and Aethelgifu will always be associated with their supposed *ménage a trois* with the king and the unsavoury image of a mother and daughter both participating in the seduction of the dissolute king. This view of Aelfgifu was certainly the one held by the twelfth-century historian, William of Malmesbury who wrote 'Eadwig was led astray by the enticements of one courtesan, and when Dunstan rebuked him most severely for his folly, he expelled Dunstan from England'.[31] William of Malmesbury also refers to Aelfgifu as a 'harlot' and a 'strumpet', hardly the usual descriptions given to a long-dead former queen.[32]

Aelfgifu's reputation, like that of Eadwig himself, rides firmly on the fact that both were members of a faction that ultimately failed to triumph at court. Whilst Dunstan and Archbishop Oda supported Edgar, Aelfgifu and her family were behind Eadwig. In the first years of Eadwig's reign, Eadwig's supporters clearly had the upper hand and he was able to politically disable several of his opponents, through methods including the exile of Dunstan to the continent and the denial to his grandmother, the powerful Queen Eadgifu, of her lands.[33] Much of the opposition to his rule that Eadwig faced was due to his marriage and the threat that this posed to the more established members of his court.[34] Like Judith one hundred years before her, Aelfgifu was certainly unfairly blamed for the political changes that her marriage allowed and Aelfgifu struggled to establish her position as queen in the face of this opposition. She is recognised as the king's legitimate wife in only one charter from his reign which, once again, shows the deep hostility of leading churchmen, who would have been responsible for drawing up and storing the charters.[35]

The depiction of Aelfgifu in the *Life of St Dunstan* was not the only attack on her marriage and character that she sustained during Eadwig's reign. Opposition to the marriage was directly connected to a rebellion in favour of Eadwig's brother, Edgar, in 957.[36] According to several sources, Eadwig ruled England so badly that, in 957, all of England north of the Thames deserted him and chose Edgar as king.[37] This must have been a major blow for both Aelfgifu and Eadwig and it seems likely that it was only the support of Aelfgifu's powerful family that helped secure the south for the king. Both the king and queen must have been concerned for the future as their position grew steadily worse over the next year.

The *Anglo-Saxon Chronicle* for 958 states, blandly, that 'here in this year Archbishop Oda divorced King Eadwig and Aelfgifu because they were related'.[38] This entry once again suggests that a charge of incest was being used against Aelfgifu to discredit her. The pretext used for the divorce was probably used to demonstrate further the king's supposed immorality and a number of sources refer to Aelfgifu and Eadwig being 'near of kin'.[39] As with the marriage of Judith of France and

Aethelbald, incest appears to have been associated with bad govern-ance. It seems likely that consanguity was deliberately chosen as the reason for the divorce in order to highlight Eadwig's unsuitability as a ruler. The fact that the couple only appear to have been related through shared great-great-grandparents does not seem to have been mentioned so prominently. It is clear that the intention was to portray the cou-ple as much more closely related. That this was used as a pretext on which to separate Eadwig from his influential wife as is demonstrated by the fact that at least one more inbred Anglo-Saxon marriage had remained unchallenged: that of Eadwig's grandfather, Edward the Elder, to his cousin's daughter, Aelfflaed. Like the earlier suggestions of incest regarding Aelfgifu and her mother, however, this charge achieved what Eadwig's opponents intended and Aelfgifu's name is irrevocably associ-ated with incest.

Aelfgifu was exiled from England following her forced divorce and she probably spent several years wandering on the continent.[40] If she had entertained any hopes of a reconciliation with Eadwig, she was to be disappointed. According to William of Malmesbury, Eadwig died of shock at seeing all the calamities that had beset him, dying on 10 October 959.[41] Although few details survive of Aelfgifu and Eadwig's relationship it can, perhaps, be inferred that they were close and Aelfgifu never married again. At some point during the reign of Edgar, Eadwig's successor Aelfgifu returned to England and she seems to have lived the life of a wealthy widow. Eadwig was buried in the New Minster at Winchester and around twenty years after his death he was joined there by Aelfgifu, who requested burial there in her own will. Perhaps she chose this site for her own burial in order to be with her husband in death in a way that she had not been able to be with him in life.

Aelfgifu of the House of Wessex backed the wrong faction at court and she paid for this both with her happiness and her reputation. Much less deserving of the smear of incest than her predecessor Judith of France, Aelfgifu's existence is still only remembered for the story sur-rounding Eadwig's coronation and both her and her mother's harlotry. By marrying the king, Aelfgifu provided Eadwig with the powerful support of her family and, as such, she was always seen as a threat to the king's more established counsellors. Unfortunately for Aelfgifu, these disgruntled counsellors were often churchmen and it was the Church who controlled what was written down, at least in the early medieval period. It was very easy for them to attack her with stories of incest and since she was female, these labels remained. Eadwig, although remembered as a weak king is not so damned for his own alleged incestuous behaviour with Aelfgifu. Sexual indecency was always less damaging to men. By contrast Aelfgifu, being a woman, was always regarded with suspicion by the chronicler monks and consequently suffered, despite the lack of truth behind the rumours.

Both Judith of France and Aelfgifu of the House of Wessex are notorious for the lives they are supposed to have led and, in particular, the charges of incest that have been laid against them. Both had very different characters, however, and responded in different ways to the charges laid against them. Judith of France appears to have actively rejected her lot and sought personal happiness over the preservation of her reputation. Aelfgifu, on the other hand, lost both. Both queens were attacked with claims of sexual impropriety and this was always a powerful way of nullifying a political queen. Despite their denouncement however, Judith of France and Aelfgifu in some ways endured a mild fate. Other Anglo-Saxon queens are remembered for even more villainous crimes such as murder and adultery.

Adultery & Murder in the
Anglo-Saxon Court

Eadburh, Aelfthryth & Edith Godwine

The poor reputations of Judith of France and Aelfgifu of the House of Wessex pale into insignificance when compared to those of certain other Anglo-Saxon queens. Even in the Anglo-Saxon period, some queens were very prominent political figures and in a male-dominated society this was seen as unacceptable. In an age when political murder and other unsavoury aspects of political life were common, men often escaped criticism in the sources provided that they remained on friendly terms with the Church and, thus, the chroniclers. The same cannot be said for female political figures. Eadburh, Aelfthryth and Edith Godwine were heavily criticised for their political activities in their own lifetimes and afterwards. They are remembered as murderesses and, in the case of Eadburh and Aelfthryth, also adulteresses, although, after 1,000 years, the truth of these claims is difficult to verify. What is certain however is that it is the queens Eadburh, Aelfthryth and Edith Godwine who are perceived as at fault, whereas their male accomplices receive only minor criticism, if any at all.

Eadburh was a very early queen and little evidence survives relating to her life. The surviving information provided the stereotype of a sinful queen and her story was used as a cautionary tale for later queens, such as Judith of France. According to several sources Eadburh's life nearly brought the whole office of queen to extinction. Her life, which apparently included both murder and dubious sexual morality, became a model for exactly how an early medieval queen was expected not to behave.

Eadburh was the daughter of the famous King Offa of Mercia, a man who could claim dominance over most of what would later become England.[1] Although no details survive of Eadburh's early life, she would have been aware from her infancy of her father's power and according to some sources, she was heavily influenced by notions of her father's eminence. Simeon of Durham, for example, claimed that when Eadburh 'was raised to so many honours, she became inflated with marvellous pride, and began to live in her father's tyrannical manner'.[2] Eadburh clearly saw her father as something of a hero and she may have seen her marriage, in 789, to Beorhtric, King of Wessex, as somewhat beneath her exalted station.[3] Although she is criticised for this attitude, it is perhaps not surprising that she was not entirely satisfied with a socially sub-status marriage.

Beorhtric had become King of Wessex in 786 and securing his overlord's daughter in marriage would have been something of a coup for him. Eadburh herself had probably been well schooled by her father in ensuring that Beorhtric remained an ally of the Mercian king. She would have been well aware that this was the primary purpose of the match from her father's point of view. She certainly appears to have had influence in shaping Wessex political policy. According to the *Anglo-Saxon Chronicle*, for example, 'Offa king of Mercia, and Beorhtric, king of Wessex, put him [Ecgbert, a claimant to the crown of Wessex] to flight from the land of the English to the land of the Franks for three years; and Beorhtric helped Offa because he had his daughter as his queen'.[4] Eadburh would have been pleased with the close alliance between her father and husband and, perhaps flushed with success, she also extended her political interests to matters concerning Beorhtric's court.

Eadburh appears to have quickly gained influence over her husband and she became a well-known figure at court. According to Asser:

As soon as she had won the king's friendship, and power throughout almost the entire kingdom, she began to behave like a tyrant after the manner of her father – to loathe every man whom Beorhtric liked, to do all things hateful to God and men, to denounce all those whom she could before the king, and thus by trickery to deprive them of either life or power; and if she could not achieve that end with the king's compliance, she killed them with poison. This is known to have happened with a certain young man very dear to the king; whom she poisoned when she could not denounce him before the king. King Beorhtric himself is said to have taken some of that poison unawares. She had intended to give it not to him, but to the young man; but the king took it first, and both of them died as a result.[5]

According to all versions of this story, Eadburh was not above using underhand methods to get what she wanted politically, although the death of her husband appears to have been accidental. It is impossible now to know the truth behind this episode, if indeed it happened at all, but it is interesting to note that Beorhtric's death also heralded in a new dynasty in Wessex with the accession of Ecgbert, the man that Eadburh's own father had helped to exile. Ecgbert was not closely related to Beorhtric and his accession did not follow the normal rules of succession. If Beorhtric was murdered at all, therefore, it would seem more likely that his murderer was Ecgbert, who would gain advantage from the death, rather than Eadburh, who could only suffer as a result. Eadburh, as a prominent and political queen who had already attracted criticism as a powerful woman, was more likely to have been a convenient scapegoat than a murderess in the death of Beorhtric. It is as a murderer however that she will always be remembered.

According to the story, Eadburh recognised Beorhtric's death as a step too far and, gathering up all the treasure that she could lay her hands on, fled to the court of Charlemagne in France.[6] Eadburh's personal charms attracted the king and, soon after her arrival, he summoned her to an audience before himself and his son. Charlemagne offered Eadburh the choice of marriage to either himself or his son. Eadburh considered this choice for some time before replying, 'if the choice is left to me, I choose your son, as he is younger than you'.[7] The choice was obviously not left to Eadburh, however, and Charlemagne, offended by her answer, sent her to rule as abbess at one of his nunneries. Ignoring her vows as a nun however, she embarked on an affair with an Englishman and was caught together with this man in a compromising situation.[8] Upon this revelation, Eadburh was expelled from her nunnery and spend her last years begging for her food and wandering around Europe.

Eadburh is portrayed in this story as a foolish and vain woman even after her flight from Wessex. Clearly this was an attempt to utterly destroy her reputation and show her as a woman willing to commit murder and other sins. The account is clearly an attack on Eadburh's integrity since events are unlikely to have occurred in the way described. Eadburh was told that she had a choice for her second husband and she cannot be blamed for choosing the man she preferred rather than bowing to flattery by selecting the father. She was then forced to live a nun's life against her will and, again, with no vocation and little likelihood of any future it is understandable that she took a lover to try and find some happiness. However the churchmen who wrote the chronicles did blame her and whatever the truth of Eadburh's activities it is the chronicles that survive to destroy her reputation. Eadburh's reputation was apparently the reason behind attempts by the kings of Wessex to limit the power of queens, furthermore to eradicate the office.[9] Eadburh was not the only Anglo-Saxon queen to be implicated in a political murder, however. Edith Godwine, the last effective Anglo-Saxon queen, was rumoured to have imitated her predecessor when seeking to dispose of a rival at court.

Edith Godwine was the daughter of the famous and powerful Earl Godwine of Wessex. Following her birth in the 1020s or 1030s she was raised for a grand marriage.[10] Edith was given a good education at the nunnery at Wilton and her father may always have had royal ambitions for her. These ambitions came to fruition in 1045 when Godwine, as the king's most powerful councillor, was able to persuade the new king, Edward the Confessor, to marry his daughter.[11] Edith herself probably shared her family's ambitions and William of Malmesbury gives a somewhat ambiguous picture of her as:

A woman whose bosom was the school of every liberal art, though little skilled in earthly matters: on seeing her, if you were amazed at her erudition, you must admire also the purity of her mind, and the beauty of her person. Both in her husband's lifetime, and afterwards, she was not entirely free from suspicion of dishonour; but when dying, in the time of King William, she voluntarily satisfied the bystanders as to her unimpaired chastity by an oath.[12]

Edith was an effective propagandist and was able to make the best of any situation in which she found herself, including claiming that her child-lessness was due, not to any incapacity on her part, but her own and her husband's sanctity and chastity. Even those chroniclers who believed Edith's claims that the marriage was not consummated, however, did not always believe her claims that this was due to holiness. William of Malmesbury, for one, implied that Edward the Confessor considered his wife foisted upon him and refused to consummate the marriage due to a dislike of her family.[13] Certainly, Edward and Edith's marriage does not appear to have been entirely happy and, in 1052, when Edward was finally secure enough to send her domineering family into exile, he also repudiated his marriage to Edith, sending her on foot with only one attendant to the nunnery at Wherwell, presumably hoping that she would remain there.[14] With the return of her family in 1053, however, Edith was also restored and remained in an unassailable position as queen for the rest of Edward's life.[15]

Edith herself commissioned a book in her widowhood in order to present her point of view to the world and the *Life of King Edward who Rests at Westminster* therefore presents Edith's own propaganda mes-sage. In this work, Edith claimed that, following her restoration to the position of queen, she 'was in all the royal counsels, as we might say, a governess and the fount of all goodness, strongly preferring the king's interests to power and riches'.[16] This is the image that Edith wanted to present to the world but Edward himself certainly does not seem to have thought that she acted only in his best interests. Edith was also intimately associated with the interests of her own favourite brother, Tostig, and it was on his behalf that she became embroiled in the politi-cal murder that mars her reputation.

Edith appears to have favoured Tostig over all her other brothers and it was both she, and her eldest surviving brother, Harold, who were able to persuade Edward to appoint Tostig Earl of Northumberland soon after her restoration to power.[17] However Edith's actions on behalf of Tostig did not end there and according to Simeon of Durham, at Christmas 1064, a certain Gospatric was 'treacherously ordered to be slain' by 'Queen Egitha for the sake of her brother Tosti'.[18] Few details survive for this murder, but Edith and Tostig were both plainly held responsible. Gospatric was a Northumbrian thegn and it is probable that he was in a position to incite unrest in Tostig's earldom of Northumbria. Certainly, Tostig appears to have been regarded as something of an interloper in Northumbria; it is possible that Gospatric was viewed as the local claimant and, thus, a dangerous rival to Tostig.

Edith was fond of her brother Tostig and, if she was indeed involved, she may have carried out the murder solely to safeguard his position. However, it is also possible that Edith might have had her own reasons behind her actions. Gospatric was probably the son of the powerful Earl Uhtred and Uhtred's wife, King Edward's sister.[19] As a nephew of the childless King Edward, Gospatric may well have been regarded as the heir to the throne and this is something that Edith could not have countenanced. Although Edith herself was childless, she gathered as many of the children with royal blood at court that she could and raised them under her own tutelage. She probably hoped this way to be able to influence a future king and the appearance of a claimant with whom she had no connection would not have been pleasant for her. If Edith was involved in the murder she probably hoped that Gospatric's murder would not be widely publicised and that his death would safeguard both her favourite brother's position and her own.

If this is what Edith hoped for, she was to be proved very wrong. Rather than pacifying the north, Gospatric's death stirred the Northumbrians into rebellion against Tostig in 1065.[20] Edith was probably infuriated by the news of the rebellion and she may have petitioned her eldest brother, Harold, to support Tostig. Harold, however, apparently realising that Tostig's position in Northumbria was unsustainable, refused to support his brother, to the chagrin of both Edith and Tostig.[21] At court, Edith must have listened to news of the rebellion with increasing anger but she would have been powerless to act. She must have been deeply angry with her brother Harold when Tostig was forced into exile in Flanders and she may not have supported Harold when he succeeded her husband, Edward the Confessor, on his death in 1066. Certainly, she came to terms quickly with William the Conqueror after the Battle of Hastings and Edith managed to sustain her position as queen dowager and live in some style until her death in 1075.[22]

Edith Godwine was implicated in the political murder of a rival and, in spite of her attempts to portray herself in a positive way, she retained a slightly unsavoury reputation until the end of her life. Whether or not she was involved in the murder is impossible now to say and, it is possible that attempts to place the blame on her were part of a wider campaign against her unpopular family. If she was involved however, it is interesting that the blames falls squarely on her rather than the equally guilty Tostig. Rumours of misconduct tend to stick more firmly to any queen or other woman involved than they do to men. Thanks partly to her own propaganda efforts, and also to the Normans' efforts to honour the widow of Edward the Confessor, Edith never gained the reputation of Eadburh and the murder of Gospatric remains something of a footnote to her life. Edith Godwine certainly had a dubious reputation, but that reputation was nothing compared to the reputation of her own husband's grandmother, Queen Aelfthryth.

Aelfthryth is one of the most notorious of any queen of England and this centres mainly on the murder of her stepson, King Edward the Martyr. Edward's murder was not the only one in which Aelfthryth's name was implicated however, and throughout her lifetime sources claim that she was involved in a number of murders designed to further her ambition. The stories surrounding her rival even those of Eadburh in their wickedness.

Aelfthryth was the daughter of a powerful thegn, Ordgar, who later became earldorman of Devon.[23] She appears to have been ambitious from an early age and a grand marriage was arranged for her to Aethelwold, the son and heir of the famous Athelstan Half-King, ruler of much of eastern England. The first murder in which Aelfthryth was implicated was that of her first husband. A number of sources suggest that Aelfthryth quickly became disaffected with her life as a nobleman's wife. According to William of Malmesbury, Aelfthryth and her parents were tricked into sanctioning the match with Aethelwold:

> The king had commissioned [Aethelwold] to visit Elfrida [Aelfthryth], daughter of Ordgar, duke of Devonshire, (whose charms had so fascinated the eyes of some persons that they commended her to the king,) and to offer her marriage if her beauty were really equal to report. Hastening on his embassy, and finding every thing consonant to the general estimation, he concealed his mission from her parents, and procured the damsel for

himself. Returning to the king, he told a tale which made for his own purpose, that she was a girl of vulgar and common-place appearance, and by no means worthy of such transcendent dignity.[24]

Aethelwold must have been relieved that the king appeared to have accepted his story and he and Aelfthryth settled down together. Whilst she was pregnant with her first child, however, Aelfthryth apparently learned the truth of the story behind her marriage from her husband's own mouth.[25] For an ambitious woman like Aelfthryth, this news must have been devastating and she apparently ceased to love her husband from that point. Edgar had also become suspicious of Aethelwold as reports of Aelfthryth's beauty had continued to reach him and he resolved to visit her, to see the truth for himself. News of the royal visit threw Aethelwold in a panic and he begged Aelfthryth to disguise her beauty in her ugliest clothes.[26] Aelfthryth, however, apparently deceived her husband and appeared before the king in her finest garments. Aelfthryth and Edgar quickly fell in love, in spite of the fact that both were married. The pair came to an understanding to marry and, soon after their meeting, Aethelwold was invited on a hunting expedition by Edgar.[27] William of Malmesbury narrates how Edgar whilst out hunting ran Aethelwold through with a javelin.[28] Soon afterwards, Edgar divorced his wife and the couple were able to marry.

The stories surrounding Aelfthryth's first marriage and her husband's death portray Aelfthryth as a dishonest, adulterous and murderous woman and one entirely unsuited to the position of queen. However, as with so many stories concerning medieval queens, there is more to the evidence than meets the eye. The story of Aelfthryth's first marriage is recorded by William of Malmesbury and Gaimar, both of whom were writing several centuries after Aelfthryth died and therefore unlikely to have had first hand evidence of her conduct. It is therefore debatable that events actually happened in that way at all and it seems more likely that stories of Aelfthryth were coloured by the later murder of Edward the Martyr. Also, even if these stories can be accepted as true, which seems doubtful, Aelfthryth cannot be entirely blamed for Aethelwold's murder. He apparently tricked her into marriage, something for which she had a right to be grieved. Aelfthryth is also not named as the murderer in either account although she receives the blame for it. The true murderer is Edgar, who escapes all blame and censure in the accounts. Edgar, unlike Aelfthryth, enjoys a good reputation despite his alleged involvement in the murder of Aelfthryth's first husband and the rebellion which led him to take the throne from his brother Eadwig. The major difference between him and Aelfthryth is that, as a man, he was expected by his contemporaries and those following to be politically active and to sometimes act with dubious morality to further his political ambition. Aelfthryth, as a woman, was not.

Aethelwold's murder was not the only accusation to be made against Aelfthryth. Chroniclers recorded a number of stories in an attempt to prove her wickedness. Aelfthryth had apparently not been faithful to her first husband, beginning an affair with the king during Aethelwold's lifetime, and, according to a number of sources, she was also not faithful to Edgar. One story in particular claims to testify both to her reputation as a murderess and an adulteress, found in the *Historia Eliensis*:

> It happened at a certain time, therefore, that the holy Abbot Byrhtnoth set out for the king's court on church business; as he was journeying on this side of "Geldedune" through the wood called the New Forest, as it is said, he sought some more secluded spot to satisfy the needs of nature; as he was a modest man and of great integrity he took care to look round on every side. By chance under a certain tree he surprised the queen, Aelfthryth, engaged in the preparation of magic potions (for, transformed, by her caprice and magic art into an equine animal, she wished to appear as a horse and not as a woman to onlookers, so that she might satisfy the unrestrainable excess of her burning lust, running and leaping hither and thither with horses and showing herself shamelessly to them, regardless of the fear of God and the honour of the royal dignity, she thus contemptibly brought reproach upon her fame).[29]

This account suggests that even a king as notoriously licentious as Edgar could not satisfy Aelfthryth's lust and, although it is likely to have been considerably embellished, shows something of the unsavoury reputation had by Aelfthryth. The story continues to relate how Aelfthryth's wickedness did not end there and, upon her return to court, she attempted to seduce the Abbot in order to ensure his silence.[30] When the Abbot refused, Aelfthryth, desperate not to be unmasked as a witch and an adulteress, summoned her ladies and, together they heated up sword thongs on the fire and murdered the Abbot by inserting them into his bowels.[31] This was a particularly horrible death and, interestingly, one that a later queen of England, and Aelfthryth's own descendant, would be accused of inflicting on her husband. This story is clearly an invention of the writer. However it does demonstrate Aelfthryth's notoriety and there was a third murder that she was almost certainly complicit in.

Although rumours of adultery and the murders of Aethelwold and the Abbot of Ely have dogged Aelfthryth's reputation for over 1,000 years, it is the murder of her stepson, Edward the Martyr, with which she is most famously associated. Edgar had been married twice before his marriage to Aelfthryth and his first marriage had produced a son, Edward.[32] Aelfthryth, however, had ambitions for her own sons by Edgar, Edmund and Aethelred, and there is some evidence that she was able to persuade Edgar to make Edmund his heir over the older Edward.[33] However any tacit agreement to make Aelfthryth's son heir to the throne died with Edmund in 970 and there is no indication that the much younger Aethelred was ever similarly designated.[34] Aelfthryth was probably not unduly concerned at Edgar's failure to nominate Aethelred as his heir. In 971, Edgar was only in his late twenties and she must have reasoned that there was plenty of time for Aethelred to grow up.

If this was Aelfthryth's plan, it was to be thrown into disarray in 975 with the sudden death of Edgar.[35] Neither of Edgar's surviving sons were adults but Aethelred, who was only about seven years old, was at a distinct disadvantage. Nonetheless, Aelfthryth and her allies appear to have made a credible case for the succession of Aethelred, as the legitimate son of Edgar, over that of his half-brother, who was born of a more dubious marriage. According to the *Life of St Oswald*, the whole country was thrown into confusion by Edgar's death and there was a great deal of debate over who would succeed him:[36]

Certain of the chief men of this land wished to elect as king the king's elder son, Edward by name; some of the nobles wanted the younger; because he appeared to all gentler in speech and deeds. The elder, in fact, inspired in all not only fear but even terror, for [he scourged them] not only with words but truly with dire blows, and especially his own men dwelling with him.[37]

Even in his early teens, Edward apparently had an unsavoury reputation and this may have increased support for Aethelred. Dunstan, who had been made Edgar's Archbishop of Canterbury early in his reign, proved to be as opposed to Aelfthryth as queen as he had been to Aelfgifu of the House of Wessex and, as England's leading churchman, he was able to insist upon Edward's accession in preference to that of Aethelred. This would have been a great blow for Aelfthryth and her supporters and it must have been doubly hard for Aelfthryth that it was her enemy, Dunstan, who was able to ensure that her son was not proclaimed king. She clearly did not abandon Aethelred's cause, however, and over the next three years both Aelfthryth and her supporters continued to scheme for Aethelred's accession to the throne.

Aelfthryth apparently saw her chance to act against Edward in 978 when he decided to pay a visit to her and Aethelred at her house at Corfe. Accounts differ as to exactly what happened but even the earliest detailed account places the murder at Aelfthryth's home and blames the men of her household for it.[38] Later accounts, such as William of Malmesbury, lay the blame for plotting the murder with Aelfthryth, and some even place Aelfthryth as one of the king's assailants. According to William of Malmesbury:

> The woman, however, with a stepmother's hatred, began to mediate a subtle strategem, in order that not even the title of king might be wanting to her child, and to lay a treacherous snare for her son-in-law, which she accomplished in the following manner. He was returning home, tired with the chase, and gasping with thirst from the exercise, while his companions were following the dogs in different directions as it happened, when hearing that they dwelt in a neighbouring mansion, the youth proceeded thither at full speed, unattended and unsuspecting, as he judged of others by his own feelings. On his arrival, alluring him to her with female blandishments, she made him fix his attention upon herself, and after saluting him while he was eagerly drinking from the cup which had been presented, the dagger of an attendant pierced him through. Dreadfully wounded, with all his remaining strength he spurred his horse in order to join his companions; when one foot slipping he was dragged by the other through the winding paths, while the steaming blood gave evidence of his death to his followers.[39]

Aelfthryth may not actually have gone out to meet the king or plunged the dagger in herself, but she was certainly nearby at the time of the murder and it is inconceivable that her followers would have acted on anything other than her orders. Aelfthryth, along with the young Aethelred, also had the most to gain from the murder and so she is an obvious suspect. She appears to have considered her actions to be natural for an ambitious mother and it has been claimed that she beat Aethelred with a candlestick on seeing him mourn for the brother who had blocked his path to the throne.[40] The memory of this beating apparently stayed with Aethelred for the rest of his life, giving him a terror of candlelight. Later accounts of the murder are certainly embellished to give Aelfthryth a more prominent and crueller role but there is little doubt that she was in the vicinity and aware of what was to happen.

By helping to plot the murder of Edward the Martyr, Aelfthryth was able to secure her greatest desire and Aethelred was quickly accepted as king and crowned. She probably ignored Dunstan's prophecies of disaster at the coronation as the mutterings of a bad loser and she may well have also ignored the strange clouds seen after the coronation that were held to auger doom for Aethelred's reign.[41] However, Aelfthryth may have quickly come to regret her actions on behalf of her child and perhaps she saw the reappearance of the Vikings a few years after the murder as a judgement on both her and her son. According to a number of reports, Aelfthryth became increasingly penitent both for the murder of Edward and that of Aethelwold and she apparently founded a nunnery at Wherwell, the site of her first husband's death.[42] Legend states that Aelfthryth also retired to that nunnery in an attempt to win forgiveness for her crimes and, whilst there, wore hair-cloth and slept on the ground in her penance.[43] This is certainly an exaggeration and Aelfthryth remained an important figure at court until almost the end of her life. However her last years cannot have been easy and she would have watched Aethelred's increasing troubles with concern. Perhaps she came to regret her ambition in the years before her death in either 1000 or 1001.

Aelfthryth was an extremely ambitious woman and she appears to have been determined to get what she wanted, even if this required adultery or murder. Her name will forever be associated with the death of her young stepson, Edward the Martyr, and she has remained notorious up to the present day. Aelfthryth was almost certainly involved in this murder and she may also have been complicit in the murder of her first husband. However, many of the details of her life have been embellished over time and the figure presented in the sources is an almost grotesque caricature of a wicked queen almost certainly very far removed from the real woman. Aelfthryth was an ambitious political woman and her own husband, Edgar, had certainly committed murder and adultery despite being remembered as one of England's best kings. Aelfthryth as a woman, however, received no rehabilitation from the male chroniclers of her own time and later and she will always be remembered as one of the worst queens England ever had, regardless of the true facts of her life.

Eadburh, Edith Godwine and Aelfthryth are all remembered for their unsavoury reputations, although it is the lives of Eadburh and Aelfthryth that are presented as truly corrupt. All three of the women are described as ambitious and, because of this, they were rumoured to have taken steps that were unacceptable for women. Eadburh and Aelfthryth survive almost as stereotypes and it is difficult to separate the fact from the fiction. Two later Anglo-Saxon queens, in particular, would have noted the effect that a bad reputation could have on a queen's position along with that of her children: Emma of Normandy and Aelfgifu of Northampton of the eleventh century used propaganda in their battles for dominance after the death of their shared husband, King Cnut. Both these women are remembered as notorious queens, though in a very different way to the stereotyped Eadburh, Aelfthryth and Edith Godwine.

Female Power Struggles

Emma of Normandy & Aelfgifu of Northampton

Many Anglo-Saxon kings can be described as serial monogamists. Kings such as Edward the Elder, Edmund I and Edgar enjoyed a succession of wives, discarding them with apparent ease. Few Anglo-Saxon kings can be said to be polygamous however and most at least divorced their wife before taking another. King Cnut is an exception to this rule. Rather than divorcing his first wife to marry his second, he simply maintained both queens, allowing them separate spheres of influence in his empire. This was a position deeply resented by the two women and for over twenty years, Emma of Normandy and her rival Aelfgifu of Northampton were locked in a power struggle with each other that made them both notorious in England. Both sought to make their own son the heir of their husband and both went to extreme lengths in doing so. Although they are blamed for this and their bad reputations are partly of their own making it must be said that Cnut himself propagated the situation with his conduct. As women they also received harsher criticism than their sons, which is clearly a biased result, considering that it was the sons who were the true rivals for the crown.

Emma of Normandy was destined for a great marriage. As the daughter of Richard I, Duke of Normandy, she would have known that her fate lay in an arranged marriage, although it was the Viking raids that determined who her husband would be. The Dukes of Normandy were of Danish descent and Emma's own mother, Gunnor, was Danish. Normandy therefore appears to have been seen as a safe-haven for the Viking raiders and it is likely that Emma's sympathies lay with them. Her father certainly appears to have favoured the Danes and this brought him into conflict with the King of England, Aethelred. In 991 the Pope brokered a peace between the two rulers in which each agreed not to harbour the others' enemies.[1] This truce appears to have had little effect, but it may have brought the courts of England and Normandy into closer contact.

The agreement between England and Normandy does not appear to have been lasting and, in 1000, the Vikings raided England before travelling to Normandy.[2] The raiders were welcomed by Emma's brother, Richard II, and Aethelred apparently decided that a more lasting relationship with Normandy was required. The oldest Emma could have been at this time is mid-teens and she is unlikely to have had any say in the negotiations for her marriage to Aethelred. She must have been daunted by the news that she was to marry a forty year-old widower with a large family of his own. However, England was larger and wealthier than Normandy and it is possible that Emma also relished the rise in status that marriage to Aethelred would bring. Certainly, there is no record that she objected and, in early spring 1002, Emma crossed the channel and soon afterwards married Aethelred.[3]

Emma was crowned as queen soon after her marriage and she was obviously accorded a great deal of respect in England, always being referred to as 'the Lady' in the *Anglo-Saxon Chronicle*, for example. However, her youth and the large age gap between herself and Aethelred means that Emma was not expected to play any political role and she appears only as a background figure in the last years of Aethelred's reign. During her marriage she bore Aethelred only three children and this suggests that the couple were rarely together. Emma may also have been viewed with suspicion in an England damaged by years of Viking raids and, certainly, she seems to have continued to associate with the Danes. The *Anglo-Saxon Chronicle* entry for 1003, for example, records that 'here Exeter was destroyed because of the business of a French churl called Hugh, whom the Lady had set up as reeve; and the raiding army completely did for the town'.[4] Whether Emma was involved in Hugh's treachery or not her alienation was apparently uppermost in English minds during her first marriage.

England had been plagued by Viking attacks since the 980s and Aethelred was unable to contend with them, earning himself the nickname 'the Unready'. He may, however, have consoled himself with the thought that the Vikings of the 980s, 990s and early eleventh century came only for plunder, leaving for the continent once they had wreaked their havoc. However, in 1013, the tenor of the Viking attacks suddenly changed with the arrival of a Viking fleet at Gainsborough led by Swein, King of Denmark, and his son, Cnut.[5] Swein had been raiding in England for several years but, in 1013, he came looking for conquest, perhaps seeing the weakened kingdom as an easy target. He certainly appears to have conquered the kingdom with ease and, soon after his arrival, much of northern England submitted to him, abandoning their loyalty to Aethelred.[6] Gratified at the ease of his conquest, Swein left his son to guard his ships and moved south.

By the time of Swein's invasion, Emma had been Aethelred's wife for over a decade and was the mother of his children. Whatever innate sympathies she had had for the Vikings were probably long gone and she must have feared for the fate of her children. Aethelred was also anxious for the safety of his younger children and his wife and, late in 1013, both Emma and her children fled to Normandy to seek sanctuary at the court of her brother.[7] Emma may have been pleased to see her home again but also acutely aware of the difficult position in which she found herself. This would have been compounded when, only weeks after she arrived, she was joined by Aethelred himself.[8] Aethelred's presence as a deposed king cannot have been welcome to either Emma or her brother and Emma may have felt concern for the future of her sons, Edward and Alfred.

In Aethelred's absence, Swein was accepted as king throughout England. However, on 2 February 1014, he died suddenly, leaving his teenaged son, Cnut, as his heir in England.[9] According to William of Malmesbury, the Danes in England immediately attempted to declare Cnut king.[10] The English, however, decided to send for Aethelred, 'declaring that their natural sovereign was dearer to them, if he could conduct himself more like a king than he had hitherto done'.[11] Emma may have been sceptical, along with much of England, about Aethelred's ability in this respect but she returned to England along with the rest of her English family, leaving Normandy for the last time in her life.

Aethelred quickly proved himself unequal to the task before him and, in the face of both rebellion by his eldest son, Edmund, and an invasion by Cnut, he died quietly in London on 23 April 1016.[12] Emma, who was in London at the time, was probably by his side.

Aethelred's death left Emma in a difficult position. For much of her marriage, Emma had probably hoped that her own son, Edward, would be chosen to succeed his father in preference to his older half-brothers. She may have been the source of a rumour that his father had named him as heir. According to one source:

> When the royal wife of old King Aethelred was pregnant in her womb, all the men of the country took an oath that if a man child should come forth as the fruit of her labour, they would await in him their lord and king who would rule over the whole race of the English.[13]

Emma later proved herself to be a proficient propagandist and it is possible that she took steps to ensure that the succession to the throne fell to her own son, as her mother-in-law, Queen Aelfthryth, had done earlier. If this had been Emma's hope, however, she would have realised in 1016 that neither of her sons were in a position to claim the crown. Soon after Aethelred's death, Emma's children were taken, once again, to her family in Normandy, although Emma, perhaps unwilling to return to Normandy as a penniless exile, remained behind in England, placing her hopes in her stepson, Edmund.

Soon after Aethelred's death, the royal council in London elected Edmund as king.[14] Emma, seeing little other hope, probably agreed with this election although she must have been uncomfortably aware that Edmund, as a mature man, already had both a wife and sons of his own. He also does not appear to have been inclined to protect his stepmother personally, and left London soon after his election in order to raise an army. Cnut quickly besieged London and Emma must have felt let down by Edmund on hearing, in the autumn, that Edmund and Cnut had agreed to divide the kingdom between them, leaving London in the hands of Cnut. When news of this division reached London, the citizens bought peace with the new king, finally lifting the siege.[15] Emma's whereabouts in the winter of 1016 are not recorded but she was presumably quickly taken into Cnut's custody. Emma probably lost all hope when word arrived soon afterwards that Edmund had died, leaving Cnut as sole ruler of England.

Emma of Normandy was an excellent propagandist and provided her own version of the year following Aethelred's death. According to an account commissioned by her, after Cnut had won the crown he 'lacked nothing except a most noble wife; such a one he ordered to be sought everywhere for him, in order to obtain her hand lawfully, when she was found, and to make her the partner of his rule, when she was won'.[16] According to Emma's *Encomium*, Cnut searched across Europe to find such a bride and found her in a great queen who was living in Normandy.[17] He did not, in reality, have to look so far afield and, in a more accurate account, the *Anglo-Saxon Chronicle* records that 'before 1 August [1017] the king ordered the widow of the former king Aethelred, Richard's daughter, to be fetched to him as queen'.[18] Emma, as Cnut's prisoner, probably had very little say in her marriage to Cnut and it is likely that she would have seen it as the best offer that she was likely to get. As she herself later claimed, it is just possible that she also obtained a promise from the king that a son of their marriage could succeed in precedence to his sons by any other wife.[19] This would certainly have been a necessary provision for Emma as she cannot have failed to know, in 1017, that Cnut was already married.

When Cnut had been left behind at Gainsborough in 1013 to guard his father's ships he did not concern himself only with military preparations. It is likely that it was during this period that he first met Aelfgifu of Northampton, a young noblewoman from a prominent Midlands family.[20] Aelfgifu belonged to the family from which Aethelred's son Edmund had taken his wife and it is clear that there were political considerations in both kings drawing their wives from the family. However, Cnut's later conduct towards Aelfgifu suggests that there was a strong personal attachment between them and Aelfgifu bore Cnut two sons in quick succession. Aelfgifu is reported to have been the mistress of the Norwegian King Olaf before her marriage to Cnut and it is likely that her sympathies were wholly Scandinavian.[21] Her own father, Ealdorman Aelfhelm, had been murdered on Aethelred's orders and she would have had no love for either the English king or his Norman wife.

Aelfgifu's whereabouts in 1016 are not recorded and she may have remained on her family's estates in the Midlands with her children. She must have been jubilant when word reached her of Cnut's victory over Edmund and it is possible that she waited to be called to London to take up her position as Cnut's queen. If this was the case, she was to be disappointed and must have been horrified to hear the news that her husband had married Emma. Aelfgifu must have feared repudiation by Cnut and relegation to life in a nunnery, the fate of earlier abandoned queens. Aelfgifu, however, seems to have had a personal hold over Cnut that Emma could never have. Although her marriage had given Cnut some political advantage in England, there was probably an additional personal element in his choice of her. Conversely Cnut's marriage to Emma was wholly political. Through his marriage to the English queen he was probably hoping both to present himself as an English king and to neutralise any support that Emma's Norman family might give to her sons. It was common practice for conquering kings to marry into an existing royal family and Cnut's own father, Swein, had married the Queen of Sweden after deposing her son.[22] Throughout her marriage to Cnut, Emma was presented as an English queen, in spite of her foreign origins; hence she is always listed in sources by her English name, 'Aelfgifu'.

Emma was more than a decade older than Cnut and, in spite of the political nature of their marriage, she appears to have quickly gained influence over him. This influence was probably cemented by the births early in their marriage of a son, Harthacnut, and a daughter, Gunnhild. Cnut certainly appears to have treated Harthacnut as his heir, perhaps obeying his promise to Emma.[23] Emma was also crowned with Cnut in 1017 and appears to have enjoyed a higher status than she had done in Aethelred's reign, even early in her second marriage.[24] It has even been suggested that she can be seen as Cnut's co-ruler.[25] Certainly, attempts were made to emphasise Emma's position as an English queen, as seen for example in a letter from 1020 in which the Archbishop of York addressed the king and queen jointly.[26]

Whilst this improvement in her status must have been pleasing to Emma she must always have been acutely aware of Aelfgifu's position as a rival in England. She had probably expected Cnut to quietly repudiate Aelfgifu soon after their marriage and it must have come as a shock to her when the king showed no signs of doing so. Aelfgifu's whereabouts are not recorded for most of Cnut's reign but it is possible that she and Emma often came into contact with each other. It has been suggested that Aelfgifu was given a household at Bosham in Sussex and, certainly, it is recorded that a daughter of Cnut drowned there and was buried in the local church.[27] If such a daughter existed, she would have been Aelfgifu's rather than Emma's. For Aelfgifu to be lodged at Bosham would have seemed uncomfortably close to Emma's own base at Winchester, although Cnut may well have liked to keep both his wives within easy access of his court. However, as the sons of both women grew up, Cnut also appears to have realised the difficulties of keeping two rival wives and, in the late 1020s, he apparently began looking around for some way of making provision for Aelfgifu and her children.

As well as being King of England and Denmark, Cnut was King of Norway. In 1029 his regent in Norway drowned which left Cnut with an opportunity to advance Aelfgifu and her children.[28] In 1030, Cnut named his eldest son by Aelfgifu, Swein, King of Norway and dispatched the boy to Norway, along with his mother who was to act as regent.[29] This appointment must have pleased Aelfgifu and is a measure of Cnut's respect for his first wife and her abilities. However the move was probably less popular with Emma and it may be significant that around the same time her son, Harthacnut, was appointed King of Denmark by his father.[30] Denmark was Cnut's ancestral kingdom rather than one of his recent conquests and Emma may have felt a sense of satisfaction in the preferential treatment accorded to her own child.

Aelfgifu seems to have adopted her role as regent of Norway with gusto. She and Swein quickly took control of the country and set about trying to mould it into a Danish kingdom, as Cnut would have wanted. According to *Saint Olaf's Saga*, the pair promptly introduced Danish laws to Norway, such as that forbidding anyone to leave the country without their leave.[31] The king and queen also introduced a number of new taxes to Norway, insisting, for example, that every man over five years of age contribute towards equipping warships as well as taxes in food which were required by the new king and his mother.[32] Although these new laws were introduced in Swein's name, it was clear to everyone that it was his mother who was the real power in Norway. Even today, 'Aelfgifu's time' is remembered as a period of misery and repression.[33] Aelfgifu was probably only carrying out Cnut's commands but in the process she made both herself and the other Danes in Norway deeply unpopular, causing a wave of Norwegian nationalism to quickly sweep through the country.

This nationalism quickly took the form of a cult that began to grow up around the grave of King Olaf, the last native Norwegian king. Aelfgifu is reported to have been Olaf's mistress in her youth and it is possible that she knew better than most how this king was no saint. However, she also recognised the dangers of this cult to Danish rule in Norway and apparently took steps to try to dispel it. *Saint Olaf's Saga*, which recounts Aelfgifu's attempts to dispel the cult around Olaf is the only source in which this shadowy queen's character is fully developed and clearly shows her as something of a clever and determined woman. According to the saga, it was decided to disinter the body of King Olaf in order to see if it showed any signs of sanctity.[34] The body was duly found to be remarkably preserved and only Aelfgifu of those assembled seems to have showed any scepticism:

> Then Alfifa [Aelfgifu] said, 'Mighty little do bodies decompose when buried in sand. It would not be the case if he had lain in earth.' Then the bishop took a pair of shears and cut the king's hair and trimmed his whiskers. He had long whiskers as people in those days used to have.
>
> Then the bishop said to the king and Alfifa, 'Now the hair and the beard of the king are as they were when he died, but it had grown as much as you can see here cut off.'
>
> Then Alfifa replied, 'That hair would seem to me a holy relic only if fire does not burn it. We have often seen wholly preserved and undamaged the hair of persons who have lain in the ground longer than this man has.'
>
> Thereupon the bishop had fire put in the censer, blessed it, and put incense on it. Then he laid King Olaf's hair into the fire, and when all the incense was burned, the bishop took the hair out of the fire, and it was not burned. The bishop had the king and the other chieftains view it. Thereupon Alfifa bade them lay the hair into fire that had not been blessed. Then Einar Thambarskelfir bade her be silent and used hard language against her. So then, by the bishop's pronouncement, the consent of the king, and the judgment of all the people, King Olaf was declared a true saint.[35]

Clearly, Aelfgifu was a tenacious woman and unwilling to admit that she had been beaten. Beaten she was, however and, by 1035, both her and Swein's positions were untenable and the pair fled back to Denmark as failures.[36] This was, perhaps, the end of Aelfgifu's ambitions for her eldest son, Swein, who died soon after their expulsion from Norway, leaving her with only one surviving child, Harold, who was living in England.

Swein's death was not the only one to rock the royal family in 1035 and that same year Cnut himself died suddenly at Shaftesbury.[37] News of the death must have come as a shock to both of Cnut's wives, although it appears to have been Emma, perhaps present at Cnut's deathbed, who acted first. Emma settled in Winchester soon after the death and quickly took possession of Cnut's treasury, presumably hoping to hold it until her son, Harthacnut, could return from Denmark to claim it. It was at this point that Emma announced that Harthacnut had been named as Cnut's successor in England, although this was strongly disputed.

The news of Cnut's death would have taken longer to reach Aelfgifu in Denmark and she must have been equally shocked at the news. She was probably well aware of Emma's hopes that Harthacnut would succeed to the throne both Denmark and England and whilst Harthacnut was already established in Denmark, she may have quickly turned to look at England with hopes for the future of her second son, Harold. Certainly with Swein's death she had little to hold her in Denmark and by the end of the year, at the latest, Aelfgifu had returned to England and been reunited with her son, Harold. Harold Harefoot is a shadowy figure and it is likely that Aelfgifu was the driving force behind his actions following Cnut's death, just as Emma was behind the actions of her own sons.

It was certainly Harold who took the initiative and, soon after his father's death, he went to the Archbishop of Canterbury and demanded to be crowned King of England.[38] It seems likely that Aelfgifu would have been behind this direct attempt to pre-empt Emma but if this was the case, she was to be unsuccessful. The Archbishop, who perhaps had already been approached by Emma, refused to grant Harold the crown. Instead he placed the coronation regalia on the high altar, prohibiting anyone from touching it. This must have been a blow to Aelfgifu's hopes and both she and Emma had to resign themselves to the succession being decided by the council.

Emma and Aelfgifu may have been present at the royal council that was held at Oxford and their presence would have contributed to the already tense atmosphere in the kingdom. Both women had certainly been busy rallying their supporters in the months since Cnut's death and it appears to have been Aelfgifu who was the more successful. At the council it was decided that although Harthacnut was his father's heir, Harold as the only son of Cnut present in England was to rule England as regent until the return of his brother.[39] This situation would not have been judged satisfactory by either of Cnut's queens but, certainly, it was Aelfgifu who had the upper hand and, around that time, Harold was also able to deprive Emma of the royal treasury, further cementing his hold on the kingdom. Rather than bringing the rivalry of the two women to an end, however, the council at Oxford appears merely to have increased the tension between them.

Numerous Anglo-Saxon and later medieval chronicles refer to suggestions that neither Swein nor Harold were sons of Cnut. Florence of Worcester, for example, claims that Swein:

> Was said to be his son by Aelfgifu of Northampton, daughter of Ealdorman Aelfhelm and the most noble lady Wulfrun; but some asserted that he was not the son of the king and this Aelfgifu, but that this same Aelfgifu wished to have a son by the king, but could not, and therefore ordered to be brought to her the newly born infant of a certain priest, and made the king fully believe that she had just borne him a son.[40]

Florence of Worcester had also heard a similar story about the birth of Harold, whom he claimed to be a foundling and the child of a humble shoemaker rather than the king.[41] Stories such as these appear to have become common around the time of Cnut's death and, tellingly, a version exists in the *Encomium* of Queen Emma herself. In this account, Aelfgifu was a 'concubine' of Cnut, rather than his wife, and Harold, the son of a servant, was taken by Aelfgifu to pass off as her child by the king.[42] It seems likely that Emma was the source of the rumours both about Aelfgifu's concubinage and the rumours of her sons' births. This was probably a deliberate policy to damage the status of Harold in the eyes of the nobility of England, thus emphasising her own legitimate marriage to Cnut and the legitimacy of her son, Harthacnut.

If Emma resorted to dirty tricks in order to denigrate the son of her rival then she was not the only one. By August 1036, word had reached Gunnhild, Emma's daughter by Cnut who was living in a Germanic state, that Aelfgifu was working to ensure the succession of Harold.[43] Aelfgifu was apparently holding feasts and offering gifts to the nobles of the kingdom in order to bring them round to her point of view. This together with fact that Harthacnut had still not materialised in England appears to have strengthened Aelfgifu's cause in relation to her rival. Emma could spread rumours about Aelfgifu and Harold but without a son present in England, there was very little that she could do to advance her own cause.

By mid-1036, Emma herself appears to have become exasperated at Harthacnut's failure to arrive and claim the English crown; for the first time in twenty years, she once again looked towards her sons by Aethelred. According to Emma's own account, written several years after the disaster of 1036, it was Harold himself who summoned her two older sons to England, forging a letter to appear to be from their mother inviting them to claim the English crown.[44] However it seems unlikely that Harold and, for that matter, Aelfgifu would have risked summoning rivals to England in 1036. A more likely candidate is Emma herself, writing to her sons, pointing out to them: 'I wonder what plan you are adopting, since you are aware that the delay arising from your procrastination is becoming from day to day a support to the usurpers of your rule'.[45]

It is unlikely that Emma expected both sons to heed her summons. Both decided to come to their mother separately and Edward arrived safely with Emma in Winchester. Alfred, however, decided to come by a less direct route and his party was intercepted by Harold at Guildford. Simeon of Durham writes:

> [Alfred] Was carried heavily chained to the Isle of Ely; but, as soon as the ship reached the land, immediately his eyes were there most cruelly torn out, and then he was taken to the monastery and delivered to the custody of the monks.[46]

Alfred died soon after his blinding and Edward, hearing the news, fled quickly back to Normandy leaving his mother alone and without sons in England once again. Aelfgifu, who was so often behind the actions attributed to her sons, may have played a role in ordering the murder of Alfred and it would have given her some satisfaction to be behind the death of the son of the rival who had deprived her of her husband and her sons of their inheritance.

The death of Alfred and Harthacnut's continued failure to return to England marked the end of Emma's hopes for the English crown for one of her sons for some time and, in 1037, Harold was finally able to claim the crown in his own name. According to the *Anglo-Saxon Chronicle*, Emma was 'driven out without any mercy to face the raging winter beyond the sea to Bruges'.[47] Once again, Emma's propagandist would appear to have been behind this account but there is no doubt that in 1037 with Emma driven to Flanders as an exile, her future looked bleak indeed. Aelfgifu, now the only queen in England, must have been jubilant and apparently set about ruling England alongside her son, Harold Harefoot.

Emma of Normandy's prospects looked bleak in 1037, but she was not defeated and from Flanders she sent once again to Harthacnut, asking him to come and claim the English crown.[48] Harthacnut, perhaps angered at the way that his mother had been treated, finally arrived in Flanders with a fleet in early 1040. Emma and Harthacunt were still in Flanders when, on 17 March 1040, Harold Harefoot died suddenly in England having reigned as king for only three years.[49] Aelfgifu of Northampton disappears from the sources with the death of her only surviving son and it seems likely that she quickly fled, knowing that her rival would return to take her vengeance. Her fate is a mystery but she cannot have enjoyed a happy old age.

Emma, on the other hand, arrived in England in triumph as the mother of the new king and quickly took up a position as Harthacnut's closest advisor. Perhaps remembering her earlier vulnerability when none of her sons were present in England, she also persuaded Harthacnut to invite his half-brother, Edward, to return to England to share his brother's rule:

> Obeying his brother's command, he was conveyed to England, and the mother and both sons, having no disagreement between them, enjoy the ready amenities of the kingdom. Here there is loyalty among sharers of

the rule, here the bond of motherly and brotherly love is of strength indestructible.[50]

This was the point at which Emma's *Encomium* ends and it was the image of a victorious queen mother that she wanted to present to the world, particularly perhaps to her rival Aelfgifu of Northampton. Whilst she was the victor in the power struggle with Aelfgifu, this was not the end of her story, however. After ruling for only two years, Harthacnut also died, leaving the throne to his half-brother, Edward the Confessor. Emma must have been pleased that the succession had been secured for her last remaining son but she did not have the same good relationship with Edward that she had enjoyed with Harthacnut. In 1043, only a short time after Edward's coronation, Emma was forcibly deprived of her lands and treasures on the orders of the new king and retired from her place at court.[51]

For the rest of her life, Emma was always treated with the respect due to her as the king's mother, but she was denied any political role and she died, almost unnoticed, on 6 March 1052.[52] It was not for a quiet retirement that either Aelfgifu or Emma had fought following the death of Cnut and, in their old age, they may both have reflected on the futility of their struggle on behalf of their sons. Both women were determined to secure the lucrative role of queen mother for themselves and both, ultimately, suffered for their attempts. It is difficult to see either as entirely blameworthy, however, and Cnut, through his failure to regulate his unorthodox marital inclinations must ultimately bear much of the blame. It was only natural that both his wives would want to see their own son on the throne and clear that, without effective provision made for all his sons, his wives would compete. Both Emma of Normandy and Aelfgifu of Northampton are remembered as notorious for their political actions and the underhand methods that they both employed; for both, these actions were ultimately futile.

PART II

POST-CONQUEST QUEENS:

ARROGANCE, REBELLION & GREED

Post-Conquest Queens

If there is doubt about the recognition Anglo-Saxons gave to the role of queen, there is no such ambiguity regarding post-conquest society. The period between the eleventh century and the end of the fourteenth saw the emergence of queenship as a major political role and the period included some exceptionally powerful queens. The period is also remembered for some of the most notorious queens that England has ever known and, once again, it is the church chroniclers and other male writers who claim to provide evidence for their wicked behaviour. There is no doubt that conditions following the Norman conquest helped to cultivate powerful and political queens who were viewed with suspicion and often hostility by many of their male contemporaries.

The Norman conquest had a profound effect on the role of the queen in England. Previously, kings tended to look for their wives amongst their own nobility, selecting their spouses from the families of the powerful men at court. The Norman conquest saw a move away from this and introduced an international flavour to queenship that had only previously been seen with women such as Judith of France and Emma of Normandy. Right up until the mid-fifteenth century, the English crown retained continental possessions separate from their lands in England and this meant that their rule was never entirely centred on England. This interest in continental affairs was reflected in the policies of these kings, in the selection of their wives and the lives that these women were expected to lead.

Post-conquest kings' wives were generally selected as part of a deliberate policy to either protect or extend continental lands. Examples include Matilda of Boulogne who brought her rich county of Boulogne to King Stephen, and Eleanor of Aquitaine who could offer Henry II Aquitaine.[1] Isabella of Angouleme, the second wife of King John, also brought her husband the country of Angouleme, so strategically important that John was forced to act to acquire her lands so that they did not fall into the hands of a rival. Not all queens brought lands with them however: Eleanor of Provence brought her husband little in the way of material benefit. However through marrying Henry III did neutralise any political advantage that his rival, the King of France, had gained from marrying Eleanor's sister, ensuring support for English interests on the continent. Similarly, Eleanor of Castile and Isabella of France were selected as brides in an attempt to ensure the protection of Gascony, and Berengaria of Navarre, the wife of Richard I, was chosen to win the support of her brother for her husband's rule in the province.[2]

Post-conquest queens were therefore chosen from across Europe rather than from the English nobility due to the advantage it gave their husbands in continental affairs. Just how marked a change this was is clear from the fact that, of all the queens who reigned between the Norman conquest and the late fourteenth century, only one was of English birth. John's first wife, Isabella of Gloucester was an English heiress and selected for her wealth rather than any political advantage she might bring.[3] However, she is certainly an exception and her marriage occurred whilst John was still a younger son with little chance of a throne. Almost as soon as John had secured the crown for himself in 1199, he began looking around for another wife and, soon after her husband's coronation, Isabella of Gloucester had been divorced in favour of the more politically glamorous Isabella of Angouleme.[4] The foreign nature of most queens in this period did however also have an effect on their reputations; Eleanor of Provence for example was often unfairly criticised and censured for her non-English birth.

A change in how queens were selected was not the only change that the Norman conquest brought to the office of queenship. Another consequence of the new interest in continental affairs was that queens were expected to play a more active political role in representing the royal family whilst the king was in another part of his empire. When William the Conqueror left Normandy for his invasion of England, his wife Matilda of Flanders remained as co-regent of Normandy with Roger of Montgomery.[5] Matilda obviously did a good job and, in 1069, she was sent back to Normandy from England. Orderic Vitalis described how 'King William sent his beloved wife Matilda back to Normandy so that she might give up her time to religious devotions in peace, away from the English tumults and together with the boy Robert could keep the Duchy secure'.[6] It seems probable that Matilda's return to Normandy was due more to the need for a member of the ducal family to keep an eye on William's affairs there than to Matilda's desire for religious devotions and, throughout her time as Duchess of Normandy and Queen of England, she spent time as regent in both countries.

Matilda of Flander's daughter-in-law, Matilda of Scotland, was also expected to play the role of regent in England during the frequent absences of her husband, Henry I. She had, in fact, been ruling England capably for two years as regent when she died in 1118 and her rule was probably used as a model of what a queen could be by her daughter, the Empress Matilda.[7] Eleanor of Aquitaine, the wife of Henry II, was also frequently left as regent in England whilst Henry visited his continental domains and she took on the role capably following the accession of her son, Richard I. It is clear, therefore, that many post-conquest queens were actively encouraged to take on political roles whilst their husbands were absent and it was only with the decline of the continental empire that this aspect of queenship declined. Even after the disasters of John's reign, however, and the loss of most of the continental possessions, queens were still called upon to act as regents from time to time when their husbands were abroad. For example, Eleanor of Provence acted as regent whilst her husband, Henry III, was campaigning in Gascony. Allowing the queen to rule as regent in her husband's absence greatly increased the responsibility given to the king's wife compared to that of the Anglo-Saxon period. However, in many respects the role was still essentially the same and queens were expected to behave in similar ways to their Anglo-Saxon predecessors.

William I presented himself as an English king and heir to Edward the Confessor following his victory at Hastings. Accordingly his wife,

Matilda of Flanders, was presented as an English queen and heir to the Confessor's wife, Edith Godwine. Matilda would have based many of her ideas of queenship on her immediate predecessors in England and she would have understood, like her predecessors, what made a good or notorious queen.

In spite of their increased political role, post-conquest queens were still expected, first and foremost, to produce an heir. Failure to produce a son could have disastrous consequences for a queen in a still heavily male-dominated society. It seems unlikely that the childless Isabella of Gloucester, for example, would have been divorced if she had borne King John a son and heir. Eleanor of Provence was also under pressure to produce an heir after several years of barren marriage and there were rumours across England that she was infertile. This must have been discomfiting for the young queen who was still only in her late teens and it must have been with relief that she finally provided Henry III with a son. Queens in the post-conquest period would have known, like Anglo-Saxon queens such as Edith Godwine, that childlessness had the power to marginalise a queen and even strip them of that role. It is unlikely that Berengaria of Navarre, queen of Richard I, for example, would have lived a life of such great obscurity had she been mother to her husband's heir. The importance of Matilda of Scotland was diminished posthumously with the death of her only son two years after her own death. Queens were always expected to be mothers; to produce healthy sons was a prerequisite for being a good queen. In the eyes of their contemporaries, particularly the male chroniclers, it was always the queen's fault if no heir was born and it was always the queen, never the king, who was criticised for that failure.

Fertility was, of course, not the only requirement of a good queen. As in the pre-conquest era, post-conquest queens were expected to be god-fearing and the most famous 'good' queens of the period are remembered as deeply pious. There were no saintly queens in the post-conquest period but, certainly, Matilda of Scotland was venerated to a near-saintly level for centuries after her death. She is also described in the sources in similar terms to those used for her saintly predecessors, St Aelfgifu and St Wulfthryth. Whilst St Wulfthryth retired from the world to avoid the repetition of the sexual act following the birth of her daughter, Matilda of Scotland appears to have found an equally successful deterrent. According to William of Malmesbury, 'the bearing of two children, one of either sex, left her content, and for the future she ceased either to have offspring or desire them, satisfied, when the king was busy elsewhere, to bid the court goodbye herself, and spent many years at Westminster'.[8] This implies that Matilda also chose to shun sexual relations with her husband in favour of a religious life. However, there were rumours that the real reason behind the couple's lack of further children after the birth of their heir was that Henry I was disgusted by his wife's kisses on the sores of lepers as part of her religious devotions and shunned her bed for fear of catching some contagion.[9] Regardless of the underlying reality, Matilda of Scotland is remembered as a good queen in a similar way to her Anglo-Saxon predecessors, that is for her religious devotions. Piety was always a very important aspect of the role of queen and every female monarch in the period between the Norman conquest and the end of the fourteenth century is remembered as a patron of the Church.

Clearly, therefore, much of what had been expected of an Anglo-Saxon queen was still the case for the post-conquest period and any who failed to live up to this model ran the risk of being labelled as a bad or notorious queen. Queens were still not expected to have political ambitions of their own and any political activity carried out by her was to be for the benefit of a male family member rather than herself. This unwritten rule caused trouble for a number of post-conquest queens who, perhaps bolstered by the greater political role they were offered, sought to extend their power even further. The Empress Matilda is a prime example of this. As a Queen Regnant she was in the unfortunate position of trying to assert her own rights without a male relative to hide behind. She can be contrasted effectively with her contemporary, Matilda of Boulogne, who, whilst also militarily and politically active, escaped much of the reprehension directed at the Empress.[10] The difference lies in the fact that Matilda of Boulogne always acted in the name of her husband and son whilst the Empress was forced, by necessity, to act for herself. As a consequence, the Empress Matilda is remembered as greedy and arrogant whilst Matilda of Boulogne is a selfless individual who fought on behalf of her family. To their contemporaries, a woman's place was as a quiet supporter of her male kin and Empress Matilda, by virtue of her position as heir to the throne could never achieve this.

By failing to live up to the ideals of queenship, however unattainable, Empress Matilda's reputation paid the price and she will be forever notorious. To modern eyes however she appears courageous in fighting for her rights when the odds were heavily stacked against her.

As with the Anglo-Saxon period, the post-conquest period produced a number of notorious queens and this was due to their perceived failure to live up to contemporary, male ideals of queenship. Empress Matilda, Eleanor of Aquitaine, Isabella of Angouleme, Eleanor of Provence, Eleanor of Castile and Isabella of France are all remembered as selfish and greedy women, often eager for power at the expense of their husbands. The period certainly produced the first queens to rebel against their husbands and it saw the murder of one king at the hands of his wife. However both Eleanor of Aquitaine and Isabella of France, who are known to have rebelled against their husbands, went through difficult times and their actions now seem understandable, even if they were not to the chroniclers. Eleanor of Aquitaine had been the greatest heiress in Europe and by the time of her rebellion she had endured over a decade of infidelity and indifference from her husband, Henry II. Isabella of France was unfortunate enough to be married as a child to the homosexual Edward II who also flaunted his male lovers at her expense during their marriage. Is it therefore surprising that Eleanor, a great heiress in her own right, and Isabella, the daughter of the most powerful ruler in Europe, were not content to simply ignore this behaviour? It is certainly true that many queens of the period would not have taken this action but both had their reasons which would have been socially acceptable if they had been men. Most of the notorious queens in the eleventh to fourteenth centuries were also very political and it was this political activity that terrified their contemporaries and caused them to attack their reputations. For all the changes that the conquest brought to queenship, the expected role of women still remained woefully stagnant.

The Empress Matilda, Eleanor of Aquitaine, Isabella of Angouleme, Eleanor of Provence, Eleanor of Castile and Isabella of France were famous and powerful women in their own lifetimes. Although the recorded stories of their lives vary, they are mostly remembered for their political activities. For their contemporaries, women were not expected to seek any political role for themselves and so this was unacceptable. The conquest changed the role of queen because the empires of the Norman and Angevin kings required trustworthy regents. These were often queens who were consequently expected to take on a prominent political role. Society does not appear to have accepted this change and the political queens of the period will always be remembered as notorious. The period between the Norman conquest and the end of the fourteenth century saw some of the most notorious queens that England has ever produced and this is a direct reflection of the fact that they were also amongst the most powerful.

Arrogance & Pride

Empress Matilda

The Empress Matilda could have been the first ruling queen of England. This was certainly the cause to which she devoted her life. Apart from a few brief months of power, she was ultimately doomed to failure. By claiming the crown of England, Matilda thrust herself into a man's world and she quickly discovered that very different standards were expected of women. Although Matilda enjoyed considerable success in her quest to win the crown of England, ultimately it was the way that her contemporaries perceived her character that led to disappointment. Matilda is remembered as a hard, proud and unwomanly queen and her 'reign' was used for over four hundred years as evidence for how women were not fit to rule. Crucially her contemporaries failed to understand that in seeking to claim the crown Matilda was trying to assert her rule because she was queen regnant, not simply a queen, and that such a role demanded the characteristics of a king. To be hard, proud and masculine were characteristics admired in a king but for Matilda as a woman they brought only criticism. Clearly, the characteristics deemed virtuous in a king could easily make a woman notorious, as Matilda found to her cost.

The Empress Matilda was forced by circumstances to enter a man's world, but to begin with her life followed the pattern of a normal medieval princess. Matilda was born on 7 February 1102, the eldest child of Henry I and his wife, Matilda of Scotland.[1] For a brief time in her infancy, therefore, she was actually heiress to England, although this changed the following year with the birth of a brother, William. No evidence survives of Matilda's early childhood. She may have been raised by her mother and it is likely that Matilda of Scotland's influence remained with her for the rest of her life. Many considered Henry's marriage to the Scottish princess to have legitimised his kingship in England and, as the great-great niece of Edward the Confessor, Matilda of Scotland brought another element of royalty to the status of her daughter. She would also have provided a powerful role model to the young Matilda since she frequently ruled England as regent during Henry's absences. Matilda of Scotland would also have been an important example to her daughter of how a woman might be able to hold and transfer a claim to the throne.

The young Matilda emerges suddenly from obscurity at the age of seven in 1109. In that year, the Germanic Emperor, Henry V, sent envoys to England to ask for the hand in marriage of Henry I's only daughter, Matilda.[2] This was a flattering offer and one that Matilda's father leapt at, lavishing a rich dowry and train on his young daughter to prepare her for the marriage. The marriage negotiations moved quickly and early in 1110 Matilda left England accompanied by an Imperial escort.[3] At the age of eight, Matilda must have been apprehensive about leaving home to marry a man old enough to be her father. She would have known that she was unlikely ever to return to her home and she never saw her mother again.

If Matilda was nervous about meeting her husband and adapting to life in the Germanic states, she was to prove more fortunate than many other medieval princesses. The Emperor, Henry V, was notorious across Europe for his part in the deposition and murder of his father. However, he proved himself to be a kind and loving husband to his little wife, apparently going through a wedding ceremony with Matilda upon her arrival in 1110, before sending her to be raised in a way fitting for a Germanic empress.[4] Matilda must have been relieved to find her husband personable and she quickly adapted to Germanic ways. In 1114, when she was finally judged old enough for a full marriage, Henry and Matilda enjoyed a grand second wedding.[5] The couple quickly became close and in 1116 they travelled to Rome together. Matilda remained in Italy after her husband left, ruling the kingdom as regent for two years and gaining her first experience of rulership.[6] Matilda probably grieved for her husband when he died in May 1125.[7] It is possible that the couple, who had appeared so mismatched at the start of their union, had grown to love each other; Matilda was popular with the Germanic peoples and retained a reputation for goodness for many years after she had left the empire.[8]

In 1125, Matilda was twenty-three years old and a childless widow. She had lived in the German Empire for most of her life and she must have been tempted to remain there, perhaps accepting one of the numerous offers of marriage that she received following her husband's death.[9] However circumstances conspired against her and soon after Henry V's death, Matilda's father sent an escort to bring her to Normandy. Her only brother, William, had drowned five years earlier and Henry I's second marriage had proved barren, leaving Matilda, as Henry's only legitimate child, of immeasurable value to him.

William of Malmesbury relates how Matilda was reluctant to leave the Germanic states when summoned and it is possible that she extracted a promise from Henry that she would be recognised as his heir if she agreed to his demands.[10] Henry quickly set about establishing her as his heir, and, at Christmas 1127, everyone present at court was induced to swear allegiance to Matilda as heir to the throne.[11] This oath was repeated at Northampton in 1131 with all the leading nobles of England agreeing to accept Matilda's claim.[12] Henry also set about arranging a second marriage for Matilda in the hope that she would provide him with grandsons to continue his line. Matilda must have realised that she would be required to marry again and she was given no more say in her second marriage than in her first.

Henry opened marriage negotiations for Matilda in early 1127 with the thirteen year-old son of the Count of Anjou, Geoffrey.[13] Matilda was furious when she heard the news of the match her father had arranged for her. This is hardly surprising for, at twenty-five, Matilda was a mature woman, already widowed, and had been the wife of an emperor. She used her title of Empress until the end of her life and it was something of which she was justifiably proud. Matilda probably felt humiliated by the news that not only was she to marry a child, but the son of a mere count. The events surrounding Matilda's second marriage give us the first hint of her fiery character. According to reports, she argued and fought against her father when she was informed, finally being locked in her room by her father until she gave in to his demands.[14] This must have been deeply humiliating for Matilda, who took out her inevitable resentment on her young husband rather than her more intimidating father.

In June 1128 Matilda was forced to travel with her father to Normandy where she was married to Geoffrey. The first meeting between the couple cannot have been easy, and Matilda, probably still seething with resentment, made no effort with her young husband. She apparently disdained her husband for his youth and inferior rank; Geoffrey himself found her proud and frosty.[15] He may also have been irked by her refusal, to the end of her life, to use the title of Countess of Anjou, instead favouring the title of her first husband.[16] Given the circumstances in which Matilda's consent for this marriage was obtained, Matilda's behaviour is hardly surprising and Geoffrey was an entirely unsuitable husband for her. It was probably little surprise to anyone when the couple spent a difficult year together in Anjou following their marriage and, in June 1129, Matilda returned to her father in Normandy. It seems likely that after a year of childless and stormy marriage, both were hoping for a divorce and Matilda must have entreated her father to help end her unendurable marriage.

Henry, who had forced the marriage upon his daughter in the first place, was at a loss as to what to do with his determined daughter and allowed her to stay with him for two years. No moves seem to have been made towards a divorce and by 1131, both Henry and Geoffrey had decided that action was necessary. Henry of Huntingdon writes:

> In the summer, Henry returned to England, bringing his daughter with him. There was a great assembly at Northampton at the Nativity of St Mary. All the leading men of England gathered there, and it was decided that his daughter should be restored to her husband, the Count of Anjou, who was asking for her. After this, the king's daughter was sent to her husband, and was received with the pomp that befitted such a great heroine.[17]

By 1131, Geoffrey was older and more mature and he must have reasoned that marriage with the greatest heiress in Europe was worth having to put up with a haughty wife. Matilda may also have reasoned that she was unlikely to be provided with any husband other than Geoffrey and, approaching thirty, she was concerned at her lack of an heir. Certainly, both Geoffrey and Matilda seem to have been determined to try to make their marriage work and on 5 March 1133, Matilda gave birth to her first child, a healthy son whom she named Henry, after her father.[18] Matilda wept throughout her son's christening and she must have felt exonerated from the stigma of childlessness. A second son, Geoffrey, was born in 1134 and two years later Matilda bore a third son, William.[19] Matilda and Geoffrey seem to have felt that, with William's birth, their family was complete and they ceased to live together, probably to both their relief.

If Matilda was pleased with the birth of her sons, her father, King Henry, was overjoyed and Matilda with her eldest two sons spent much time with him during the last years of his life.[20] However the relationship between Matilda and her father does not appear to have mellowed and their relationship remained tempestuous. Henry of Huntingdon, for one, even suggests that Matilda's behaviour was partly responsible for Henry's sudden death on 1 December 1135:

> In the thirty-fifth year, King Henry stayed on in Normandy. Several times he planned to return to England, but he did not do so, being detained by his daughter on account of various disputes, which arose on a number of issues, between the king and the Count of Anjou, due to the machinations of none other than the king's daughter. The king was provoked by these irritations to anger and bitter ill-feeling, which was said by some to have been the origin of the chill in his bowels and later the cause of his death.[21]

The charge that Matilda contributed to her father's death is unjustified. Matilda, as Henry's heir, but Geoffrey's wife, was in a difficult position and would have been expected to obey both men – an impossible task when they were in conflict. In leaving her father, Matilda was criticised when he died but, if she had stayed with her father, she would almost certainly have been accused of disobeying her husband. Despite the criticism of the chroniclers, Henry does not appear to have blamed Matilda and, as he lay dying, he confirmed to those present that he wished his daughter to succeed him.[22]

England had never had a female ruler before Matilda and Henry, aware of the difficulties that she would face, had tried to prepare the way for Matilda's accession through requiring oaths in her favour from his court. One of the most prominent of the oath takers was Henry's nephew, Stephen of Blois, who was the son of his sister Adela. In spite of his oaths in support of Matilda, Stephen appears to have had his eye on the English throne for some time and, as soon as word reached him of his uncle's death, he hastened to England and had himself crowned king.[23] News of Stephen's actions caught Matilda by surprise and Stephen may have been the last person Matilda suspected of betraying her. Stephen appears to have been an affable man, with one chronicler praising him as 'rich and at the same time unassuming, generous, courteous; moreover, in all the conflicts of war or in any siege of his enemies, bold and brave, judicious and patient'.[24] Stephen and Matilda may have been closer than usual for cousins and a legend exists that Matilda's eldest son, Henry, was the product of an adulterous affair between them.[25] If so Stephen's betrayal would have been doubly hard for Matilda to accept. However, once again, it would seem that this story was an invention designed to blacken Matilda's name rather than represent the truth. Certainly, Geoffrey never seems to have doubted that Henry was his child and Matilda later displayed a savagery towards Stephen that belied any proximity between them. Stephen's betrayal must have deeply angered Matilda, but there was little she could do. At the time of her father's death she was expecting her third son and unable to return to England to personally claim the crown. All she could do in 1135 was occupy a small number of castles in Normandy and allow Stephen to consolidate his position almost unopposed.

In spite of Stephen's actions, Matilda was not prepared to simply return to Anjou and forget her grand inheritance. It was for England and Normandy that she had consented to leave her comfortable life in the Germanic states and she was not prepared to relinquish her royal prerogative. She was, however, forced to bide her time whilst Stephen enjoyed an initial surge of popularity in England. By 1138 certain English lords had tired of Stephen's rule and once again began looking to Matilda. In that year her illegitimate half-brother, Robert, Earl of Gloucester came to her in Normandy and offered his help in securing the English crown.[26] Earl Robert was one of the most powerful lords in England and Matilda was eager to receive his help, sailing with her brother to England in October 1139.[27] Matilda went directly to Arundel Castle, which was being held by her stepmother, Queen Adeliza. There she was besieged by Stephen who eventually however was true to his affable and often foolish nature. He was persuaded to allow Matilda to leave and travel to her brother's supporters at Bristol.[28] Matilda quickly made the West Country her base, receiving homage there as queen and making laws and minting coins.[29] She would always have been painfully aware, however, that she was not the only person claiming to rule England.

Matilda's return to England sparked a civil war that would last for the next fifteen years. Although Matilda never led an army, she was probably intimately involved in planning her campaign. It seems likely that Matilda hoped for a swift campaign and, according to John of Worcester, she was 'ecstatic' in early 1141 when she heard that Stephen had been captured by her supporters at Lincoln.[30] Stephen was brought to Matilda at Bristol and she must have felt that the crown was finally within her grasp.[31] Certainly, many of Stephen's supporters made their peace with the Empress and Stephen's own brother, the Bishop of Winchester, became an important supporter. The Bishop of Winchester was also the papal legate in England and his support was essential in establishing Matilda's rule in England. She travelled to see him at Winchester soon after Stephen's capture and the pair made a pact. According to the *Gesta Stephani*:

> When they had jointly made a pact of peace and concord he [Winchester] came to meet her in cordial fashion and admitted her into the city of Winchester, and after handing over to her disposal the king's castle and the royal crown, which she had always eagerly desired, and the treasure the king had left there, though it was very scanty, he bade the people, at a public meeting in the market-place of the town, salute her as their lady and their queen.[32]

On that day in Winchester, Matilda was accepted as England's first reigning queen. This was her greatest moment of triumph. However it is also at this time that many sources begin to turn overtly hostile towards Matilda and this sudden unpopularity is often attributed to her conduct as queen.

The *Gesta Stephani* describes how following her accession Matilda quickly showed herself to be capricious and headstrong.[33] Stephen's wife, Matilda of Boulogne, came to Matilda personally and begged for the release of her husband in order that he could live quietly in retirement with her.[34] Instead of heeding the woman's pleas, Matilda abused her in 'harsh and insulting language', causing Stephen's wife to take up arms on her husband's behalf.[35] Regardless of any promises he made to her, it is to be expected that Matilda would not have willingly released Stephen, a known oath-breaker, from captivity. There is no doubt that this source, which is a life of King Stephen, was deeply biased. However, this and other charges of arrogance may have thwarted her attempts to fully establish herself in 1141. In the sources Matilda ungraciously received those lords who had supported Stephen, even though they came offering their allegiance and this may well have caused these men to turn once again to Stephen.[36] Even more damningly, she apparently began to behave in a proud and disdainful manner towards even her own most loyal supporters. In the *Gesta Stephani* she insisted on remaining seated even when her greatest supporters King David of Scotland, Robert of Gloucester or the Bishop of Winchester entered, requesting them to kneel in her presence.[37] Furthermore she:

> Repeatedly sent them away contumely, rebuffing them by an arrogant answer and refusing to hearken to their words; and by this time she no longer relied on their advice, as she should have, and had promised them, but arranged everything as she herself thought fit and according to an arbitrary will.[38]

As a reigning queen, Matilda was in a difficult position. It was natural for the monarch to receive supporters on bent knee while remaining seated, and to expect to rule themselves rather than be ruled. It is certainly hard to imagine Matilda's grandfather, William the Conqueror, for example, receiving criticism for similar behaviour and a kingly manner in male rulers was praised. However, as a woman, any attempt by Matilda to behave in the manner of a ruler was seen as both unwomanly and insufferably arrogant. Matilda's understandable attempts assert her authority as a monarch therefore damned her queenship in the eyes of her contemporaries It was accusations of arrogance that led to the ultimate loss of all she had won in England.

Although she had been recognised as ruler in England in 1141, Matilda still needed to be crowned to ensure her position. She therefore travelled to London soon after her meeting with the Bishop of Winchester, to prepare for her coronation and consequent formal recognition as queen. London had been loyal to Stephen throughout the early years of the civil war and Matilda must have realised that she faced a struggle to win the Londoners' support. However most sources claim that instead of approaching the situation in a conciliatory manner Matilda stormed into the city and alienated the population almost immediately. For example in the *Gesta Stephani*, Matilda arrived in London with an army, but was welcomed by the Londoners, anxious to create good relations with their new queen.[39] Matilda was in no mood to be sympathetic to the supporters of her enemy and demanded large amounts of money from the city. When the Londoners aswered that they could not pay, Matilda acted in the following way:

> With a grim look, her forehead wrinkled into a frown, every trace of a woman's gentleness removed from her face, she blazed into unbearable fury, saying that many times the people of London had made a very large contribution to the king, that they had lavished their wealth on strengthening him and weakening her.[40]

Matilda was justified in pointing out that the Londoners had spent all their funds for the sake of a usurper. Kings were expected to display fortitude and Stephen for example was often criticised for being too soft on his enemies. Matilda, however, could never be a king in the eyes of her contemporaries and to the churchmen who recorded history she was dangerously unwomanly. The Londoners were probably also seeking any excuse to abandon their new queen and Matilda's reply to them was not the most tactful. Her behaviour certainly alienated the Londoners and the city's leaders instead joined with Stephen's wife, who was busy raising an army in Kent.[41] Matilda does not appear to have noticed the increasing ill feeling towards her in London and continued making the arrangements for her coronation. Her likely opinion was that she was acting exactly as a ruler should. Nevertheless this behaviour in a queen was unacceptable in a male-dominated society.

Matilda's relationship with the Londoners became apparent one day as she was sitting down to have dinner at her base outside the city walls.[42] According to the *Gesta Stephani*,suddenly:

> The whole city, with the bells ringing everywhere as the signal for battle, flew to arms, and all, with the common purpose of making a most savage attack on the Countess [Matilda] and her men, unbarred the gates and came out in a body, like thronging swarms from beehives.[43]

Matilda was apparently caught completely unawares by this dramatic assault on her camp and was forced to flee the city, leaving her belongings to be plundered.[44] Matilda's expulsion from London signalled the end of her hopes of a coronation and soon after she had gone Stephen's queen took possession of the city for the king. In retaliation, Matilda ordered Stephen to be placed in chains in his dungeon.[45]

Although Matilda had suffered a setback at the hands of the Londoners, Stephen was her prisoner and she could still lay a claim to the title of 'Lady of the English'. She must have been angered to hear that soon after the fall of London, the Bishop of Winchester also abandoned her cause. Matilda and her supporters moved quickly to Winchester and besieged the bishop in his castle.[46] This proved to be the greatest mistake of Matilda's brief reign. Hearing of the bishop's situation, Stephen's wife mustered a force of Londoners and rushed to attack the besiegers.[47] Matilda was able to flee but her half-brother, and most important supporter, Robert of Gloucester, was captured by Stephen's queen.[48] For all the accusations of arrogance against Matilda, she recognised the fact that she relied on her brother and he was ransomed for Stephen in November 1141, bringing Matilda's reign to an end.[49]

In spite of Stephen's release and re-establishment as king, Matilda did not end her campaign to win the English throne and she returned to the West Country to gather her forces, still determined to assert her authority as queen. Stephen was equally determined to capture his rival. In September 1142 Matilda found herself besieged in Oxford Castle.[50] Matilda had no intention of surrendering to her cousin and it was during the siege that she showed something of her courage and determination. A number of sources state how Matilda decided to make her escape one snowy December night. Dressed in white as camou-flage against the snow, Matilda and three knights left the castle, sneaking through the ranks of the besiegers.[51] This journey must have been an ordeal for the whole group and they walked six miles through the snow to Wallingford, crossing the frozen River Thames on foot.

Matilda must have been relieved to return to the relative safety of her own territory in the West Country and she would have been cheered by the arrival soon after her escape from Oxford of her eldest son, Henry.[52]. Henry was still too young to play an active role in the campaign but as Matilda's heir his presence must have boosted morale amongst Matilda's supporters. By the late 1140s, Henry was almost an adult and Matilda appears to have decided that it was time to pass her claim on to the next generation. In 1148, she left England for the last time and sailed to Normandy, where she would remain for the rest of her life. She prob-ably followed the course of Henry's wars in England closely and must have felt triumphant when, on 6 November 1153, Henry was finally recognised as heir to the throne by Stephen.[53] She must also have felt that her activities in England were vindicated when on the death of Stephen just under a year later Henry was proclaimed King of England. Remembering her own problematic relationship with England how-ever, Matilda acted wisely and did not attend Henry's coronation in England.

Matilda lived out the rest of her life in Rouen, effectively ruling Normandy as an unofficial regent for her son.[54] She remained a strong influence over her son until her death and she must have felt proud of all she had done to secure the throne of England for him. We can speculate that Matilda privately regretted that she had been unable to secure her own coronation. According to one chronicler, 'she was swollen with insufferable pride by her success in war, and alienated the affections of nearly everyone'.[55] Perhaps in her old age she came to regret the way she behaved when the crown was within her grasp but realistically it is doubtful that she could have acted in any other way. The facts of Matilda's life proved clearly that a woman could not be both a queen regnant and enjoy a spotless reputation. Matilda found herself in a unique position as a female claimant to the throne and she discovered, to her cost, that women were simply not expected to behave in the same way as men.

Matilda died on 10 September 1167 at the venerable age of sixty-five. Her attempts to fulfill what was considered a man's role wrecked her reputation and she remains notorious today. For four hundred years after her death her story was held up to demonstrate the dangers of female rule and even today she is portrayed as an unnatural and unwomanly figure. The actions of Empress Matilda have been damned through allegations of arrogance and pride. In the twelfth century, England was simply not ready for a reigning queen and, in the end, the best Matilda could do was keep the voice of legitimacy alive long enough for her son to grow into a man and claim the throne. As a queen regnant, Matilda was unable to rule through a male relative, at least nominally, and was therefore held up as an oddity and an unnatural woman. This is a view that still persists and the her name will always bear this notoriety. This can also be seen with the reputation of Matilda's daughter-in-law and contemporary, the famous Eleanor of Aquitaine.

Adultery & Rebellion

Eleanor of Aquitaine

Eleanor of Aquitaine was the most famous woman of her generation. No other medieval woman has commanded such enduring interest and numerous biographies have been written about her. Certainly, her fame exceeded even that of her mother-in-law, Empress Matilda, and Eleanor became a legend in her own lifetime. Like Matilda, Eleanor's fame was perhaps not entirely welcome and even to this day she retains a slightly unsavoury reputation. In her youth, Eleanor was portrayed as a selfish and domineering woman, who would become an adulteress, then a rebellious and disloyal wife and finally simply a woman who did not know her place and would not let go of the empire she had ruled for nearly fifty years. Eleanor's long and active life defied attempts to classify her, so to the conservative chroniclers she was someone to be feared. Eleanor was a woman living in a man's world and unlike many other queens of England, she excelled in it, to the chagrin of many of her contemporaries.

Much of Eleanor of Aquitaine's notoriety comes from her marriages and relationships with husbands and children. It is probable that much of her behaviour was a result of her unorthodox upbringing. Eleanor's childhood would have been dominated by her grandfather, Duke William IX of Aquitaine. A flamboyant figure, he overshadowed her father, William X. William IX was notorious across Europe for his abduction of the beautiful Viscountess of Chatelerault, who appears to have been more than willing to accept the position of the Duke's official mistress, driving his wife to seek refuge in a nunnery. Despite the protests of the duchess, William's relationship with his Viscountess was lasting and after several years his mistress was able to persuade him to marry his son to her daughter.[1] Eleanor's mother, Aenor, is a shadowy figure and was probably very young at the time of her marriage. Nonetheless, she bore William three children; Eleanor in 1122, followed by Petronilla and William Aigret. In 1130 when Eleanor was eight, both her mother and her brother died, leaving Eleanor as her father's heir.[2] It is unlikely that William X intended to be succeeded by his daughter. In 1136 he became engaged to Emma of Limoges but before the wedding could occur, she was kidnapped and forced to marry her abductor, William of Angouleme – yet another example of an unconventional marital arrangement in Eleanor's childhood.[3] In 1137, William X, who had still not remarried, died suddenly of food poisoning.[4]

As he lay dying, William confirmed Eleanor as his heir and entrusted her guardianship to his overlord, Louis VI of France. Louis VI immediately seized the opportunity presented by William X's death and, on 18 June 1137, his sixteen year-old son, Louis, set out with a large escort for Aquitaine in order to marry Eleanor.[5] Young Louis had been born as a second son and was raised by the Church. This made him deeply religious and somewhat unsuited to the role of heir to the French throne, which was presented to him on his brother's death.[6] Throughout her lifetime, Eleanor showed an interest in romance and it is likely that she was expecting a warrior in the same vein as her father and grandfather. Louis proved to be a constant disappointment for her. He arrived in Aquitaine in July and married Eleanor at Bordeaux on 25 July 1137. The new Duke and Duchess of Aquitaine were crowned there before moving onto the ducal capital of Poitiers.[7] Eleanor was as tall as Louis and attractive, with red or auburn hair.[8] Louis appears to have been overawed by his wife throughout their marriage and from the outset Eleanor was the dominant partner.

Whilst Louis and Eleanor were still becoming acquainted, word arrived at Poitiers that Louis VI of France had died, leaving his kingdom to his son, Louis VII. This must have been a shock to the young couple. For Eleanor, the news meant that she would have to leave her homeland for the first time in her life. The young king and queen immediately set out from Aquitaine for Paris in order to claim their crown. It is likely that Eleanor was as disappointed in Paris as she was in her husband and they found the city palace in a state of disrepair.[9] Eleanor immediately began remodelling the palace, probably in the style of the more opulent palaces she had known in Aquitaine.[10] She was crowned queen at Christmas 1137 but had little role in government, appearing only rarely in charters during Louis' reign, something that must have been another disappointment for her.

Despite her lack of a defined political role, Eleanor had a great deal of influence over Louis. Eleanor's grandmother had been the heiress to Toulouse, but the territory had been usurped by a kinsman. Eleanor maintained her claim to Toulouse throughout her lifetime and, in 1141, persuaded Louis to invade Toulouse on her behalf.[11] It is possible that she was trying to mould her unpromising husband into a warrior but if so her encouragement failed. The campaign proved to be a disaster for Louis and it is likely that Eleanor again felt a deep disappointment in her husband.

Eleanor's influence over Louis did not end with the Toulouse disaster and in 1143 Louis was again embroiled in a war at Eleanor's behest. In 1142, Eleanor's sister Petronilla fell in love with the nobleman, Raoul de Vermandois, and Louis gave his permission to the match despite the fact that Raoul already had a wife.[12] Petronilla and Raoul were duly married and Raoul's discarded wife was sent back to her uncle, the Count of Champagne. It is likely that Eleanor, who is known to have appreciated the ideals of courtly romance, was pleased that her sister had married for love and she proved a loyal supporter of the couple. However the marriage did not please everyone and the Count of Champagne immediately appealed to the Pope demanding that his niece be reinstated as Raoul's wife. The Pope responded by declaring the marriage invalid and excommunicating Raoul and Petronilla. Eleanor and Louis reacted angrily to this sentence and in January 1143 Louis invaded Champagne and laid waste to the province, probably once again at Eleanor's behest.[13]

Eleanor's influence in Louis' actions is plain to see and this campaign, like the invasion of Toulouse, proved to be a disaster. When Louis' army reached the town of Vitry in Champagne, the townspeople sheltered in the church. Flames from the burning town caught the church roof and, as Louis watched in horror, the church burned to the ground with the people of Vitry inside.[14] Louis' captains found him shaking and unable to speak following the disaster at Vitry and he remained in a trance-like state for two days.[15] Louis finally emerged from his trance a changed man and in later summer 1143 appears to have had a further breakdown. He ordered that his hair be shorn like that of a monk and he took to wearing monastic habits and spending hours at prayer.[16] For Eleanor, this change in Louis must have been intolerable and it is possible that the real problems in their marriage date from the Vitry disaster.

Eleanor had troubles apart from those concerning Petronilla. Early in her marriage, Eleanor is known to have miscarried a child.[17] Following this Eleanor does not seem to have conceived and by 1144 she was concerned. On 10 June Eleanor met privately with the churchman Bernard of Clairvaux and asked for his help in lifting the excommunication on Raoul and Petronilla. Bernard reproved Eleanor for interfering in politics and she burst into tears saying she only did so because she had no child. Bernard then offered her a deal: if she desisted in her interference in politics, he would ask God to send her a child.[18] Eleanor accepted this and in 1145 she bore a daughter, Marie. A daughter was not Eleanor preference but this was, at least, proof that she was able to bear children.

Following Vitry, Louis grew steadily more pious and, at Easter 1146, he undertook to go on crusade.[19] Eleanor, who had by then spent several uneventful years in France, must have been anxious to be included in this campaign. Insisting on taking part, Eleanor took the cross and one legend holds that she and her ladies dressed as Amazons and rode through the crowd, to encourage others to join the crusade.[20] It is likely that Eleanor saw the crusade as a way of leaving behind the monotony of her life in France and her unsatisfactory marriage to Louis. Certainly she threw herself into preparing for the crusade and a number of her personal vassals took the cross. Louis and Eleanor set out for the Holy Land in 1147.[21] It was not unusual for women to go on crusade in this period, although it has been suggested that Louis loved Eleanor so much that he could not bear to leave her behind.[22] It is, of course, possible that he did not trust her enough to leave her behind unsupervised. There is no doubt that by 1146 any love Eleanor had felt for Louis had evaporated.

The French army followed the route towards Constantinople that Conrad of the German Empire had taken a few months earlier.[23] Throughout her life Eleanor seems to have enjoyed travelling and it is likely that she was excited about visiting Constantinople. In Constantinople Eleanor and Louis were entertained lavishly by the emperor and his wife, being taken to visit shrines and other sites.[24] The emperor was, however, anxious to be rid of his French guests and Eleanor and Louis soon set off again for the Holy Land. It must have been very disconcerting for them when, soon after leaving Constantinople, they heard news that the Germanic army had been decimated in the Holy Land. The French army came into contact with several Germanic survivors and was joined in November 1147 by the injured Germanic emperor, Conrad himself. Despite the worry caused by the Germanic defeat, the French had no option but to follow the same route towards Antioch.[25]

In order to reach Antioch the French had to cross Mount Cadmos, where the Germans had sustained their heavy defeat. Eleanor appears to have ridden in the vanguard of the army, which was led by one of her Aquitainian vassals.[26] The vanguard carried little luggage and so was able to move swiftly. On the day of the crossing, the vanguard reached the proposed campsite early and decided to press on to the other side of the mountain. The rear of the army, which was much slower, reached the original campsite as night was falling and were disconcerted to find that the vanguard was not there. The Turks, seeing that the French army was split in two, attacked the rear, causing heavy losses. Louis' royal guard were killed and Louis himself, who fought bravely, was only spared because his simple clothes meant he was not recognised.[27] Louis was forced to spend the night hiding in a tree before limping back to join the vanguard in the morning with the few other survivors. The vanguard was oblivious to the fate of the rest of the army and Eleanor must have spent the night worrying about what had befallen Louis. The defeat was a disaster for the crusade but also for Eleanor's reputation. Almost immediately, she was personally blamed for the ambush, with rumours that her enormous amount of luggage hampered the rear of the army's progress.[28] This claim seems unjustifiable since it is impossible that one woman's luggage could have slowed down an entire army. To the churchmen who were struggling to establish what had gone wrong on the crusade, Eleanor, as a woman of already dubious reputation, was a convenient and easy target. There would have been nothing Eleanor could have done about this portrayal of her and, regardless of her true actions and the weak leadership of the French army, she will always be remembered as the cause of the French misfortunes.

The army was left with no food or water following the Mount Cadmos defeat and the remainder of the crossing must have been an ordeal. When the army finally reached Adalia, it was found that there was no food there either. Louis at first refused to abandon his army to travel to Antioch by ship, but was forced by his barons to do so.[29] The royal couple sailed away from Adalia leaving thousands of their men behind, most of whom starved or converted to Islam.[30] It must have been a relieved Eleanor who stepped ashore at Antioch in March 1148.[31] Antioch was ruled by Eleanor's uncle, Raymond of Aquitaine who like her father and grandfather was a handsome and warlike man – a contrast to Louis, and he and Eleanor seem to have spent a great deal of time together. Such conduct led to rumours and John of Salisbury claimed that 'the attentions paid by the prince to the queen, and his constant, indeed almost continuous, conversation with her, aroused the king's suspicions'.[32] It is not impossible that Eleanor and her uncle were lovers; there is no doubt the scandal accompanied Eleanor throughout her life. Eleanor certainly preferred the company of Raymond to that of Louis and during their stay she told Louis she wished to remain in Antioch and have their marriage annulled.[33] This seems to have been the first time divorce was mentioned and Louis was deeply shocked. He consulted his counsellors and was told that he would be shamed if he left his wife behind. The French therefore left Antioch secretly at night, taking Eleanor with them as a prisoner to Jerusalem.

Eleanor must have been furious at her treatment by Louis and seems to have remained in disgrace throughout her time in Jerusalem. The king and queen finally set sail for home with the 300 men remaining in their army in April 1149, having failed to win any military victories.[34] It is perhaps indicative of the state of the royal marriage that Eleanor and Louis sailed in separate ships.

On the way back to France, the couple visited the Pope at Tusculum. Their purpose may have been to discuss their marriage and the Pope took it upon himself to reconcile them, even going so far as preparing a special bed for them.[35] Louis, who previously seems to have been uninterested in sexual intercourse, took this as a sign of God's approval and, in early summer 1150, Eleanor bore a second daughter, Alix.[36] The birth of another daughter was something of a blessing to Eleanor and even Louis' council began to suggest that Louis take a new wife who could bear him a son. To the male councillors it was, of course, entirely Eleanor's fault that Louis had no son although, in only a few years, Eleanor would be able to demonstrate that the problem was not hers.

Events began to move more quickly for Eleanor in August 1151 when Geoffrey, Count of Anjou, and his son, Henry FitzEmpress, arrived in Paris to perform homage for Normandy. Henry was over ten years younger than Eleanor and does not appear to have been handsome, being described as having a reddish, freckled complexion, large head and stocky build.[37] However, to Eleanor, he must have seemed an interesting proposition. According to William of Newburgh, 'Eleanor was extremely irritated by the habits of the king, and claimed that she had married a monk, not a king'.[38] Upon meeting Henry, she apparently longed to divorce Louis and marry him.[39]. It seems unlikely that Eleanor and Henry had the privacy to commit adultery in Paris but it is likely that some agreement to marry in the future was reached between them. It was claimed by Gerald of Wales that Henry 'basely stole Queen Eleanor from his liege lord, Louis, king of the French, and then married her', implying that an understanding had been reached between Henry and Eleanor before her divorce.[40]

One person who was apparently against the proposed marriage was Henry's father, Geoffrey. Capgrave describes in his *Chronicle of England*:

> Geoffrey Plantagenet warned Henry his sone that he schuld in no wise wedde Helianore the qwen of Frauns, for he told him in very treuth that whan he was steward of Frauns, and dwelled with the kyng, he had comounde with the same qwen oftetyme.[41]

Several other sources assert that Eleanor and Geoffrey committed adultery with each other. The evidence for this is even more tenuous than for Eleanor's supposed liaison with Raymond of Antioch. It seems likely that rumours of an affair between Eleanor and her future father-in-law were based on her notorious reputation and the belief of contemporaries that she was capable of any sexual sin, rather than the facts. To her contemporaries, she had already proved herself an incestuous adulteress with her uncle and it was not a great stretch of the imagination for them to believe that she had had an affair with her future father-in-law. Eleanor was probably as unconcerned with these rumours as her predecessor Judith of France had been; similarly would she discover just how firmly rooted negative associations could be for a female.

Following Henry's departure, Eleanor again raised the suggestion of divorce. This time Louis was prepared to consider the matter and, on 21 March 1152, Eleanor and Louis' marriage was annulled on the grounds of consanguity.[42] The separation appears to have been amicable and Louis retained custody of their daughters. He did not know of Henry and Eleanor's plans and allowed Eleanor to return home to Aquitaine. Louis and Eleanor were never to meet again. Following the divorce, Eleanor set out home to Poitiers. She must have travelled with a considerable escort, as Eleanor was once again the most desirable heiress in Europe. En route she learnt of two separate ambushes laid for her, one by Theobold of Blois and the other by Henry's own brother, Geoffrey.[43] Both men meant to kidnap and forcibly marry her and Eleanor must have known she was in considerable danger. She probably uncomfortably remembered the fate of Emma of Limoges and she cannot have relished the possibility of being forced into yet another arranged marriage. It must have been a great relief to arrive back in Aquitaine safely.

Henry was also journeying secretly to Aquitaine and he arrived in Poitiers in mid-May, where he and Eleanor were married. It is actually unlikely that the marriage was a love match and it seems to have been based on political considerations. However, Eleanor probably reflected that Henry would make a more fulfilling husband than Louis had been. The marriage was conducted with great secrecy. Louis had clearly been unaware of their intentions. He had agreed to divorce Eleanor on the basis of consanguity because he believed their marriage was against God's will. However, Eleanor and Henry were much more closely related to each other than she and Louis and the latter was furious when word reached him of the marriage. Louis apparently claimed that Henry had basely stolen his wife and immediately invaded Normandy, only to be quickly repelled by Henry and forced to retreat impotently to Paris.[44]

Eleanor must have known how hurt Louis would be upon hearing of her marriage and it is possible that there was an element of revenge in her choice of Louis' greatest rival.[45] The marriage also provided personal fulfillment for Eleanor because on 17 August 1153, she gave birth to her first son.[46] For Eleanor, at thirty-one, this must have been a major source of satisfaction and a major reproof to Louis.

The first years of Eleanor and Henry's marriage were dominated by his struggle for the crown of England and they were often apart. The death of King Stephen's son, Eustace led to Henry being named heir to England and this was a major triumph for the couple. In June of 1154 Eleanor joined Henry in Rouen then on the death of Stephen in December sailed for England.[47] Henry and Eleanor were crowned together at Westminster on 19 December 1154 and in February 1155 Eleanor bore her second son, Henry.[48] Eleanor must have felt triumphant.

Henry and Eleanor ruled vast lands in England and on the continent and Eleanor was expected by Henry to play an active political role. Early in 1156, Henry crossed to Normandy leaving Eleanor as co-regent in England with Richard of Luci.[49] Eleanor obviously performed the role satisfactorily and was left as regent again when Henry travelled to Normandy in 1158.[50] Eleanor also had some influence over Henry, encouraging him to invade Toulouse on her behalf in 1159.[51] This campaign proved a failure but demonstrates Eleanor's continuing preoccupation with the county.

Despite the importance of Eleanor's political contribution, her main purpose during the early years of her marriage was to bear children. Her eldest son, William, died in 1156 but in June of that year Eleanor bore a daughter, Matilda.[52] This birth was followed at Oxford in September 1157 by Richard and then Geoffrey one year later. Daughters Eleanor and Joanna were born in 61 and 65 and Eleanor's last child, John, was born on Christmas Eve 1166. After years of childlessness and disappointment Eleanor must have been delighted with her children. Richard appears to have been Eleanor's favourite and she named him heir to Aquitaine at his birth.

Henry was also pleased with the births of his children and proved to be a fond father. Like Eleanor, he also had great plans for their futures and attempted to arrange grand marriages for them. In August 1158, Henry crossed to France and swore fealty to Louis for his French possessions. Whilst he was there, he betrothed young Henry to Marguerite, Louis' eldest daughter from his second marriage. This betrothal was made for political reasons and it is clear from its terms that Louis had not yet forgiven Eleanor. It was usual for a betrothed girl to be raised by her future husband's mother, but Louis stipulated that Marguerite should not be placed in Eleanor's care, instead being raised by a mutually acceptable Norman family.[53] Even in his provisions for his daughter, however, Louis was to be thwarted. In 1160 Henry had the two infants brought together and married prematurely in order to claim Marguerite's dowry for himself.[54] Marguerite was then given over to Eleanor's care.

In the early years of their marriage Eleanor and Henry worked together as an effective team in ruling their empire. However, relations between them began to sour quickly, perhaps as a result of Henry's adultery. In around 1165 Henry began his famous and lengthy affair with Rosamund Clifford.[55] The Christmas of that year was the first Eleanor and Henry had spent apart, with Eleanor at Angers and Henry at Oxford. Eleanor probably deeply resented Rosamund Clifford who proved a more enduring rival than Henry's earlier more fleeting affairs. It was rumoured that Eleanor even went so far as to murder Rosamund in her jealousy: according to legend, Henry, concerned for Rosamund's safety, built a specially designed maze in which to hide his mistress. Eleanor discovered the way through the maze with the use of a thread and, in the centre, offered Rosamund the choice of a dagger or poison with which to kill herself; Rosamund chose the latter.[56] This story is clearly fantasy and Rosamund is known to have retired to a convent after her affair with Henry. However, it does suggest that Eleanor's feelings against Rosamund were strong and it is possible that this affair turned Eleanor against Henry. At Christmas 1167, Eleanor informed Henry of her decision to return to Aquitaine, a move that signified an informal separation. Eleanor spent the years 1168 to 1173 ruling Aquitaine personally.

In spite of the apparently amicable nature of the separation, over the years animosity grew between Eleanor and Henry. In 1170 Henry succeeded in having young Henry crowned as his heir at Westminster and Eleanor does not appear to have been invited to the coronation. Eleanor was ambitious for all her children and probably resented this keenly. Henry was also fond of his children but, unlike Eleanor, was unable to accept that they had grown up and needed to be given independence. This led to a growing resentment between Henry and his sons and, in April 1173, they rose against him. Most contemporary sources make it clear that Eleanor was considered a ringleader in the revolt and, when Henry summoned her to join him at Easter 1173, she refused.[57] The Archbishop of Rouen also threatened Eleanor with excommunication if she refused to join her husband but still she remained in Aquitaine, conspiring with her children and her ex-husband. There is no doubt that Eleanor, as Henry's wife, received the greater share of the blame for the revolt and this was very damaging to her reputation. Eleanor was certainly guilty of conspiring against Henry but he had also treated her badly through his affairs and her actions seem, to modern eyes, understandable, even if they were not so excusable to her contemporaries.

By June, the rebellion had spread throughout Henry's French lands, with his sons, young Henry, Richard and Geoffrey, as active participants. In August Henry struck back and soon recaptured his lands, making peace with Louis in September. Eleanor was left without support in Poitiers as Henry marched towards her. She cannot have relished being captured by her husband and she would have known that she could expect no mercy from him. In September she was captured trying to escape to France dressed as a man and brought as a prisoner to Henry.[58] This must have been one of the darkest moments of Eleanor's life and it would have been doubly worse for her knowing that the man who had brought her so low was her own husband, the hated Henry. Perhaps at this point Eleanor looked back on her time as Queen of France and considered that Louis had not been so bad after all. Henry took Eleanor over to England with him where she was confined at Salisbury.

Eleanor's fortunes reached their lowest ebb in 1173 and she must have felt that the future looked bleak. Henry talked openly of divorcing her and, in 1175, the papal legate was sent to her to persuade her to retire to Fontevrault Abbey as its Abbess.[59] This would have allowed Henry to both remarry and keep control of Eleanor's lands. As such this was unacceptable to Eleanor, despite the only chance of freedom it offered. Eleanor totally refused to agree to a divorce and remained in captivity. She must have had little hope as, at eleven years Henry's senior, she was unlikely to survive him.

Eleanor spent the rest of Henry's reign a prisoner. It is likely that news did reach her in her prison but she was isolated from the world. In 1179 Louis died. Whilst Eleanor is unlikely to have grieved from him, news of his death must have reminded her of her own mortality and her own bleak future. A bigger blow reached Eleanor in June 1183 when Henry the younger fell ill and died suddenly on the continent. It is reported that his last request was for his father to show Eleanor mercy but she remained a captive. In 1186 Eleanor suffered a further blow when her third surviving son, Geoffrey, was killed in a tournament in Paris.[60]

Eleanor must have realised that she would never be released in Henry's lifetime and probably resigned herself to die in prison. The years of rebellion by his sons had affected Henry adversely, however. During the winter of 1188 and 1189, Richard was in open rebellion in alliance with Philip Augustus, the young king of France. By July 1189 Henry was ill and finally defeated by his son. As part of the terms of his surrender, Henry asked for a list of names of those who had rebelled against him. On seeing that the first name was that of his favourite son, John, Henry turned his face to the wall and died.[61]

Eleanor is unlikely to have mourned for Henry and she probably welcomed his death. Her favourite son, Richard, succeeded to his father's lands unchallenged and immediately sent word to England for Eleanor to be released and appointed regent in his absence.[62] This proved unnecessary; once word of Henry's death reached England, Eleanor's gaolers released her, presumably recognising that the new king was unlikely to favour those who imprisoned his mother. After years of inactivity, Eleanor threw herself into preparing England for Richard's arrival. Richard was not a familiar personage in England and Eleanor immediately carried out a number of acts in his name with the aim of increasing his popularity. One of these acts, probably also close to her own heart, was to order the release of all prisoners in England.[63] She also ordered the removal of royal horses from religious houses, thereby removing an expensive and hated burden.[64]

Richard landed at Portsmouth on 13 August 1189 and met Eleanor at Winchester. They had not met for several years and it must have been an emotional reunion. Richard and Eleanor then travelled slowly to London for his coronation. Richard was crowned on 3 September in Westminster Abbey. Eleanor had arranged a splendid ceremony and she took a prominent place, dressed in silk and furs.[65] It is clear that Eleanor was happy to resume her role of queen and was not prepared to relinquish her position to anyone. Nevertheless this probably suited Richard as he knew little of England and relied on Eleanor to help govern his new kingdom. He also had no intention of remaining in England for long and quickly set about raising money to fund his crusade.

Eleanor's release also saw her reunited with her youngest son, John. It has often been suggested that Eleanor hated John and certainly she seems to have preferred Richard. However, the surviving evidence suggests that Eleanor was as ambitious for John as she was for the rest of her children and was prepared to support his interests. When Richard was ready to go on crusade he asked his brother John and Henry II's illegitimate son, Geoffrey, to take oaths swearing that they would stay out of England for three years.[66] Richard of Devizes writes how Eleanor begged Richard to release John from his oath – hardly the actions of a mother who hated her son.[67] Nonetheless her actions do seem to have focused on her eldest surviving son. Soon after Richard left England for the Holy Land in December 1189, Eleanor set out for Navarre to fetch Berengaria, a sister of the King of Navarre, to marry Richard. They then travelled together to Sicily where Eleanor left Berengaria with Richard before rushing back to England where her presence was badly needed.

With both Richard and Eleanor absent, John had begun to call himself the king's heir and had himself appointed supreme governor of England in Richard's absence.[68] He also ordered that all the castles in England be turned over to him, ignoring all Richard's provisions for the regency. Eleanor landed at Portsmouth on 11 February 1192. On hearing of his fearsome mother's arrival, John attempted to flee to France but Eleanor swiftly prevented him. According to Richard of Devizes 'with all her strength she wanted to make sure that faith would be kept between her youngest sons, at least, so that their mother might die more happily than their father, who had gone before them'.[69] Eleanor arrested John's Flemish mercenaries and closed the channel ports to prevent any further support arriving for John.[70] Following her arrival she also called a number of councils and took control of the government of England.

Eleanor must have eagerly awaited Richard's return to England in order to put an end to John's pretensions. However, in January 1193, the devastating news reached England that Richard had been captured on his way home from the crusade. Eleanor immediately dispatched the Abbots of Boxley and Robertsbridge to the Germanic states to find out where Richard was being held.[71] From them, Eleanor learnt that Richard had been captured by the Duke of Austria and handed over to the Emperor Henry VI. Eleanor called a council at St Albans in June 1193 to discuss the terms of Richard's release and to appoint officers to collect the ransom demanded by the emperor. She threw herself into securing Richard's release and personally selected 200 hostages from amongst the nobility to be sent to the Germanic states.[72]

Eleanor also wrote two remarkable letters to the Pope, begging for his aid and expressing her grief. The first began:

> To the reverend Father and Lord Celestine, by the Grace of God, the supreme Pontiff, Eleanor, in God's anger, Queen of England, Duchess of Normandy, Countess of Anjou, begs him to show himself to be a father to a pitiable mother. I have decided to remain quiet in case a fullness of heart and a passionate grief might elicit some word against the chief of priests which was somewhat less than cautious, and I was therefore accused of insolence and arrogance. Certainly grief is not that different from insanity while it is inflamed with its own force. It does not recognise a master, is afraid of no ally, it has no regard for anyone, and it does not spare them – not even you.[73]

The second letter continues on the same theme of grief and touched upon Eleanor's dead sons:

> My insides have been torn out of me, my family has been carried off, it has rolled past me; the Young King [young Henry] and the earl of Brittany [Geoffrey] sleep in the dust – their mother is so ill-fated she is forced to live, so that without cure she is tortured by the memory of the dead. As some comfort, I still have two sons, who are alive today, but only to punish me, wretched and condemned. King Richard is detained in chains; his brother John is killing the people of the prisoner's kingdom with his sword, he is ravaging the land with fires.[74]

These letters show more about Eleanor's character than any other. They demonstrate her passionate nature and the great grief she felt. Even by the 1190s, Eleanor had outlived her generation and many of the younger generation. These letters show clearly that she keenly felt her age and the losses which time had inflicted on her. They also show her as a very effective propagandist.

Despite her pleas, Eleanor received little help from the Pope. Nonetheless by 1194 the ransom was raised and Eleanor and the Archbishop of Rouen were summoned by the emperor to bring the ransom to Speyer.[75] Eleanor's hopes of seeing Richard again were dashed, however, on 17 January when the emperor announced that he had received an alternative offer from King Philip Augustus of France and John to keep Richard in prison. It took all her negotiating skill to secure Richard's release later that month by convincing Richard to declare himself the emperor's vassal. She then returned in triumph with Richard to England where he was ceremonially recrowned at Winchester.

Soon after the coronation, Eleanor and Richard crossed to Normandy where Eleanor engineered a reconciliation between Richard and John. Eleanor must have felt pleased about the work she had done for her sons but she began to feel her age around this time. Soon after the reconciliation she retired to the Abbey of Fontrevault where she must have hoped to live quietly until her death. Eleanor rarely appears in sources between 1194 and 1199 and appears to have lived a secluded religious life.

She did not, however, cut herself off totally from the world and was ready for action in April 1199 when she received word that Richard was lying dangerously wounded at Chalus. Eleanor travelled day and night to be with him but he was beyond help when she arrived. He died in her arms on 6 April 1199, having named John as his heir.[76] Despite the deep grief she must have felt, Eleanor immediately threw herself into securing the throne for John. The succession was disputed between John and her grandson Arthur, son of her dead son Geoffrey of Brittany. Eleanor was acting as John's chief advisor in 1199 and advised him to go at once to Chinon to secure the royal treasury before meeting with her at Niort. John then crossed to England to be crowned whilst Eleanor toured her lands in Aquitaine to ensure their support for John. In mid-June she even travelled to Tours where she did homage to Philip Augustus for Aquitaine in order to ensure that Arthur could have no claim to the duchy.

Soon after the Christmas of 1199, John and Philip met to discuss a truce. It was agreed that in order to secure the truce, John would supply a bride for Philip's son. Eleanor therefore set out on the long journey to Castile to select one of her daughter Eleanor, Queen of Castile's, daughters. There she spent several months, no doubt reacquainting herself with her daughter and meeting her grandchildren, before selecting the youngest daughter, Blanche. Eleanor and Blanche then began to journey to Normandy, parting company when Eleanor unexpectedly decided to return to Fontevrault. It seems likely that Eleanor, at the age of seventy-eight, had begun to feel the effects of an arduous journey and could go no further. Blanche continued to Normandy where she was met by her uncle, King John, and married to the dauphin of France.[77] Eleanor must have been pleased with the work she had done in securing her and Henry's empire for their last surviving son.

Eleanor's story does not end with her second retirement, however. Arthur of Brittany still posed a major threat to John and must have been a source of worry to his grandmother. In May 1202 Eleanor decided to travel to Poitiers to help John in his war against Arthur. When Arthur learnt that his grandmother had left Fontevrault, he immediately set out in pursuit in an attempt to capture her and Eleanor found herself besieged in the flimsy castle of Mirebeau.[78]

Eleanor sent an urgent message to John at Le Mans before trying to delay Arthur with attempts at negotiation. This tactic had limited effect however and by the time John arrived Eleanor was trapped in the keep with the rest of the castle occupied by Arthur's men. John had force marched the eighty miles from Le Mans and caught Arthur by surprise. He swept into Mirebeau and won his only victory on the continent, rescuing his mother and taking Arthur prisoner.[79] Eleanor must have been relieved to see John and seems to have gladly returned to her retirement at Fontrevault. She is unlikely to have been sympathetic about the fate of Arthur following his attack on her at Mirebeau. He disappeared into John's dungeons and was probably murdered soon afterwards.[80]

Eleanor never emerged from her third period of retirement at Fontevrault. At some point in 1204 she slipped into a coma and died on 1 April 1204, aged eighty-two.[81] Her death meant John lost his most able advisor and it must have been painful for Eleanor to watch him gradually lose the Angevin empire from her retirement at Fontevrault.

She died at an ancient age by the standards of the time and she may have reflected, in the end, that she would be remembered as a great queen. Certainly, Eleanor of Aquitaine was a powerful and influential queen and brought much to the role. However, she did not always conform to the behaviour expected of a queen and, as such, has a somewhat ambiguous reputation.

Eleanor of Aquitaine was a legend in her own lifetime and her story is still of immense interest to readers today. But Eleanor has never been universally admired. To medieval writers, she was a woman who interfered in politics when they did not concern her. The fact that she was the ruler of an independent state which was larger than the country ruled by her first husband was immaterial to her contemporaries. As a married woman, it was for her husband to rule her lands and for Eleanor to placidly obey and bear children. In her refusal to do this, Eleanor attracted unwelcome attention from the male chroniclers; influential churchmen, such as Bernard of Clairvaux, were no friends to her. As a powerful and independent woman, Eleanor was a threat to male rule, just as her first threats of divorce to Louis directly threatened his dignity and kingship. To her contemporaries, Eleanor was an oddity and they could easily believe that she was an adulteress and disloyal wife with ambitious and unwomanly characteristics. Like her mother-in-law, the Empress Matilda, Eleanor of Aquitaine was a woman in a man's world and consequently her reputation suffered. She is therefore remembered as a notorious queen and an example of what a queen should not be. Eleanor, as one of the most vivid women of the medieval period, probably would not have cared. Like the Empress Matilda, Eleanor is not universally criticised in the sources, and it is admitted that she had some positive traits. Her daughter-in-law, Isabella of Angouleme, on the other hand, is recorded to have had no redeeming features whatsoever and, unlike her more famous mother-in-law, is portrayed as a model of true queenly wickedness.

'More Jezebel than Isabel'

Isabella of Angouleme

Isabella of Angouleme has one of the most grim reputations of any queen of England. She led a tumultuous life that was filled with high drama and intrigue and she was infamous across Europe even during her lifetime. Isabella is remembered today as an adulteress, a disloyal mother and a poisoner. One contemporary writer even went so far as to describe her as 'more Jezebel than Isabel'. Today, Isabella is considered dishonourable like her mother-in-law, Eleanor of Aquitaine, but with none of the older woman's admirable qualities. In short, she is seen as the sort of consort that her husband, King John, deserved. There is no doubt that Isabella was hated and feared but how much she deserved this amoral characterisation is debatable. Isabella was the wife of the disastrous and highly unpopular King John and it is not surprising that much of his bad reputation infected hers. She lived in turbulent times and, as a prominent landowner in her own right, Isabella often found herself at the mercy of the changing fortunes of the English and the French on the continent. Therefore it is not entirely surprising that she sometimes sought to play the two off against each other in an attempt to preserve her lands. Although Isabella has been unfairly blamed for the loss of English lands in France, in reality she suffered as much for this disaster as anyone. She merely provided a useful scapegoat for criticism of royal policy.

Isabella was the only child and heiress of Aymer, Count of Angouleme. Her date of birth is not recorded, but her parents cannot have been married before 1184. They are first recorded as married in 1191 and it is likely that Isabella was very young at the time of her marriage to John in 1200.[1] She is often described as being twelve years old in 1200 but since this was the legal earliest age for marriage, this may have been an official age. It has been suggested that Isabella was as young as eight or nine in 1200.[2]

Isabella's father technically held Angouleme as a vassal of the duchy of Aquitaine. However, in reality, he had a great deal of independence. He had caused trouble during the reign of Richard I of England, claiming independence and doing homage directly to Philip Augustus.[3] Count Aymer is known to have entered into a more formal alliance with Philip Augustus soon after John's accession.[4] As part of this agreement, he abandoned his claims to the neighbouring county of Le Marche in favour of Hugh de Lusignan.[5] Isabella's future was also tied up in this agreement and, in early 1200, Isabella was betrothed to Hugh de Lusignan and sent to live in his household until she was old enough to be married.[6] A marriage between Isabella and Hugh posed a serious political threat to John, who was at that time still trying to impose his authority on his empire. The merging of the counties of Angouleme, La Marche and Lusignan would split the lands of the duchy of Aquitaine in half, dividing Gascony from Poitou.[7] It was therefore very much in John's interests to stop the marriage between Isabella and Hugh.

It is often claimed that John's marriage to Isabella was driven by lust with all the criticism of Isabella that this implies.[8] In the summer of 1200 John set out on a progress through Poitou. During his progress he visited the Lusignans at Le Marche.[9] John saw Isabella for the first time there and, according to reports, immediately lusted after her, desiring her as his wife. Isabella was, at most, twelve years old at this visit but she is depicted by contemporaries as a young temptress, fuelling the king's lust with her beauty and betraying her fiancé, Hugh de Lusignan. This is clearly unrealistic; Isabella had had no say in her betrothal to Hugh, nor did she in her betrothal to John. Having met Isabella, John spoke to Count Aymer discreetly about the match and Aymer, eager for his daughter to become a queen, agreed to recall his daughter.[10] John then sent Hugh de Lusignan to England on official business before returning secretly to Angouleme with the Archbishop of Bordeaux.[11] On 23 August 1200, Isabella was informed by her parents that she was to marry John the next day. Her feelings concerning this are not clear and she must have been bewildered at the sudden change in her fortunes. Both Hugh and John were considerably older than her and she is unlikely to have been emotionally attached to either man. It has been claimed that she wept and protested[12]; equally, it has been suggested that she greatly desired to be a queen.[13] Whatever her feelings, Isabella would have had no option but to go through with the marriage and she was married on 24 April 1200 at Bordeaux.

Following the marriage, John and Isabella crossed the channel and were crowned together in Westminster Abbey on 8 October 1200.[14] By the end of 1200 John probably felt he had reason to congratulate himself on the way he handled his marriage. The Lusignans initially did nothing and Hugh accepted Matilda of Angouleme, Isabella's cousin, as an alternative bride.[15] Matilda was no compensation for the loss of Isabella's county, however, and the insult rankled the Lusignans. In 1201, trouble broke out in Poitou and John charged the Lusignans with treason. The Lusignans turned to Philip Augustus for support and, in 1202, Philip declared that John had forfeited Aquitaine, Poitou and Anjou and gave them to John's rival, Arthur of Brittany.[16] John seems to have blamed Isabella for the loss of his French possessions and apparently told her this in 1205.[17] Sources also blame Isabella, claiming that following their marriage John and Isabella would lie in bed together rather than attend to business, again suggesting that Isabella's precocious charms kept the king from his proper duties.[18] No sensible blame can be attached personally to the very young Isabella and she is treated only as a useful scapegoat in these sources. As a woman, Isabella would always be viewed with suspicion by both the political leaders at John's court and by male clergymen, and it was convenient to blame a helpless child who in reality had been forced into an arranged marriage. If anyone should bear the blame for the defection of the Lusignans it is John and the underhand way in which he married Isabella. Isabella herself was never an active participant in this but, as a woman, she was an easy target and the rumours of John's sexual misconduct would always attach themselves more to Isabella than to the king. Isabella never attained a political role in John's reign but her name will always be associated with the loss of the Angevin Empire due to the actions that others took on her behalf.

As well as being linked with the disasters on the continent, Isabella was also caught up personally in the war. In January 1203 she was besieged by rebels whilst staying at Chinon Castle. This must have been terrifying and she sent frantic messages to John begging for rescue. John set out to rescue her but, after reaching Le Mans, he became fearful of being captured and instead sent mercenaries to Chinon.[19] This must have been a frightening time for Isabella and she must have felt a great deal of relief at the arrival of John's mercenary force. However it is just possible that John's failure to come to her aid in person hints at trouble in the royal marriage. Only the year before, John had gone personally to Mirabeau to free his mother when she was similarly besieged but, in 1203, he apparently rated his personal safety higher than any dramatic gesture. John certainly did have reason to fear for his personal safety and it is possible that this induced John and Isabella to leave Normandy in December 1203. John claimed that he went to England to gather more resources for his continental wars, but he never returned, leaving the bulk of the Angevin Empire to the French king.[20] John and Isabella must have spent a sombre Christmas at Canterbury that year. In March 1204 they received news that Normandy had fallen.[21]

Isabella spent much of the next few years travelling around England with her household and was not given any role in government. In 1202 Count Aymer had died and Isabella inherited Angouleme. She took little part in its government, however, with first her mother and then John's officials controlling the county. She did visit Angouleme during John's expeditions to Poitou in 1206 and 1214 but it is likely that this was merely to establish an Angevin presence in the county.[22] Certainly Isabella had no active position in Angouleme during her marriage to John and it is unlikely that this would have been permitted. She also played no role in John's dispute with the papacy and her thoughts on his excommunication in 1209 are unknown.[23] This event together with the Interdict imposed on England between 1208 and 1214 provide examples of the political turmoil of John's reign.

John and Isabella's personal relationship also does not seem to have been a success. John is known to have had several illegitimate children with at least two born to noblewomen.[24] In 1214 John abducted the noblewoman Matilda FitzWalter, forcing her to become his mistress.[25] It is likely that this action both aroused Isabella's jealously and stirred up baronial opposition to John in England. Sources also refer to John's 'lady friends', one of whom he sent roses to in June 1212.[26] It seems probable that John took mistresses throughout his marriage to Isabella, something that a woman as strong-willed as Isabella cannot have accepted easily. For her contemporaries of the opposite sex however male infidelity was acceptable and Isabella would have been expected to simply ignore John's conduct. The only reason he was chastised for his affairs was his preference for abducting noblewomen, the implication being that he could have relations with women of lower status with impunity. However as is the norm for the medieval period, there was one standard for men and quite another for women. Although John has largely escaped censure for his affairs, a great deal of Isabella's poor reputation stems from her supposed infidelity. A contemporary, Matthew Paris, described her as guilty of adultery, sorcery and incest.[27] One suggested lover is Isabella's own half-brother, Peter de Joigny, and this would account for the accusation of incest. Peter visited England in 1215 and possibly 1207 so Isabella and her brother may have formed a close relationship with each other.[28] However Isabella was mostly pregnant during his visits and it is a mark of her unpopularity that this suggestion has been made. A further story grotesquely narrates how John had one of Isabella's lovers strangled and his corpse suspended over her bed.[29] There was probably little affection between John and Isabella. She was not mentioned in his will and, after his death, Isabella issued three perfunctory charters for his soul then never mentioned him again.[30] She may also have taken lovers during their marriage; if so, she was no more at fault than her husband but because of her sex, such accusations were enough to damn her.

Isabella had little contact with her children by John. It is unclear whether this was her choice or not but she never seems to have built a relationship with them. The eldest, Henry, was placed in the household of the Bishop of Winchester in 1212 and was joined by his youngest sister, Eleanor, in 1216.[31] Neither were her second son, Richard, and daughter, Isabella, raised by their mother. During John's Poitou campaign in 1214 Isabella also lost custody of her final daughter, Joanna. As part of a peace agreement with Hugh de Lusignan, Joanna was betrothed to Hugh's son, Hugh the Younger, and sent to be raised in Le Marche as Isabella had been.[32] Isabella was never given the opportunity to be a mother to her children in their formative years. These early separations and, perhaps, dislike of their father, may have been major factors in Isabella's subsequent conduct towards her children.

The last few years of John's reign were racked by civil war in England. It has been suggested that Isabella was imprisoned by John during these years but it is more likely that this refers to her being guarded for her own protection.[33] Isabella was one of the most unpopular figures in John's regime and under considerable threat from the people of England. Isabella spent the last years of John's reign in the relative safety of the West Country.[34] In early 1216 John's relations with his barons took a turn for the worst when they held a council in which they decided to elect the Dauphin, Louis of France, as king.[35] Louis landed at Thanet on 20 May 1216 and quickly took Rochester Castle. He was received with joy in London and by autumn 1216, controlled most of southern England.[36] News of Louis' progress must have filled Isabella with dread as she waited in Bristol. In the midst of this chaos, John died on 18 October 1216 and was buried at Worcester.[37]

When news reached Bristol of John's death, Isabella immediately showed the strength of character that would underpin her widowhood. Isabella travelled at once to Gloucester where her nine-year-old son, Henry III, had been brought. He was hastily crowned on 28 October, with one of Isabella's gold collars.[38] Despite this decisive action, Isabella was not given a position in the regency and William Marshall was appointed regent at a council the following day.[39] This must have been galling for her but it is, once again, a measure of her unpopularity in England and a demonstration of her inability to build a political party of her own during her time as Queen of England. Certainly, Isabella's position in England following John's death does not appear to have been good. Denied any political role, Isabella also seems to have had trouble securing her property.[40] This explains Isabella's decision to return to Angouleme in June 1217, leaving her children in England.

Isabella's behaviour on her return to Angouleme in 1217 illustrates her forceful and independent character. She quickly established her lordship in Angouleme, gaining control over Cognac even, a region which had been lost to Angouleme in the 1180s.[41] The English minority council seem to have expected Isabella to govern Angouleme for the benefit of Henry III, but, in 1220, Isabella once again demonstrated her self-direction, marrying Hugh de Lusignan, son of her former fiancé and the man betrothed to her own daughter, Joanna. Isabella appears to have had no qualms about robbing her daughter of her fiancé and she may have reasoned that the same had happened to her when she was a young girl and that, after years of a loveless marriage to John, she deserved a little happiness. It is likely that Isabella's second marriage was based more on personal liking than her first. The elder Hugh had been a widower with children when he was betrothed to Isabella and the young Isabella may well have got to know the younger Hugh when she joined his father's household. Perhaps they remembered each other fondly and, in any event, Isabella would have known the value of an alliance between herself and Hugh territorially. Isabella would also have known that her marriage would not be looked upon favourably in England and her letter to Henry III, explaining her actions, provides a strong indication of her character:

> We hereby signify to you that when the Counts of March and Eu departed this life, the lord Hugh de Lusignan remained alone and without heirs in Poitou, and his friends would not permit that our daughter should be united to him in marriage, because her age is so tender, but counselled him to take a wife from whom he might speedily hope for an heir; and it was proposed that he should take a wife in France, which if he had done, all your land in Poitou and Gascony would be lost. We, therefore, seeing the great peril that might accrue if that marriage should take place, when our counsellors could give us no advice, ourselves married the said Hugh, count of March; and God knows we did this rather for your benefit than our own.[42]

The reasons Isabella gives to explain her marriage seem implausible. It is clear that it was Isabella's own desire to marry Hugh and her excuses were merely an attempt to avert Henry's anger and try to persuade him that she was actually acting in his best interests. By marrying Hugh, however, Isabella created the very political crisis that John sought to avert by marrying Isabella in 1200. It is possible that, in her second marriage, Isabella also allowed herself to enjoy a little revenge at John's expense and, certainly, she had never been well treated in England. It is therefore easy to see why she might not have proved loyal to a country where she had been so unhappy.

Isabella's excuses convinced no one and her marriage caused anger in Henry's minority council, who responded by confiscating Isabella's dower. In retaliation, Isabella refused to release her daughter Joanna, Hugh's jilted fiancée, until her rights were reinstated, essentially keeping the girl as a hostage.[43] The dispute dragged on until October 1220 when Henry III finally agreed to reinstate Isabella's dower. Hugh then escorted Joanna to La Rochelle where she was taken back into English custody.[44] The negotiations following Isabella's marriage show her to be a shrewd negotiator. The incident was also the first indication of the troubled and manipulative relationships Isabella would have with her English children and it is clear, from her behaviour, that she saw Joanna as a bargaining chip in her attempts to get what she wanted. Again, however, she had also never been allowed much contact with her English children and she may well have reasoned that they could fend for themselves without their mother, as they had always done. In any event Isabella's relationship with Henry's minority council was tense; in 1224 she and Hugh defected to the French and Isabella was granted a pension in return for her dower lands forfeited in England. In 1230 Isabella entered into another agreement with France at Henry's expense, increasing the size of her pension.[45] There is evidence that, from 1228, Henry III's government were petitioning the Pope to annul Isabella's marriage to Hugh. This, however, came to nothing.[46]

It is likely that Isabella's second marriage was more satisfying than her first. She and Hugh enjoyed a more equal relationship, issuing charters together.[47] Isabella also had a great deal of influence over Hugh. For example in June 1241 Hugh swore fealty to the French candidate for Count of Poitou, a title to which Henry III also laid claim.[48] This enraged Isabella, who had also been slighted by the Queen of France when she attended court at Poitiers; she was not inclined to make any further agreements with the French crown.[49] Furious at her husband's conduct, Isabella stripped Lusignan Castle of its furnishings and returned to her own castle at Angouleme with Hugh's possessions. Hearing of his wife's activities, Hugh followed, but Isabella would not admit him to the castle for three days, forcing him to sleep in a building in front of the castle.

When Hugh was finally admitted, Isabella abused him for supporting an alternative Count of Poitou to her son Henry.[50] This obviously had an effect – at Christmas 1241, Hugh declared himself against the French and persuaded Henry to join a military expedition to Poitou.

The English army, led by Henry III and his brother Richard, sailed on 9 May 1242. No evidence survives of Isabella's reunion with her two English sons. It seems likely that it was a tense meeting given the twenty-five years since she had last seen them and her political activities during that period. Certainly Henry and Richard are likely to have turned against their mother during the campaign, when Hugh deserted them for the French. The English campaign was a disaster and Henry barely escaped with his life, returning to England defeated. Henry's disastrous campaign opened Isabella's eyes to the reality of the political situation in Europe and she resigned herself to the fact that her sons could not defeat the French for her. Isabella therefore decided to take matters into her own hands and, in 1244, assassins were captured in the royal kitchens trying to poison Louis IX's food. When questioned, the men confessed that they had been sent by Isabella and there is no evidence that Isabella ever attempted to deny this charge.[51] Isabella would have known that a military campaign against Louis was no longer a possibility without English backing and she may have considered that the death of Louis would enable her to hold her lands more securely. Poisoning, however, was a grievous sin and Isabella would have realised that with the crime discovered she would be hunted down. When Isabella was informed of the arrests she threatened to kill herself with a dagger before being restrained.[52] She then fled to Fontevrault Abbey, seeking sanctuary from her pursuers. Isabella spent her last years safely immured in the Abbey and died there on 4 June 1246.[53]

In England, news of Isabella's death was met with a brief display of mourning. It is, however, unlikely that Isabella's English children felt real grief although Henry did extend a warm welcome to some of Isabella's children by Hugh who arrived in England in 1247.[54] The eight children Isabella bore Hugh de Lusignan proved a major source of tension in England during the reign of their half-brother Henry III and it is as their mother that Isabella is now primarily remembered.[55] Isabella's children by Hugh also seem to have been born with Isabella's gift for political intrigue, which Henry III failed to inherit, and they were to prove to be major political rivals to Henry's own queen, Eleanor of Provence.

Isabella of Angouleme is not the most ill-famed of English queens but she is remembered as among the worst. Bad King John and Isabella of Angouleme were described in the sources as a well-matched couple – both were portrayed as devious and self-interested figures. Isabella of Angouleme's legacy is so disreputable that it is now difficult to see the real woman behind this characterisation. There is no doubt that Isabella often acted in a self-interested way, sometimes at the expense of her own children, but she was born into a difficult political situation in Europe. She had to fight to maintain her position throughout her life-time, a situation likely to incline most people towards selfishness. Until she arrived in Angouleme in 1217, Isabella was essentially powerless in every aspect of her life. She had no say in her first marriage, no say in the upbringing of her children and she had no say in the government of her husband's kingdom or her own lands. It is therefore not surprising that she grasped her freedom eagerly. She proved her capacity for effective ruling in Angouleme. It is also possible to see Isabella attempting to help her eldest son in her later life, even if these attempts, such as encouraging Henry's ill-fated campaign and trying to murder the King of France, were ultimately harmful. When the facts of Isabella's life are analysed she can, perhaps, be said to have been an unsuccessful queen, rather than a wicked one. Presumably recognising her failure in the role in 1217, she resolved to build a life for herself even if it further damaged her reputation. There is no doubt that Isabella was hated and whatever the truth of her life, to the chroniclers and later writers she had few of the redeeming features of her daughter-in-law, Eleanor of Provence, who although notorious, is noted for her devotion to her family, or her granddaughter-in-law, Eleanor of Castile, who enjoyed a remarkably happy marriage. Although these women were attributed with dubious morality, neither suffered the iniquitous image borne by Isabella.

Nepotism & Greed

Eleanor of Provence & Eleanor of Castile

Far from now representing the most ill-famed of English queens, Eleanor of Provence and her daughter-in-law, Eleanor of Castile, are remembered favourably, the latter having often been presented as the model of a good queen since the late medieval period. However this has not always been the case. Their unpopularity did not surpass that of women such as Isabella of Angouleme and Isabella of France, but during their lifetimes in England they were two of the most scorned English medieval queens. Eleanor of Provence was physically attacked by a London mob and Eleanor of Castile was the subject of much grumbling from the population throughout her reign. The ostracisation of both women derived from ideas of their foreign birth, together with the immigrants that their presence attracted to England. Eleanor of Provence was remembered for the many penniless relatives who joined her in England and whom she attempted to advance through patronage; nor was nepotism an alien concept for Eleanor of Castile. Both are also portrayed in sources as insatiably greedy, stripping the country of resources for their own profit. Although two very different women, their stories and the problems they encountered establishing themselves in a foreign country run parallel. With the loss of the Angevin Empire, England had become more insular with more strongly defined ideas of what constituted a 'foreigner'. As natives of France and Spain respectively, both Eleanors were considered foreign in England and they experienced all the suspicion and disapproval this brought.

Eleanor of Provence was the second of four daughters born to Count Raymond Berengar of Provence and his wife, Beatrice of Savoy.[1] The four sisters were all legendary beauties and this attracted high-ranking suitors, ensuring that all four became queens. Eleanor's elder sister, Margaret, married Louis IX of France when Eleanor was still young and this marriage served to increase Eleanor's own value on the marriage market. Although nothing survives of Eleanor's early life, legend suggests that she attempted to take her future into her own hands. According to one account, Eleanor composed a romantic poem about a legendary Cornish hero which she sent to Richard, Earl of Cornwall, the brother of Henry III of England.[2] If Eleanor did indeed write this poem her intention may have been to bring herself to the attention of one of the most powerful men in Europe and, if this was the case, it succeeded. The story continues: Richard was impressed by the poem and, knowing that his elder brother had been unsuccessful in finding his own bride, suggested that he marry the beautiful Eleanor. The idea appealed to Henry and he was so impressed with reports of Eleanor's beauty and character that he privately instructed his envoys to negotiate a marriage contract even if she brought no dowry.[3]

Eleanor was approximately thirteen at the time of her marriage and must have been apprehensive when she landed at Dover in January 1236.[4] Her family was unusually close and she must have missed her parents and sisters. She may have had some consolation from the fact that her uncle, William of Savoy, accompanied her to England and she quickly tried to show her gratitude towards him. Perhaps at Eleanor's request, William became one of Henry's chief counsellors and Henry also attempted to make him Bishop of Winchester.[5] For Eleanor, it must have seemed only natural to attempt to advance her relatives in her new home. However, almost from the outset there appear to have been hostile undercurrents about Eleanor's foreign birth and the strangers she brought with her. Eleanor, however, would not have been aware of this on her arrival in 1236 and she must have been anxious to meet her new husband. Henry was over twice Eleanor's age but made an effort to ensure that his young wife was comfortable and happy. The pair quickly became close. Eleanor must certainly have been hopeful for the future when she and Henry were married at Canterbury on 14 January 1236.[6] Eleanor was crowned soon afterwards in Westminster Abbey, appearing richly adorned in the jewels that Henry had given to her.[7]

Eleanor and Henry quickly settled into married life and, throughout their lives, they were renowned for their exceptionally happy marriage. In spite of her youth, however, Eleanor quickly came under pressure to produce an heir and there were rumours across the country that she was infertile.[8] Such accusations cannot have been easy for the young Eleanor to deal with and it is likely that she came to look more and more to her husband and relations for support. She must have been relieved when, in June 1239, she gave birth to a healthy son who was baptised Edward after Henry's favourite saint, Edward the Confessor.[9] Eleanor must have felt vindicated and the following year she also gave birth to a healthy daughter, named Margaret after Eleanor's older sister, the Queen of France. These births were followed in quick succession by two further healthy children, Beatrice and Edmund.

As well as being renowned for their happy marriage, Eleanor and Henry are also remembered as being loving parents to their children. Eleanor had enjoyed a close and loving family life in childhood and she took steps to replicate this for her own children. Edward, Eleanor's eldest son, remained devoted to his mother throughout his lifetime and Eleanor also retained a close relationship with her daughters even after their marriages. In 1253, for example, Henry wrote to Alexander of Scotland, the husband of their daughter Margaret, asking him to send Margaret south whilst both he and Alexander were absent abroad so that she could visit her mother.[10] Eleanor must have been greatly grieved when this request was refused. She and Henry were also distraught when their youngest child, Catherine, was born with a disability in 1253. The extent of Catherine's disability is not clear but both her parents gave generous gifts to the church to pray for her health.[11] They also provided their daughter with a fine memorial when she died before her fourth birthday. The illness and death of her youngest child must have had a profound effect on a woman as devoted to her family as Eleanor and it may have made her more determined than ever to promote the welfare of her remaining children, at whatever cost.

Certainly, Eleanor's actions towards her children did, on occasion, damage her reputation still further in England. In 1255, for example, when Henry and Eleanor received news that their daughter, Margaret, was being badly treated in Scotland, the couple immediately dropped everything and set off for Scotland at the head of an army.[12] They then brought the Queen of Scotland to England whilst they negotiated for her better treatment. This action demonstrates Eleanor's devotion as a mother and was entirely understandable, but it was also rash. This is also shown in the 'Sicilian Business', a scheme in which Eleanor became involved in 1254.[13] During that year the Pope contacted Eleanor and Henry offering the crown of Sicily to their younger son, Edmund, if they would only conquer the island for him. The prospect of a crown for her son was too much for Eleanor to resist and she was a major driving force behind the scheme, ensuring that Edmund was officially invested as King of Sicily at Westminster Abbey in October 1255.[14] However not everyone in England was as convinced as Eleanor by the merits of this expensive scheme. Nonetheless she could not have acted without Henry's support and should not be held wholly responsible for the scheme. It must have been a great disappointment when in November 1255, her uncle, Thomas of Savoy, acting as her envoy in the matter was captured and imprisoned in Turin. Eleanor immediately set about raising the ransom, but the setback signalled the end of the Sicilian Business.

The Sicilian Business damaged Eleanor's reputation but, by the mid-1250s, she was already deeply unpopular. Throughout her lifetime, Eleanor showed herself anxious to advance her relatives and this was noted and commented on from early in her marriage. Eleanor was particularly close to her mother's family, the Savoyards, and on her marriage they flocked to England. Over 170 Savoyards are known to have visited England during Eleanor's marriage and at least 70 settled, making them a powerful group amongst the higher ranks of society in England.[15] Eleanor encouraged Henry to patronise her relatives and he appears to have been willing to do so. In 1243 Eleanor's mother, Beatrice of Savoy visited and she was rewarded with a generous pension by her son-in-law.[16] Eleanor's uncles, Amadeus of Savoy and Thomas of Savoy were also granted pensions by Henry in the 1240s; in 1244 another uncle, Boniface of Savoy, was appointed as Archbishop of Canterbury.[17] These grants sparked jealousy amongst the English nobility and the honours were not merely limited to a financial nature. Eleanor's most able uncle,

Peter of Savoy, became one of Henry's most trusted advisors and he was also given rich grants of land. Eleanor encouraged the English nobility to arrange marriages with the Savoyards, perhaps playing a part in the marriage of her younger sister, Sanchia, to Henry's brother, Richard of Cornwall.[18] On a personal level, this marriage brought Eleanor's much loved sister into her daily life however it also caused discontent amongst the English nobility, which she does not appear to have noticed.

The growing Savoyard community in England congregated around Eleanor and she considered herself the leader of the Savoyard faction at court. She would have been perturbed when, in 1247, Henry's four Lusignan half-brothers and a half-sister arrived in England, seeking their brother's protection and patronage.[19] Henry openly welcomed his mother's children and quickly set about showering them with patronage as he had previously done with Eleanor's family. One half-brother, William of Valance, was permitted to marry the heiress of the Earl of Pembroke and another, Aymer de Lusignan, became Bishop of Winchester. Alice de Lusignan was also married to the heir to the Earl of Surrey, further strengthening the Lusignans' position in England. Neither Eleanor nor her closest ally, Peter of Savoy, welcomed these newcomers and the court divided into Lusignan and Savoyard factions. Both sides resorted to dirty tricks to rid themselves of their rivals and it is possible that the Lusignans stirred up trouble in Eleanor's close marriage. According to Eleanor's contemporary, Matthew Paris, when the Lusignans were exiled from England in 1258, they asked the King of France for permission to enter his kingdom:

> But the King of France refused, being exasperated by a complaint made against these Poitevins [the Lusignans] by the Queen of France to the effect that they had shamefully scandalised and defamed her sister, the Queen of England.[20]

This was probably Eleanor's revenge on the Lusignans but it is likely that their defamation caused Eleanor's reputation further damage.

Eleanor's interest in the Savoyard faction and her opposition to the Lusignans gave her a political position at court and she retained an interest in politics throughout her lifetime. In 1253, Henry left England in order to command a military expedition to Gascony and, a complement to his wife's abilities, left her as co-regent of England with his brother, Richard of Cornwall.[21] Eleanor threw herself into this role enthusiastically, raising troops in England to join Henry in his campaign against the King of Castile's invasion of Gascony. Perhaps eager to aid Henry's campaign on the continent, Eleanor also began to strictly enforce tax on cargoes loading and unloading at Queenhithe in England and to insist upon her right to Queen's gold payments from fines owed to the crown.[22] These extra payments would have bolstered Henry's finances in his campaign but they also increased the hostility of the Londoners towards the queen, a hostility that Eleanor would later come to experience more directly. In any event, Eleanor's rule as regent was not destined to last long and, in April 1254, she set out from England with her eldest son Edward to play her part in the peace Henry had negotiated for Gascony, exchanging war for a marriage.

The crisis in Gascony had arisen when Alfonso X, King of Castile, claimed the territory by virtue of his descent from Eleanor of Aquitaine, through her daughter, Eleanor.[23] Castile's claim to the province had been intermittently raised for half a century by the 1250s but, in late 1252, Alfonso renewed his claim, invading the province. Henry III was not a warlike king and, although he travelled to Gascony to conduct a campaign, on 15 May 1253, he instructed his ambassadors to try to arrange a marriage with Castile in order to avoid hostilities.[24] After long negotiations, it was decided that Henry's eldest son, Edward, would marry Alfonso's twelve-year-old half-sister, Eleanor. Eleanor of Castile must have waited with apprehension for the arrival of Edward and his mother but, unlike many other medieval princesses, she was apparently lucky in the husband chosen for her and the couple quickly became close, marrying at Burgos in Castile on 1 November 1254.[25]

Soon after the wedding, Eleanor of Castile and Edward returned to Gascony where they spent a year getting to know each other and adapting to married life.[26] It is possible that Eleanor of Castile perceived her mother-in-law's poor reputation and she may have deliberately limited the number of Castilians who accompanied her to England in October 1255. Nevertheless her arrival did stir up another wave of xenophobia in England. Henry III, eager for his young daughter-in-law to be comfortable, had taken advice from Eleanor's half-brother, Sancho of Castile, to furnish her apartments in Castilian fashion.[27] Eleanor was probably grateful for the carpeted rooms she received from Henry III but even this gesture stirred up trouble with fear that Eleanor's arrival would be accompanied by an influx of foreigners as her mother-in-law's had done. In reality her foreign birth was damning and it seems likely that any action carried out by Eleanor would have been wrong in the eyes of the English.

Eleanor of Castile appears rarely in sources between 1250 and 1260 and she may have spent much of this time growing up, learning the customs of her adopted country. She may have had some influence over Edward, and it is possible that she approved when, in 1258, he finally broke away from his mother's Savoyard faction and began allying himself with the Lusignans.[28] This was a deliberate act of rebellion against his controlling parents and Eleanor of Provence must have been deeply worried by her son's actions. Her distress would have increased when, in October 1259, Edward announced that he was now allying himself with his uncle, Simon de Montford, the leader of the barons who entered into rebellion against Henry III's rule in 1258.

Henry, like his father, King John, had had trouble with the barons for much of his reign. This hostility erupted dramatically in 1258, perhaps catching both Henry III and Eleanor of Provence by surprise. In two parliaments of that year, Henry was forced to agree to the demands of the barons, as his father had done, and to exile his half-brothers, the Lusignans.[29] Eleanor of Provence must have been relieved to see the back of the hated Lusignans but that would have been a small consolation. Eleanor herself was also seen as an enemy by the barons and her lands and castles were seized.[30] Eleanor and Henry deeply resented the dominance of the barons but there was little they could do. In 1260, Simon de Montford was in a strong enough position to have Peter of Savoy removed from the royal council, something which must have been deeply worrying for Eleanor. One consolation must have been Edward's return to his parents' cause but, even with his support, Henry and Eleanor were forced to employ foreign mercenaries and, in June 1263, they withdrew to the Tower of London.[31]

Locked in the Tower of London together, the future must have seemed bleak for Eleanor and Henry and they appear to have quarrelled about the best way to approach the situation. The couple were in a hopeless situation and matters can only have been made worse by the fact that they had no money with them and nobody in London would agree to give them credit.[32] Eleanor, who was always active herself, may well have felt frustrated at Henry's lack of activity and, when word reached her that Edward had taken matters into his own hands and stolen money from the New Temple in London, she apparently decided to abandon her husband and throw in her lot with her son.[33] According to the *Annals of Dunstable*:

> The queen left the Tower by the Thames on her way to Windsor by boat and came to London Bridge; when the Londoners assailed her and her men shamefully with foul and base words and even casting stones; so that freed with difficulty by the mayor of London and driven by necessity she went back to the Tower.[34]

Eleanor must have been horrified by the Londoners' reaction to her and perhaps this was the first moment in which she truly realised how unpopular she was. No English queen either before or after her was actually attacked by a mob and Eleanor must have emerged dishevelled and bruised from her ordeal. The indignities of the day were not over for Eleanor, however, and, when she arrived back at the Tower she found the gates barred against her on Henry's orders.[35] It must have been a furious and distraught Eleanor who was finally taken to lodge at the Bishop's palace, although she and Henry appear to have been reconciled soon afterwards.

As in other perilous times, Eleanor immediately turned to her family for help and, in September 1263, her brother-in-law, Louis IX, summoned Henry, Eleanor and their sons, along with Simon de Montford, to present their cases before him in France.[36] The barons forced Henry and Eleanor to swear oaths that they would return to England, but Eleanor clearly had no intention of keeping her oath. Henry and Eleanor laid a number of complaints about de Montford before Louis, but there was little he could do. Soon after the meeting, Henry and Edward returned to England but Eleanor and Edmund, in violation of their oaths, refused to return.

Henry and Edward were not idle on their return to England and both set about raising an army in an attempt to defeat the barons.[37] On 14 May 1264 a royal army, four times the size of the force commanded by de Montford, met the barons in Battle at Lewes. Both Eleanor of Provence and Eleanor of Castile would have waited anxiously for news of this battle, hoping for word of a royal victory. It was not to be, however, and the Battle of Lewes proved to be a great disaster for Henry III. By the end of the day Henry III, his brother, Richard of Cornwall, and Edward were all prisoners and it was left to Eleanor of Provence alone to continue the struggle against the barons.[38] The royal women were clearly considered a potential danger by the barons and this is likely to be due to Eleanor of Provence's reputation as a formidable woman. They took no chances and Eleanor of Castile was ordered to join Henry III in his imprisonment so that the barons could keep an eye on her.[39]

The barons were right to be worried about Eleanor of Provence's activities and, soon after news of the Battle of Lewes reached her, she began collecting troops in order to invade England.[40] News of this deeply troubled the barons and the *Annals of Dunstable* describes how 'the king on their advice had his letters sent to all the shires of England commanding all the adjacent sea coasts of England to be guarded by an ample force of armed men against adversaries coming from foreign parts'.[41] News of this probably only spurred Eleanor on and she also persuaded the King and Queen of France to approach the Pope to annul the baron's actions and to excommunicate them.[42]

In spite of the difficulties of her position, Eleanor pressed on with gathering her forces and, by autumn 1264, she was based on the Flemish coast with a large army.[43] Eleanor was probably confident of victory against the barons and must have imagined that she would land in England in triumph. However, once again, bad luck dogged her and storms kept her trapped on the coast for several months. Eleanor must have watched anxiously as she quickly ran out of money and, with the last of her funds, her army drifted away, leaving her unable to do anything for Henry and Edward except watch, impotently, from France. For a woman as active and resourceful as Eleanor of Provence, this must have been difficult to bear and it would have been with relief, in May 1265, that she finally heard that Edward had escaped his captors and was raising his own force in England.[44] On 4 August 1265 Edward and the barons met in battle at Evesham and, during the day, Simon de Montford was killed, crushing the baron's resistance and restoring Henry III to power.[45] Eleanor of Provence landed at Dover on 1 November 1265 to be reunited with her husband and son and to be restored to her position as queen.[46]

Although glad to return, Eleanor of Provence was never to regain the same influence that she had had before the baron's revolt. She may, perhaps, have been content with this and to allow her daughter-in-law, Eleanor of Castile, more influence. Certainly, after the birth of her first son, John, in July 1266 and a second son, Henry, in May 1268, Eleanor of Castile's position in England was secured.[47] The births of these sons, as well as a number of daughters, also seems to have united the two Eleanors and both Henry III and Eleanor of Provence were doting grandparents, taking custody of their grandchildren when Edward and Eleanor of Castile decided to go on crusade in 1270.

As the story of Eleanor of Castile's own ancestress, Eleanor of Aquitaine shows, it was not unheard of for women to accompany their husbands on crusade and Eleanor of Castile was adamant about accompanying Edward. According to legend, when attempts were made to dissuade Eleanor from going, she replied that no one ought to separate husband and wife and that, in any event, Syria was as near to Heaven as England and Spain.[48] Whether or not these were Eleanor's exact words, she probably said something to that effect and Edward and Eleanor of Castile were devoted to each other throughout their marriage. Eleanor certainly suffered emotional and physical hardships whilst in the Holy Land, giving birth to two daughters during the campaign.[49]

The crusade is notable for a legend that has grown up around Eleanor of Castile. Whilst they were in the Holy Land, Edward was stabbed twice by an assassin with a poisoned dagger before he was able to overpower his assailant and kill him.[50] Edward was grievously injured in this attack and, according to some reports, it was Eleanor herself who saved him. Camden wrote:

> When her husband was treacherously wounded by a moor with a poyson'd sword, and rather grew worse than receiv'd any ease by what the Physicians apply'd to it, she found out a remedy, as new and unheard of, as full of love and endearment for by reason of the malignity of the poison, her husband's wounds could not possibly be clos'd: but she lick'd them dayly with her own tongue, and suck'd out the venomous humour, thinking it a most delicious liquor. By the power whereof, or rather by

the virtue of a wife's tenderness, she so drew out the poisonous matter, that he was entirely cur'd of his wound, and she escap'd without catching any harm. What then can be more rare than this woman's expression of love? Or what can be more admirable? The tongue of a wife, anointed (if I may so say) with duty and love to her husband, draws from her beloved those poisons which could not be drawn by the most approv'd Physician, and what many and most exquisite medicines could not do, is effected purely by the love of a wife.[51]

The story of Eleanor sucking out the poison from Edward's wounds is one of the most enduring that surrounds her. However, no version of this story is contemporary with Eleanor. In fact, those contemporary sources which mention the assassination attempt on Edward present a very different picture of a hysterical Eleanor having to be carried from Edward's tent so that his surgeons could operate. The story of Eleanor sucking the poison from Edward's wounds fits well with the almost saintly posthumous reputation that has grown up around her. However, the image of a hysterical Eleanor fits more accurately with the reality of her character. It is also entirely understandable and Eleanor, who was completely dependent on Edward and appears to have loved him, must have been terrified.

The assassination attempt in June 1272 marked the end of Edward's interest in crusading and, as soon as he was well enough, the couple set out to return to England.[52] Eleanor was probably relieved. The couple moved in leisurely stages towards England and it was whilst they were staying in Sicily they received the news that their eldest son, John, and Edward's father, Henry III, had died. Edward apparently took the death of his father much harder than the death of his son although Eleanor's feelings are not recorded. By 1272, she had already lost several daughters and the death of an infant son that she had not seen for two years may have had little effect on her. Certainly, both Edward and Eleanor seem to have reasoned that they still had one surviving son and that they were also still young. In any event, during the journey back to England, Eleanor bore a third son, Alphonso. Edward and Eleanor finally arrived back in England on 2 August 1274 and were crowned together in Westminster Abbey.[53]

Eleanor of Provence took the deaths of her grandchildren harder than their parents did. She retained custody of her grandson, Henry, after his parents returned to England and she was with him when he died on 14 October 1274.[54] This was in stark contrast to his parents who, although staying in London at the time of their eldest surviving son's death, did not bother to make the short trip to visit him at Guildford.[55] They also did not commission any memorial masses for their next eldest son, Alphonso, when he died in 1284, a very unusual omission for that time.[56] Eleanor of Castile spent the majority of her marriage in childbearing and bore around fifteen or sixteen children.[57] To modern eyes, at least, neither she nor Edward appear to have been fond parents and they had little involvement in their children's upbringing, for example, sending their daughter, Joan of Acre, to be raised in Ponthieu by Eleanor's mother.[58] It is true that Edward and Eleanor's court was extremely mobile, constantly moving around the country. However, Henry III's court had also been mobile and he and Eleanor of Provence had always shown an interest in their children in a way that Edward I and Eleanor of Castile did not.

The children were, however, a source of common interest between Eleanor of Provence and Eleanor of Castile in a relationship that might otherwise have been tense. After Henry III's death, Eleanor of Provence still retained a keen interest in politics and it is possible that her influence over Edward irked Eleanor of Castile. Certainly, Eleanor of Provence was unable to let go of her children, even when they were well and truly grown up, as one letter that she wrote to Edward shows:

> Know, dear sire, that we are most desirous to have good news of your health and how things have been with you since you left us. We are letting you know that we are in good health, thanks be to God. We have left Gillingham sooner than we expected, because of the noisomeness of the air, and the thick clouds of smoke which rise in the evenings and have come to Marlborough, arriving on the Friday after Michaelmas. Thanks be to God we are in good health, and we greatly desire to know the same of you.[59]

After the loss of her two daughters in 1275, Eleanor of Provence was probably extremely anxious to know of the health of her surviving children. Her letter, however, shows a single-mindedness and forcefulness that Eleanor of Provence exhibited throughout her life and one that never made her popular. This possessiveness was also exhibited in her relationships with her grandchildren and, in 1285, the two women certainly came into conflict when Eleanor of Provence insisted that her granddaughter, Mary, become a nun at Amesbury, in spite of the protestations of Mary's mother to the contrary.[60] Eleanor of Provence lived at the nunnery of Amesbury for most of the time after 1276 and, in 1287, became a nun herself.[61] She probably wanted Mary to keep her company but such a move certainly did not make her popular with her daughter-in-law.

Although Eleanor of Castile's main activity during her marriage was childbearing, she is also chiefly remembered for her acquisition of land. This began early in her marriage and she was apparently determined to carve out a large landholding in England at whatever cost. Even before she was queen, Eleanor had an excellent grasp of the landholdings in the country and was relentless in pursuing what she believed belonged to her. A letter by Eleanor in 1265 to John of London shows something of this aspect of her character:

Know that our lord the king gave us the other day the manor of Berewic with its appurtenances, at the solicitation of Sir Roger de Leyburn, and because it is appurtenant to the guardianship of Cantilupe, my lord has given it to another, so that nothing of it is remitted to us, but there is another manor close by in the county of Somerset, which is at the town of Heselbere, which belonged to Sir William the Marshal, who is dead and held it of the king in chief. Wherefore we would desire that you should ask of Sir John de Kyrkbi if the guardianship of that manor is granted, and if it is not, them that you should pray Sir Roger de Leyburn and the Bishop of Bath on our behalf that they should procure from our lord the king that he grant us the manor until the coming of age of the heir of Sir William. And, if it is given, there is another manor in the county of Dorset, which is called Gerente, which belonged to Sir William de Keenes, who is dead, and he held it in chief of the king, wherefore we would that if we cannot have the other, you should pray them on our behalf that these should apply to the king to allow us this one; the manor of Heselbere is worth less. And if neither, pray Sir Roger in this way. Tell him that the manor of Berewic that the king gave us at his suggestion has been taken from us, for this will tend to make us seem less covetous; and say the same to the bishop of Bath.[62]

If Eleanor hoped that she would not be seen as covetous in her acquisition of land, then she did not succeed but quickly gained a reputation across England for greed. One popular rhyme of the period sums up the mood in England at the time, saying 'the king he wants to get our gold, the queen would like our land to hold'.[63] Eleanor disregarded the popular perception of her, neither did she heed Archbishop Pechan of Canterbury when he admonished her for the sin of usury and warned her that Edward's harsh rule was being blamed by the people squarely on her influence.[64] The second charge was not reasonable since Eleanor of Castile never managed to achieve political influence over her husband. However, she was certainly guilty of usury and greed and the details of her land acquisitions do not make easy reading.

Eleanor appears to have been happy to use any methods possible in her quest for land and she was not averse to bending and even breaking the law in order to increase her own wealth. In 1278, for example, she was able to acquire Leeds Castle in Kent from William Leyburn by taking over a debt which he owed to a Jewish moneylender.[65] Once she had acquired the debt, Eleanor immediately repossessed the castle, which had been used as security, giving the owner only minimum compensation for his loss. Eleanor's land acquisition was very tied up with Jewish moneylenders and, in 1283, Edward granted her the goods and chattels of condemned Jews.[66] This certainly helped Eleanor increase her wealth but it did not increase her popularity and her name came to be associated with the hated Jewish moneylenders.

Eleanor's agents also committed a number of harsh acts in her name and Eleanor, although not personally involved, would have known what was happening and her silence suggests that she approved of her officials' actions. At Havering, for example, Eleanor's agents limited local hunting rights by extending her rabbit warrens. When twelve tenants protested, they were imprisoned.[67] Eleanor's agents also seized a house on another estate and had the owners imprisoned on trumped up charges. Their baby was then dumped in its cradle in the middle of the road.[68] Eleanor was apparently unconcerned by these actions and on the only recorded occasion that she dismissed an official it was for his failure to generate sufficient revenue.[69]

Eleanor of Castile also had a reputation for having a fierce and implacable temper. In 1279 Archbishop Pechan wrote to the nuns at

Headingham who were refusing to admit a friend of Eleanor's to their nunnery.[70] The Archbishop, who apparently knew Eleanor well, warned them that they would do well not to cross the queen. In 1283, Eleanor also threatened to prosecute the Bishop of Worcester for a debt she claimed he owed her.[71] The bishop was equally adamant that there was no debt but Edward's chancellor advised him to pay her anyway if he knew what was good for him. Clearly, Eleanor of Castile was known as a domineering woman. Sometimes even Edward felt she had gone too far, forcing her to relax a fine she had imposed in 1283.[72] Even Eleanor herself later came to realise that she had been unjust and, on her death-bed, begged Edward to make amends for her actions for the good of her immortal soul. Eleanor's acquisitiveness went beyond that of most other medieval queens. It must also be pointed out that Edward benefited from his wife's acquisitions and he did not work very hard to encourage moderation in her behaviour. Her policies suited him, but it is Eleanor who bears the full blame. Similarly with Edward's harsh rule. It seems that to the people of England, Edward as a popular and English king was incapable of doing wrong except at the instigation of his unpopular foreign queen.

Eleanor continued to acquire land right up until the end of her life and it was an abiding interest for her. During 1290, it became clear that Eleanor's health was deteriorating. In November 1290, the court set out north on a progress and Eleanor insisted on accompanying Edward, as she had always done, not wanting to be parted from him. The court made slow progress, however, and, it seems likely that this was due to Eleanor's poor state of health. They tried to reach Lincoln but, due to Eleanor's illness, were forced to stop at the manor of Harby and it was there, on 28 November 1290, that Eleanor of Castile died.

Edward I was devastated by the death of his wife and resolved to give her the grandest memorial of any English queen. He had her body transported slowly to Westminster and, at every place her body stayed for the night, he erected a cross in memorial to her, constructing twelve in all.[73] According to Camden, the crosses were 'a monument which King Edward I erected in memory to Queen Eleanor, the dearest husband to the most loving wife'.[74] These twelve crosses, the most famous of which was erected at Charing Cross, in London, served as a testament to Edward's devotion and caught the imagination of people for several centuries afterwards. It was on the basis of these crosses that Eleanor achieved a posthumous reputation completely remote from that which she had enjoyed in life and, after her death, she was portrayed as a pious queen.[75] This is not how she was viewed in her own time, however, and her reputation, during her lifetime, was of one of the most notorious and unpopular queens that England had ever had, just as her mother-in-law, Eleanor of Provence, was also perceived.

Eleanor of Provence survived her daughter-in-law by just over six months, dying at Amesbury on 24 June 1291.[76] She had also been unpopular during her lifetime but, unlike her daughter-in-law, was survived by no husband to provide an extravagant memorial to her. In her day she was seen in a negative light by the people of England and through her association with the troubles of Henry III's reign they would never have judged her to be a successful monarch. To modern eyes, at least, she appears as one of the most personally likeable of all medieval queens. For both women it is clear that their real crimes were their foreign births. There is no doubt that at points they acted unwisely and even harshly, but similarly did their husbands and many other contemporaries. The difference is that, by the thirteenth century, kings were beginning to be considered as Englishmen. Queens on the other hand, who were generally brought from the continent, were not. They were therefore alien to the increasingly insular country and, as such, useful scapegoats and easy targets.

Eleanor of Provence and Eleanor of Castile were deeply unpopular during their lifetimes and were scorned as poor queens by their contemporaries. Over the years Eleanor of Castile's reputation completely altered, such that by the later medieval period she was used as a model of queenly virtue for other women to follow. It was only much later that a more accurate picture of her life and reputation was able to emerge, providing a much less likeable, but much more human, picture of the queen. Eleanor of Provence, on the other hand, received no such attestation of her husband's devotion and retained an image of an unloved and unsuccessful queen until recently. Her reputation has improved in recent years and she shows a likeable quality in her devotion to her family. Neither queen, however, was a success in their time and this was largely due to their foreign birth and their apparent avariciousness.

Eleanor of Provence was certainly acquisitive for her family, procuring honours and wealth for them at the expense of others, and Eleanor of Castile was acquisitive for herself. It amounted to the same thing in their contemporaries' eyes, however, and both queens were always ill-famed for their greed. However in comparison with Eleanor of Castile's own daughter-in-law, Isabella of France, this was a small matter and the two Eleanors' notoriety pale in comparison to that of the She-Wolf of France.

The She-Wolf of France

Isabella of France

With the exception, perhaps, of Aelfthryth, Isabella of France has the worst reputation of any queen of England. However, until 1325, Isabella's career was that of a traditional queen consort and her career after 1330 was mostly that of a traditional queen dowager. Isabella's sullied reputation rests on the years between 1325 and 1330 and the extraordinary course that she took during that period, leading to Isabella and her lover establishing themselves as rulers of England behind a puppet king. There is no doubt that Isabella went much farther than any other medieval queen and she rightly attracted a great deal of attention. However it is also necessary to look at the circumstances that caused Isabella to take the action she did in 1326 and it is clear that Isabella was sorely tried. For years, Isabella attempted to play the role of a good and dutiful queen and it was only after years of provocation that she finally snapped and took unprecedented, and to many, damning action. It should also not be forgotten that she received the support of the country in her endeavours. It was only later as her situation degenerated that she became the victim of her own fame with the irretrievable loss of her reputation. Isabella of France carried out some cruel and terrible actions but she was driven into these and supported, at least for a time, by the entire country, only later being transformed from 'Isabella the Fair' into Isabella the She-Wolf of France.

Isabella of France was the only surviving daughter of Philip IV of France and his wife, Jeanne, Queen of Navarre. As the daughter of two monarchs, Isabella would have been raised to have the highest opinion of her own status and she was thoroughly spoiled by her adoring father. Isabella enjoyed a cosseted upbringing and she would have known, from her youth, that she was destined to be a queen. Relations between France and England were often tense and, in 1298, the Pope proposed a double marriage to cement an alliance between England and France, with Edward I marrying Isabella's aunt, Margaret, and his son marrying the infant Isabella.[1] The first marriage occurred soon afterwards, but Isabella's was postponed until she was older. Isabella was formally betrothed by proxy to Prince Edward in May 1303.[2] Isabella probably enjoyed being the centre of attention at the ceremony and she must have wondered what her absent future husband was like.

Edward, who was twelve years older than Isabella, showed no interest in his future bride and was only interested in the political advantages of the match. Isabella, as the daughter of two sovereigns, was the most eligible princess of her generation. According to Froissart, she was also 'one of the greatest beauties of her time' and she must have been confident in her ability to please her husband.[3] She came from a very good-looking family and both Isabella and her father Philip were nicknamed 'the Fair'. Throughout her lifetime everyone praised Isabella's beauty and her charms and she cannot have doubted that she would be anything other than adored by Edward, as she was by everyone else.

Edward I of England died in 1307 and Edward II decided to delay his coronation until he could share it with Isabella. Soon after his accession, Edward crossed to France and was met at Boulogne by Isabella and her father, Philip, as well as many other members of her family. Philip had provided Isabella with a magnificent trousseau for her wedding, including seventy-two headdresses and two gold crowns.[4] Isabella also wore a rich wedding dress, which she preserved all her life. Edward and Isabella were married with great ceremony at Boulogne on 25 January 1308.[5] Isabella must have seen her wedding as the culmination of her destiny and she had been preparing herself to be Queen of England since her infancy. She is likely to have been pleased with Edward as he was, by all accounts, a handsome and charming man. It is unlikely that, at first, she noticed anything unusual about Edward's behaviour towards her, although some of his actions may have caused concern to her father and her other relatives present. Certainly, the fact that Edward sent his wedding presents to his favourite, Piers Gaveston, in England did not go unnoticed by the French.[6]

Piers Gaveston had been a member of Edward's household since 1300 and he quickly became Edward's most intimate companion.[7] Their relationship had caused Edward I much concern and, in February 1307, he had banished Gaveston, only for Edward II to immediately recall him on his accession. Edward II is known to have had an illegitimate son who was born before 1307 and so he clearly did, at least on one occasion, have a mistress.[8] There has been much debate over the exact nature of the relationship between Edward and Gaveston. However, several contemporary sources hint at an intimate relationship and most modern historians believe that there was a homosexual relationship between them. Edward relied on Gaveston and had left him regent of England when he travelled to France to marry Isabella. It is unlikely that Isabella knew of this before her marriage although she may quickly have come to suspect the truth after her arrival in England.

Edward and Isabella sailed for England soon after the wedding. Isabella must have eager to visit her new country and she would have been shocked to discover the extent of Edward's feelings for Gaveston when they landed in England. As soon as the ship docked, Edward ran off the ship and flew to embrace Gaveston who was waiting in the harbour.[9] Isabella had been escorted to England by her uncles, the Counts of Valois and Evreux and they were dismayed by this incident, writing indignantly to her father in France.[10] It is likely that this was the first Isabella knew of Edward's relationship with Gaveston and this, along with the events of the next few weeks, must have made her increasingly uneasy.

The royal couple travelled to London where they were crowned together in great ceremony. This event must also have been marred for Isabella, however, as Gaveston played a prominent role in the ceremony and caused offense amongst the English barons by carrying the royal crown before the king.[11] Edward also sat with Gaveston at the coronation banquet that followed, rather than with Isabella.[12] Isabella was always keenly aware of her royal dignity and these slights would have weighed heavily on her mind. It was also around this time that Isabella

Right: 1 A nineteenth-century interpretation of the murder of Edward the Martyr giving a prominent role to Queen Aelfthryth.

Below: 2 The brooding ruins of Corfe Castle, the scene of the murder of Edward the Martyr.

3 Queen Emma's mortuary chest at Winchester Cathedral, which she shares with her husband, King Cnut.

Above left: 4 Queen Emma with her sons, Edward the Confessor and Harthacnut.

Above right: 5 The Empress Matilda, the English Crown's first female claimant.

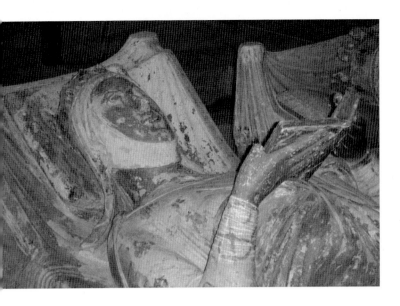

6 The tomb of Eleanor of Aquitaine at Fontevrault where she lies buried next to her estranged husband, Henry II.

7 The tomb of Isabella of Angouleme at Fontevrault.

8 An image of Eleanor of Castile on the Eleanor Cross at Waltham Cross.

9 The Eleanor Cross at Waltham Cross.

Above: 10 The marriage of Isabella of France and Edward II.

Here sheweo how Jan fane Duches of Bretayn doughter of the kyng of Nabern, and now wedded wyf to Henry the iiij kyng of England was Crowned Quene of this noble Rame of England

11 The coronation of Joan of Navarre, the only English queen to be punished for witchcraft.

Above: 12 Margaret of Anjou with her husband, Henry VI.

Left: 13 Elizabeth Woodville, the unlucky queen of Edward IV.

Above left: 14 Anne Boleyn, second wife of Henry VIII.

Above right: 15 Engraving representing Catherine Howard, the fifth wife of Henry VIII.

Left: 16 Traitors' Gate, through which Anne Boleyn and Catherine Howard passed on their way to their deaths.

17 A romantic nineteenth-century interpretation of Lady Jane Grey's acceptance of the Crown.

18 Mary Tudor, England's first effective queen regnant.

noticed Gaveston wearing the jewels her father had given to Edward as a wedding present, something that she wrote indignantly to her father about.[13]

Isabella was not the only person to notice and resent the prominence of Gaveston. Her uncles, the counts of Evreux and Valois returned to France soon after the coronation bringing reports of the poor reception Isabella had met with in England. Edward also faced opposition in England and, according to the Chronicle of Lanercost:

> The people of the country and the leading men complained loudly at his [Edward's] coronation against the aforesaid Piers, and unanimously wished that he should be deprived of his earldom; but this the king obstinately refused. The rumours increased from day to day, and engrossed the lips and ears of all men, nor was there one who had a good word either for the king or for Piers. The chief men agreed unanimously in strongly demanding that Piers should be sent back into exile, foremost among them being the noble earl of Lincoln and the young earl of Gloucester, whose sister, however, Piers had received in marriage by the king's gift.[14]

From early in his reign with regard to this there had been much opposition to Edward and in June 1308 he was compelled by parliament to send Gaveston into exile.[15]

Isabella must have been elated to hear of Gaveston's exile, and she spent more time with Edward during Gaveston's absence.[16] Isabella and Edward also seem to have reached an understanding with each other and even after Gaveston's return they were often together. She also seems to have been on good terms with Gaveston. It is probable that Isabella was prepared to accept Edward's relationship with Gaveston in return for the status of queen. By 1311 she was probably aware of the homosexual nature of Edward's relationship with Gaveston but was prepared to ignore it in return for good treatment and the trappings of queenship. She and Edward also developed some kind of relationship during this period and by early 1312 she was pregnant.

Despite the rapprochement between Isabella and Gaveston, his presence was deeply resented by the English nobility. Gaveston was seen as an upstart by the more established nobility and hated for his close relationship with the king. By 1312, the barons were actively working towards the destruction of Gaveston. The two leading barons, the Earls of Lancaster and Leicester were the maternal half-brothers of Isabella's mother and it has often been suggested that they acted as their niece's champions in the destruction of Gaveston.[17] However, the evidence of Isabella's pregnancy and her improved status suggest that she had come to accept the presence of Gaveston. She does not appear to have identified with her uncles' policies at this stage of her queenship.

Midway through 1312, Isabella, Edward and Gaveston set out northwards for York.[18] Whilst there they heard the news that Thomas of Lancaster was secretly marching north with an army, so they fled to Newcastle. Isabella would have known that she was not the focus of Lancaster's anger but the escape must have been an ordeal for her. Soon after their arrival, Edward and Gaveston took ship to Scarborough, leaving Isabella unprotected at Newcastle.[19] Isabella left Newcastle soon afterwards, travelling to the safety of Tynemouth Castle to await events. She must have been very anxious about what the future would hold for her unborn child and, perhaps, angry at Edward and Gaveston's desertion of her.

Isabella was not the focus of the baron's wrath, however, and instead they set off in pursuit of Gaveston. Soon after their voyage to Scarborough, Edward and Gaveston separated. They were never to see each other again. Gaveston was quickly attacked and captured by Lancaster and he was turned over to the control of the Earl of Pembroke.[20] On 19 July 1312, he was taken out to the crossroads at Blacklow Hill, near Warwick, and beheaded by the barons without trial.[21] Edward was furious at the death of his favourite but powerless to take any immediate action against the barons. Isabella's feelings about the death of Gaveston are unclear, but it is likely that she was not displeased with his now permanent absence from Edward's side. Some time after the murder, Isabella travelled slowly south towards Windsor.

Isabella of France gave birth to her eldest child on 13 November 1312 at Windsor Castle.[22] According to John Capgrave 'many Frensch lordis, that were aboute hir, wold a clepid him Philippea, aftir the kyng of Frans: the Englisch lordes wold have him Edward. The king had so grete joy of this child new born, that his heavinesse for Petir [Gaveston] cesed some'.[23] Isabella must have been triumphant in the birth of her son, even if she was unable to name him Philip. By 1312 her career followed that of a traditional medieval queen and the birth of a son cemented her role. She also gained a much greater political role following her son's birth and demonstrated a politically independent streak on a number of occasions over the next few years.

Isabella set herself up as a peacemaker during Edward's troubled reign. In early 1313 she is mentioned in sources with the Earl of Gloucester, presiding over peace negotiations between Edward and the nobility.[24] Isabella attempted to reach a compromise between the opposing sides in the dispute in order to restore a measure of stability in England. In 1318 she is recorded again as a peacemaker in concert with the Earl of Hereford. Isabella and the earl appear to have achieved a measure of success in their endeavours and the peace negotiations led to a Treaty with Lancaster.[25] For much of her queenship, Isabella quietly promoted Edward's policies and ensured that some measure of stability was maintained.

Isabella did not only work for Edward, however because she also had her own political interests during the middle part of Edward's reign. This can be clearly seen in her actions concerning the election of the Bishop of Durham in 1317.[26] Lancaster suggested one of his clerks for the position and Edward also supported his own candidate, Thomas de Cobham. Isabella, ignoring the wishes of both her uncle and her husband, supported Lewis de Beaumont, a kinsman of hers and a member of her household. When the monks of Durham elected one of their own monks, Isabella appealed to Edward on her knees on de Beaumont's behalf. Edward yielded to her pleas and refused to elect the monks' candidate, securing the election for de Beaumont. Isabella busied herself with securing Church appointments for her supporters and, in 1316, is known to have petitioned the Pope in an attempt to secure the election of her confessor to the see of Rochester.[27] She also enlisted the support of the King of France, despite the fact that Edward had already written to the Pope supporting his own candidate. Clearly, Isabella was used to getting her own way, and was determined in what she wanted.

Isabella also remained an important political figure in relations with France. In May 1313, she and Edward visited the French court at Paris and Isabella played an important role in political negotiations between the two countries. Isabella must have been pleased to see her family again after five years since she is known to have been fond of her family.

Isabella's visit may, however, have been tainted by her concern regarding the behaviour of her three sisters-in-law, Margaret, Blanche and Jeanne of Burgundy.[28] During the visit, Isabella gave her three sisters-in-law silk purses that she had embroidered herself. In July 1313, following their return to England, Isabella and Edward held a banquet attended by several French knights. During the banquet, Isabella noticed the purses that she had given to Margaret and Blanche hanging from the belts of two knights.

In February 1314, Isabella returned to France without Edward in order to negotiate a treaty.[29] It is likely that she mentioned her suspicions to her father whilst there and, soon after her return to England in April, scandal rocked the royal family in France. Margaret and Blanche of Burgundy were found to have been having affairs with the two knights, aided by their sister, Jeanne. The knights were tortured and executed on the orders of Isabella's father and Margaret and Blanche sentenced to life imprisonment. Isabella's eldest brother, Louis, immediately annulled his marriage to Margaret and disinherited his young daughter. Isabella was not present in France whilst these events occurred but she was considered by contemporaries to have been directly involved in events and was vilified for her disloyalty to her sisters-in-law.[30] The scandal led to the earliest criticism of Isabella in the sources and she certainly does not come out of this incident as an entirely attractive figure when it is viewed in the light of her own subsequent conduct. But at the time she probably believed that she had served her family and saved the prestige of the French royal house. It is also understandable that Isabella, who was fond of her family, would not have wanted to stand by whilst her brothers were cuckolded, particularly when the succession to the throne of France was at stake.

Isabella's marriage during this period was, by contrast, scandal-free. Isabella conceived children only occasionally and it appears that she and Edward were rarely intimate with each other. She did however bear him three further children after after the birth of Edward.[31] Isabella's influence over Edward during this period appears to have been widely recognised and, in 1319, attempts by the Scots to capture Isabella whilst she was staying near York highlight the importance she was seen to have in Edward's government.[32]

Nonetheless Isabella's position in government was always tenuous as demonstrated by the rise of the Despensers. In the years immediately after Piers Gaveston's death Edward did not have a favourite at court. After a few years, he became notably fond of a father and son, both called Hugh Despenser. The elder Despenser had been an important figure in government since the reign of Edward I but his rise and that of his son proved dramatic under Edward II. Some contemporary sources hint at the relationship between Edward and the younger Despenser and the actions of Isabella herself towards her rival suggest strongly that their relationship was homosexual. The rise of the two new favourites cannot have been welcome to Isabella and was the catalyst for the breakdown of her marriage.

The Despensers viewed Isabella as a rival and their attitude towards her was consistently hostile. In 1320, the elder Despenser refused to pay Isabella money that he owed her from the manor of Lechlade and, in 1321, the younger Despenser refused to pay Isabella rents he owed her from Bristol.[33] These were calculated slights against the queen and Edward refused to act on Isabella's protests. Isabella must have felt that her influence over Edward was slipping away and she became increasingly marginalised in English politics and court life. She nevertheless remained loyal to Edward throughout the early 1320s despite increasing baronial opposition.

In February 1321 the barons met with Lancaster in order to enlist his support against the Despensers. Isabella must have been anxious about the rise in baronial discontent and retired to the Tower of London in July to bear her youngest child, Joan.[34] This must have been an ordeal for Isabella but she still remained loyal to Edward and in October 1321 she played a major role in providing a pretext for him to make war on the barons.

Isabella departed on a pilgrimage to Canterbury in late 1321 and, on 2 October, she approached Leeds Castle, which was part of her dower, intending to stay the night. Upon arrival, Isabella's stewards were denied entry to the castle by the wife of the castellan and, when they insisted, the castle guards became violent, killing some of Isabella's attendants.[35] The castellan was a known supporter of the barons and it is likely that Isabella had been sent to Leeds in order to provide an excuse for Edward to attack him. However, it is also likely that Isabella was genuinely shocked at the violent response she met and may have harboured resentment towards Edward for sending her there, effectively using her as bait. When Edward heard of Isabella's experience at Leeds he set out with an army of Londoners to capture the castle. The castle quickly fell and the castellan was hanged from the gates.[36] Edward then marched north where he met the barons in battle at Boroughbridge to win a stunning victory. Isabella's uncle, Thomas of Lancaster, was taken prisoner and executed, poignantly in the same manner used upon Gaveston.

Isabella's feelings on the death of her uncle were probably mixed. He had been a thorn in the side of Edward's rule for years and she may have believed that he deserved to die. However, as his kinsman she was bound to be affronted by the manner of his death and must have been uneasy at the power Lancaster's death would give to the Despensers. Certainly, Isabella's treatment in England deteriorated rapidly after Lancaster's execution.

Relations between England and France had been difficult for some years during Edward's reign and, in 1324, Isabella's uncle, Charles of Valois, overran the English possession of Gascony.[37] Edward retaliated on 28 September by seizing Isabella's lands and those of foreign monasteries.[38] Suspicion fell on Isabella as a Frenchwoman and Edward and the Despensers exploited this to gain more control over the queen. Her allowance had already been cut dramatically and, in late 1324, Isabella's three youngest children were removed from her custody.[39] The younger Despenser's wife was also 'appointed, as it were, guardian of the queen, and carried her seal; nor could the queen write to anybody without her knowledge: whereat my lady the queen was equally indignant and distressed, and therefore wished to visit her brother in France to seek a remedy'.[40] Isabella must have been furious at Edward's treatment of her after sixteen years of loyal marriage and this, in addition to all Edward's other bad conduct towards her, would be an entirely understandable motive for her to hate him. She had, after all, done no wrong and had been a loyal queen of England. Her imprisonment, on the pretext that she was a Frenchwoman, would therefore rightly have infuriated her.

Isabella kept her resentment hidden and Edward's actions show that he did not regard her as a threat, entirely underestimating his dynamic wife. Isabella had acted as a negotiator between England and France on a number of occasions and Edward does not seem to have recognised the danger in sending her again on 9 March 1325.[41] According to the *Chronicle of Lanercost*:

> The King of England sent his consort the queen to her brother, the king of France, hoping that, by God's help, peace might be established between himself and the king of France through her, according to her promise. But the queen had a secret motive for desiring to cross over to France; for Hugh Despenser the younger, the king's agent in all matters of business, was exerting himself at the pope's court to procure divorce between the king of England and the queen.[42]

There is no other evidence that Edward was considering a divorce and it is unlikely that he considered going so far. However, there was clearly very bad feeling between Isabella and the Despensers and Edward always sided entirely with his favourites rather than his wife.

Isabella must have felt a great sense of freedom and relief as she arrived in France. Isabella landed at Boulogne and was lavishly entertained there before travelling to Paris where her brother, King Charles, welcomed her.[43] Charles secretly promised Isabella aid and she clearly felt confident enough to act against Edward. Soon after her arrival she was also able to persuade Edward to send their eldest son, young Edward, to her in Paris to do homage for Gascony.[44] Young Edward's arrival meant that Isabella held a trump card against her husband and she began to attract English exiles to her in Paris, the most significant of these being Edmund, Earl of Kent, her husband's own brother. She was also joined by Roger Mortimer, a nobleman who had escaped from the Tower of London some years previously.

With young Edward in her possession and her brother's aid, Isabella finally showed her true intentions and the anger that must have been building within her for years and she refused to return to Edward in England. The *Chronicle of Lanercost* relates how there were rumours in England that Isabella, young Edward and Kent intended to invade to exact revenge upon the Despensers, who they blamed for Lancaster's death. However, there were also 'contradictory rumours in England about the queen, some declaring that she was the betrayer of the king and kingdom, others that she was acting for peace and the common welfare of the kingdom, and for the removal of evil counsellors from the king'.[45] Reports of Isabella's actions sent Edward and the Despensers into panic and proclamations were read in London calling Isabella and her son traitors.[46] They also sent bribes to France, attempting to have Isabella and young Edward returned to England.

Isabella's brother was also under increasing pressure to return her to England, especially as rumours began to emerge regarding Isabella's relationship with Mortimer. The pair became lovers during their stay in Paris and Isabella would remain devoted to Mortimer for the rest of her life. It is likely that she revelled in Mortimer's attentions after escaping her loveless marriage and she may well have seen no harm in her actions given Edward's own relationships with his male favourites. Certainly, their relationship appears to have had a fiery passion that Isabella's own marriage had lacked. During their time in France, Isabella and Mortimer are reported to have quarrelled, with Isabella threatening to leave Mortimer and return to her husband.[47] Mortimer responded by threatening to kill her if she tried to leave him. This was, of course, a disturbing incident but, for Isabella, it may have been taken as proof of the depth of Mortimer's feelings towards her. She does not seem to have threatened to leave him again.

Although her relationship with Mortimer gave Isabella personal satisfaction, the rumours about her relationship did nothing to help her and women were always more heavily censured for adultery than men. Finally, disturbed by the scandal she was causing, her brother asked her to leave France, allowing her and the other exiles to travel to Hainault. Isabella found a warm reception in Hainault and arranged a treaty with the Count of Hainault for military aid in return for the marriage of her son, Edward, to one of the count's daughters.[48] Isabella must have been pleased with this alliance and eager to return to England with her army, in spite of the uncertainty of her enterprise. She clearly saw her own cause as righteous and the Despensers as the enemy, writing to the Bishop of Exeter in one letter that 'we can see clearly that you are in league with the said Hugh and more obedient towards him than towards us'.[49] She could have been writing these lines to Edward.

Isabella and her fleet landed at Harwich on 24 September 1326.[50] Isabella had always been popular in England and she exploited this on arrival, insisting that she had come only to rid Edward of his evil counsellors. In a proclamation issued soon after their arrival, Isabella, young Edward and Kent insisted that they had 'come to this land to raise up the state of the Holy Church and of the kingdom, and of the people of this land against the said misdeeds and grievous oppressions, and to safeguard and maintain, so far as we can, the honour and profit of the Holy Church, and of our said lord the king'.[51] It is unclear what their actual intentions were upon arrival in England but it seems unlikely that Isabella would have considered returning to Edward even if the Despensers were removed. She must have been too angry with the memory of his treatment of her to countenance this and, again, this is an entirely understandable position, to modern eyes at least.

Upon landing, Isabella sent word to London asking for aid and the city rose to support her.[52] The mob seized the king's treasurer, the Bishop of Exeter, and murdered him in the street before capturing the Tower and placing Isabella's young son, John of Eltham, as its warden.[53] Isabella must have been anxious to hear that her youngest son was unprotected in London but jubilant at the popular support for her cause in England. She must also have been anxious to capture Edward and the Despensers who had fled London upon hearing of her landing.

Isabella and her army set out for Bristol a few weeks after landing. The town was being held by the elder Despenser and he was quickly captured following a siege. Isabella must have been pleased to take him into custody although the younger Despenser was the true focus of her hatred. Under Isabella's orders, the elder Despenser was executed and his corpse chopped up and fed to dogs.[54] There is no doubt that she approved of this treatment of the elder Despenser and this is the first real indication of a bloody streak in Isabella's character.

Following the execution of the elder Despenser, Mortimer and Henry of Lancaster set off in pursuit of Edward and the younger Despenser. They were found wandering around Wales and Edward was despatched to Kenilworth Castle.[55] The younger Despenser was taken to Hereford where he was brutally executed. Amongst the punishments meted out on him was castration, an indication of Isabella's belief about his relationship with her husband. The younger Despenser was Isabella's greatest enemy and she must have been jubilant at his death. Certainly with Edward a prisoner and the Despensers both dead, Isabella must have thought her and Mortimer's future was secure.

Isabella must have spent a triumphant Christmas at Wallingford in 1326, before entering London on 4 January 1327.[56] She called a meeting of parliament a few days later and played a prominent role in its proceedings.[57] At the parliament it was agreed that Edward II would be replaced on the throne by his son, Edward III. This must have been the culmination of Isabella's dearest hopes and she was also able to use the parliament to further her own position. According to the Chronicle of Lanercost, 'it was further ordained that our lady the Queen, for the great anxiety and anguish she had suffered as well this side as overseas, should stay queen all her life'.[58] This must have reassured Isabella that she would not be forced back to live with Edward II, a prospect she cannot have relished. Isabella sent embassies to Edward II asking him to abdicate and, as soon as they obtained a favourable answer, her four-teen-year-old son was crowned as Edward III. Isabella is recorded as having wept throughout the coronation, although it is likely that these were imitation tears rather than the symptom of any grief at her hated husband's fate.[59]

Edward III's youth meant that Isabella and Mortimer were able to set themselves up as the real rulers of England. Isabella was able to wield more power than any earlier queen of England and assigned herself a magnificent dower, leaving the crown itself in relative poverty.[60] Isabella probably wanted this money to help safeguard her position and the existence of her deposed husband in England must have been a worry to her. Isabella had no wish to see him again and, when he requested that she visit, she refused, saying that the lords would not allow her to see him.[61] Edward presents a pitiful figure in his imprisonment, recorded as weeping when he was asked to abdicate and requesting visits from his wife and children. It is possible that Isabella also felt some pity for him and she sent him gifts and clothes.[62] It seems more likely, however, that, like her tears at Edward III's coronation, Isabella's gifts were really just to maintain the appearance of a dutiful wife. She certainly recognised that he was a threat to her regime and she would have believed, as most people in England did, that he was the architect of his own downfall and deserving of his fate.

Edward II did not long survive his deposition. His death was shrouded in secrecy and precise details are difficult to discover but late in 1327, Edward was brought to Berkeley Castle and, on the night of 21 September, he was murdered. The exact manner of his death is unknown but the most common story is that he was killed when a red-hot spit was inserted into his rectum, to ensure that no mark should be seen on his body.[63] There is no contemporary evidence to support this manner of death but it is now irrevocably associated with the murder of Edward II. Isabella's exact involvement in the murder is unclear. However, as ruler of the kingdom it is unlikely that such a momentous step would be taken without Isabella's approval, even by the domineering Mortimer. Certainly, Isabella and Mortimer benefited most from Edward's death and this, taken with Isabella's later obvious remorse at his death, suggests strongly that she was involved. Isabella's reputation is irreparably tarnished by the death of Edward II and the misrule over which she and Mortimer presided.

Isabella and Mortimer quickly became unpopular rulers. Their most unwelcome action which later led to their downfall was their instigation of peace with Scotland. The Scots hoped to take advantage of the confusion in England following Edward II's deposition and invaded, ravaging the north. Isabella, Mortimer and Edward III headed north and the unwilling king was forced to agree to a peace agreement in Scotland, sealed by the marriage of his sister Joan to David of Scotland.[64] The marriage was celebrated at Berwick and attended by Isabella and Mortimer. Edward III, however, refused to attend. Isabella may have been perturbed by this evidence of her son's disapproval of her policy but she failed to heed the warning. She probably considered him to still be a child and she and Mortimer certainly treated him like one.

Isabella remained devoted to Mortimer throughout their period of rule and he became increasingly domineering. In 1329, Isabella and Mortimer felt strong enough to move against the Earl of Kent, the king's uncle. Kent had been one of their most important supporters in the invasion of England but he quickly became disillusioned with Isabella and Mortimer's rule. In 1329, Kent was told that his brother, Edward II, was still alive and imprisoned at Corfe Castle.[65] He sent a friar to Corfe to see whether the rumour was true and swore to release his brother if it proved to be so. It seems likely that this rumour had been created by Mortimer to incriminate Kent. Certainly, Isabella and Mortimer made use of Kent's conduct and, at a parliament soon after, Kent was arrested for conspiracy to restore Edward II. Kent was sentenced to death and executed, against the wishes of his nephew, Edward III.[66] The execution of the son of a king sent shock waves throughout the nobility and any remaining support for Isabella and Mortimer evaporated with his death. Isabella and Mortimer appear to have remained indifferent to their unpopularity, perhaps believing that they still maintained the support of the king.

Isabella and Mortimer's rule was certainly not condoned by the king, however, and Edward III had grown increasingly resentful of his treatment by his mother and her lover. Events came to a head when Mortimer called a parliament at Nottingham in 1330. Edward III believed that Mortimer was shown too much honour there and heard a rumour that Mortimer wished to depose him and become king himself.[67] Edward decided that the time was finally right for him to assume royal authority and, one night, he and some friends entered Nottingham Castle secretly through a hidden tunnel:

> Having rushed out of the underground passage and subterranean route, the king's friends advanced with drawn sword to the queen's bedroom, the king waited, armed, outside the chamber of their foes, lest he should be seen by his mother. As the conspirators charged in, they killed Hugh de Turpinton, knight, as he tried to resist them, Lord John de Neville of Hornby directing the blow. Then they found the queen mother almost ready for bed, and the Earl of March [Mortimer] whom they wanted. They led him captive into the hall, while the queen cried 'fair son, fair son, have pity on gentle Mortimer'; for she suspected that her son was there, even though she had not seen him.[68]

This must have been the most traumatic event of Isabella's life and she never saw Mortimer again. She must have realised, in an instant, that her reign was over and that both she, and Mortimer, were in danger.

Edward III wasted no time in establishing his authority after his coup against his mother and Mortimer. Mortimer was sentenced to death, despite Isabella's pleas, and was hanged, drawn and quartered.[69] Some accounts suggest that the shock of Mortimer's death drove Isabella mad although, given the evidence of her later lucidity, this seems unlikely. It must certainly have deeply affected her, however. Edward never countenanced putting his mother to death but immediately after the coup she was placed under house arrest and stripped of her lands and goods. Isabella spent two years under guard in isolation at Castle Rising in

Norfolk.[70] She was granted greater freedom later but she never regained Edward's trust.

After the harshness of her imprisonment was lessened, Isabella was given permission to travel and to play a role as a member of the royal family. In 1338 she spent time at Pomfret Castle and in 1344 she attended Edward's birthday celebration in Norwich.[71] Isabella all but disappears from the sources after 1330 and her time as a political figure of note had ended. She spent the remainder of her life living quietly, mainly at Castle Rising. Isabella fell ill on 22 August 1358 and died later that same day at the age of sixty-two, venerable for the time.[72] She was given a royal funeral and, according to legend, she was buried, at her own request, wearing her wedding dress and clutching Edward II's heart in a silver casket.[73] This demonstrates that, with the passing of time, Isabella had learnt to feel remorse for all that had occurred in her marriage and the terrible way in which it ended. It is perhaps more significant, however, that when Isabella chose her burial place she selected Greyfriars in London, the burial place of her beloved Mortimer.

Isabella of France is the most vilified of all the queens of England and, although she was known as 'Isabella the Fair' in her own lifetime, she is now better remembered as the 'She-Wolf of France'. The poem, *The Bard*, by Thomas Grey perhaps best sums up the reputation that Isabella has left to history:

> The shrieks of death, thro' Berkley's roofs that ring,
> Shrieks of an agonising king!
> She-wolf of France, with unrelenting fangs,
> That tear'st the bowels of thy mangled mate,
> From thee be born, who o'er thy country hangs
> The scourge of Heav'n what terrors round his wait![74]

Isabella was among the most powerful of all medieval queens. No other English queen invaded and won a country, openly took a lover or murdered her husband. Isabella of France was unique and between 1325 and 1330 pursued a role very far from the ideal expected of a medieval queen. Her reputation was black and the story of her life would have cast a dark shadow over many of the later medieval English queens as they strove not to emulate her. However, it must be remembered that the period 1325 to 1330 was only a small part of her long life and her actions were certainly driven by years of mistreatment and unhappiness. It was not, after all, Isabella's fault that she found herself married to Edward II and most other kings would have adored her. Isabella had been cosseted throughout her childhood and she tried to make the most of her difficult and loveless marriage. It is perhaps understandable that in the end Isabella snapped and took drastic action to secure her own happiness. Some of her actions are likely to have been driven by revenge but these are understandable. Isabella of France had been the most desirable princess in Europe and to find herself an unloved and disparaged wife must have affected her. She tried to endure and, when that failed, she took action, at terrible cost to her own reputation.

PART III

LATER MEDIEVAL & TUDOR QUEENS

WITCHCRAFT, WAR & AMBITION

Later Medieval & Tudor Queens

In 1399, Henry Bolingbroke usurped the throne from his cousin Richard II, ushering in a century of intermittent conflict as different branches of the royal family vied for the throne. This conflict is known as the Wars of the Roses and it impacted directly not just on the lives of the kings concerned but also on the lives of the queens and the nature of their office. The fifteenth- and sixteenth-century queens were, in general, markedly less powerful than their earlier post-conquest predecessors as queenship to some extent reverted to its pre-conquest antecedents. With a few notable exceptions, the fifteenth-century kings were almost entirely focussed on England and, by the mid-fifteenth century, all but Calais of the once vast continental empire had been lost. This meant that kings had no option but to focus on England, which led to a diminished scope for queenly political power. At a time when kings could be made and deposed by noblemen, queens, whose power was dependent on these kings, were in as vulnerable a position as they had been before the Norman conquest. This vulnerability continued into the sixteenth century and the Tudor period.

In spite of the great changes to society, queenship in the fifteenth and sixteenth centuries remained superficially similar to what had gone before. As in earlier periods, queens were, first and foremost, expected to be fertile and produce an heir. This was always the primary function of a queen in medieval England and it was no exception for late medieval queens. Margaret of Anjou, who was the queen of Henry VI, was in a very difficult position until she finally bore a son after seven years of marriage and she must have been relieved to prove to her critics that she was not sterile. Anne Neville, the wife of Richard III, also found herself in danger following the death of her only child in 1484 when her husband's attitude abruptly changed towards her. Rumours quickly emerged that Richard meant to divorce his sickly wife to marry a more fertile woman and, by Christmas 1484, it was whispered around that Richard was even trying to hasten his wife's death.[1] Richard may have spread the rumour that his wife was already dead in the hope that the shock would kill her. *Hall's Chronicle* describes its version of the event:

> When the quene heard tell that so horrible a rumour of her death was sprong emongest the comminallie she sore suspected and judged the world to be almost at an ende with her, and in that sorofull agony, she with lamentable countenaunce of sorofull chere, repaired to the presence of the kyng her husband, demaundynge of hym, what it should meane that he had judged her worthy to die. The kyng aunswered her with fake woordes, and with dissimulynge blandimentes and flattering lesynges comforted her, biddynge her to be of good comforte, for to his knowledge she should have none other cause.[2]

Anne lost her husband's love and respect with the death of her only child and, in early 1485, she died unlamented by Richard. A good queen was one who produced healthy sons in the late medieval period, just as had always been the case in England. The most extreme example of this was the six wives of Henry VIII and his willingness to dispose of wives who could not bear sons. As a number of later medieval queens found to their cost, to be a good queen was to be a fertile one.

The expectation of conspicuious piety in good queens also continued into the later medieval period. This position did, however, become more complex in the Tudor period. With the Reformation, it became possible to be pious in the wrong religion. Catherine of Aragon and her successor, Anne Boleyn, for example, are good examples of this.

Anne Boleyn is known to have had Protestant sympathies and, as a heretic, she was chastised by Catholics. However, to the Protestants of her daughter's reign she was seen almost as a saint, challenging the superstitions of Catholicism. Catherine of Aragon is also today remembered for her piety but, to Protestants in the sixteenth century, she was seen as both superstitious, ignorant and certainly not someone to admire. Catherine's daughter, Mary I, was also very pious and to some she was a great queen. However, to the majority of her Protestant subjects, she was seen as a dangerous fanatic in her attempts to restore Catholicism, just as her predecessor, Lady Jane Grey, might have been seen by her Catholic subjects had she lived longer. To be a good queen in the late medieval period was still to be a pious one. However, the Reformation added another layer to this and it was also necessary to be religious in the accepted way. Henry VIII's last queen, Catherine Parr, is a particularly good example of this and, in 1546, was nearly arrested for heresy due to her radical Protestantism.[3] Only Catherine's intelligence saved her and she claimed to the king that she had only been outspoken in her religion in order to engage him in conversation so that she could learn from him.[4] Clearly, therefore, it was possible for a queen to be too religious in the Tudor period and Mary I's notoriety, for example, is linked to her religious faith.

Changes to religion were not the only changes to occur in England during the fifteenth and sixteenth centuries and, on the whole, the country was a much more insular nation than it had previously been. Although Henry VI very nearly conquered France in the early fifteenth century, by the middle of his son's reign all that remained of England's continental possessions was Calais. The loss of the continental territories meant that, unlike their earlier post-conquest predecessors, fifteenth- and sixteenth-century kings had less reason to leave England and so there was also less scope for their wives to be called upon to become regents. Henry IV and Henry VI, for example, remained in England throughout their reigns and Edward IV, Henry VI's successor, only left England once voluntarily, for a brief campaign in France. On this campaign he did indeed leave his wife, Elizabeth Woodville, as regent, but this proved to be only a brief period of authority bearing little resemblance to the long regencies of her predecessors such as Matilda of Scotland and Eleanor of Provence. Richard III and Henry VII did not leave England during their reigns although Edward

IV's grandson, Henry VIII, also left England on two brief campaigns in France, leaving his wives, Catherine of Aragon and Catherine Parr, as regents in turn.[5] A queen was still considered to be a suitable regent in late medieval England but the lack of opportunities for regencies meant that, in reality, any political power that they might have would be limited. Moreover a regency was by no means certain and, when Henry VI came to the throne when he was less than a year old, it was never even suggested that his mother, Catherine of Valois should rule for him – instead she was kept firmly in the background.

The lack of opportunities for regencies also meant that queens were no longer expected to have a political role. Consequently a development can be seen in the ideas of what made a good queen and what made a bad queen. Elizabeth of York, for example, is remembered very favourably and this is largely due to her apparent lack of personal ambition, modestly accepting the crown matrimonial rather than asserting her own right to the crown as heiress of England.[6] Elizabeth of York is always compared favourably to Margaret of Anjou, for example, and Margaret's bad reputation is based largely on her political activity. However, even the mild Elizabeth of York was viewed as a potential political threat by her husband and, according to Francis Bacon, 'it lay plain before his eyes, that if he relied upon that title [claiming the throne through Elizabeth], he could be but a king at courtesy, and have rather a matrimonial than a regal power; the right remaining in his queen, upon whose decease, either with issue, or without issue, he was to give place and be removed'.[7] Mary I was also extremely popular until she was forced to become a fully political figure. Immediately she appeared unwomanly to her people and is remembered as a corrupt queen, just as her predecessor as queen regnant, the Empress Matilda, had been. In late medieval England, therefore, good queens were expected to be domestic and pious, something that most of the notorious queens of the period were decidedly not.

The change to a more insular style of kingship also had another effect on the power of the queen and reflects a partial return to the Anglo-Saxon style of queenship. Anglo-Saxon kings generally selected their wives from the nobility and this reflected the fact that their interests primarily lay in England. This changed dramatically in the post-conquest period and, between the late eleventh century and the fourteenth century, royal wives were mostly selected from continental families in an attempt to safeguard foreign possessions. By the late fifteenth century, however, there were no English possessions on the continent and kings appear to have looked increasingly to gaining English wives. Edward IV, for example, selected the English Elizabeth Woodville for his bride. Whilst this marriage caused scandal, the fact that it happened at all does highlight a change in ideas of both kingship and queenship. Edward's brother, Richard III, followed his brother's example in marrying the English Anne Neville. Anne had previously been married to Edward of Lancaster, Prince of Wales, which highlights her perceived suitability to be a queen of England. Edward IV's grandson, Henry VIII also followed this idea enthusiastically, marrying four Englishwomen and doing more than any other king to demonstrate the potential for an Englishwoman who attracted the king. This policy did have a down side, as many English queens discovered. An English queen did not, by definition, have a powerful foreign family to protect her in times of trouble and this can be seen clearly, once again, in a comparison of Catherine of Aragon and Anne Boleyn. Catherine of Aragon, as the aunt of the Holy Roman Emperor, was merely divorced by Henry. Anne, as the daughter of Sir Thomas Boleyn, was executed. As with their Anglo-Saxon predecessors, English-born queens in the later medieval period must have quickly come to realise that their position also made them uniquely vulnerable to the whims of their husbands and enemies.

The fifteenth and sixteenth centuries were therefore dangerous times for queens. The fate and reputation of many queens were tied up with the Wars of the Roses. When Henry Bolingbroke usurped the throne in 1399, becoming Henry IV, he set in motion a conflict that would last for a century. Henry IV was the son of Edward III's third son and took the throne from the only descendant of the first son. However, the second son, Lionel of Antwerp, had produced a daughter and by the reign of Henry VI, who was Henry IV's grandson, that daughter's claim was represented by her descendant, Richard, Duke of York. York was able to exploit Henry VI's ineptitude to highlight his own superior claim to the throne and, after years of conflict, his son, Edward IV, was able to snatch the throne from his cousin. In 1483, on Edward's own death, the throne passed to his young son, Edward V, but the throne was again usurped, this time by the boy's uncle, Richard III. Finally, in 1485, the last remaining Lancastrian claimant, Henry VII, took the crown, marrying Elizabeth of York and uniting the two warring houses. The descendants of the couple never felt entirely safe on their thrones. Henry VIII and his children persecuted their relatives to ensure the stability of their own position.

The Wars of the Roses characterised the fifteenth and sixteenth centuries, causing violence and confusion in the fifteenth century and then fuelling Tudor paranoia in the sixteenth. The conflict also had a major effect on the reputations of the queens of the period, with some such as Margaret of Anjou sometimes forced to take an active and unpopular course. However the conflict also had another, less foreseeable outcome: by the mid-sixteenth century there were very few people alive who possessed a credible claim to the throne. When Edward VI cast around for someone to succeed him in 1553, all the plausible candidates proved to be female, making it inevitable that England would finally have its first effective queen regnant.

Queenship during the fifteenth and sixteenth centuries was often insecure and the office itself was changeable. It was still based firmly on its Anglo-Saxon and post-conquest foundations but in the turbulent times of the fifteenth century, queens often had to adapt to fulfil a more varied role. By the mid-sixteenth century, England was moving away from the medieval period into the early modern period. However, queens such as Mary Tudor still consciously looked back at the medieval past for a model of queenship, proving that, even in adverse and unprecedented circumstances, English queenship remained a recognisable office with guidelines on how to be a good queen and avoid notoriety. Joan of Navarre, Margaret of Anjou, Elizabeth Woodville, Anne Boleyn, Catherine Howard, Lady Jane Grey and Mary I are all remembered as notorious and they all, at least according to their contemporaries, failed to live up to the ideal of a good queen. As with the earlier queens, however, there was often a motive behind the attacks on the women, usually tied up in the politics of the day. Due to the difficulties of the period in which they lived, all of these women found themselves in dangerous situations and, as their own party diminished in power they were actively attacked, leading to the destruction of their reputations. Once again, in the fifteenth and sixteenth centuries, women proved particularly vulnerable to attack and the mostly English queens of this period proved as vulnerable as any, to their considerable cost.

Witchcraft

Joan of Navarre

Joan of Navarre has the distinction of being the only English queen to ever be punished for witchcraft. Joan was disliked in England during her time as queen and was heavily criticised for her foreign birth. During the reign of her stepson, Henry V, her reputation took a dramatic turn for the worse when she was accused of plotting to murder the king through sorcery and spent several years in prison. Little evidence was ever presented to explain Joan's arrest and, as the example of Joan's stepdaughter-in-law Eleanor Cobham shows, an accusation of witchcraft was a convenient way of attacking a royal woman in the fifteenth century. Joan was certainly no witch but, as a foreigner in a troubled period, she was an easy target, just as her predecessors, such as Eleanor of Provence and Isabella of France had found. For a woman to be accused of witchcraft was for her also to lose her place in society. Joan of Navarre's reputation has never been able to shake off the stigma of the charges against her and it is clear that they were used as an easy way of robbing her of her property. Henry V, the architect of Joan's misfortunes, would have known the power that his accusations of witchcraft could have and Joan, as a woman and a foreigner, was his helpless victim. When he was overcome with remorse at the treatment of the queen, it was already too late. As earlier queens had found, a tarnished name is difficult to lose.

To modern eyes, the charges against Joan appear to have been unprovoked but she may already have had a sinister reputation by association.

Her father Charles the Bad, King of Navarre, was known across Europe for his unsuitable behaviour. Charles was the son of the dispossessed heiress of France, Jeanne of Navarre; as such he had political ambitions towards that country. It is possible that his wife, Joan of France, was offered to him as a way of neutralising his claim but if so the policy failed.[1] Joan of Navarre was born in 1368 in Normandy and had a turbulent childhood.[2] In 1381, Charles was once again at war with France, and Joan and her two elder brothers were lodged in one of Charles's castles in Normandy.[3] The regents of France, exasperated by Charles's behaviour, captured Joan with her brothers and took them to Paris as surety for their father's good behaviour.

Joan must have been shocked to find herself a hostage but the terms of her captivity are unlikely to have been onerous. The regents of France were Joan's maternal uncles and it is likely that they treated Joan and her brothers kindly. Despite this, Charles was anxious for the return of his children and attempted to poison the regents. This only increased French anger towards Charles and it was only through the intervention of the King of Castile that she and her brothers were released.[4] Joan's feelings on her captivity and release are unclear. Given the uncertainty of life as the daughter of Charles the Bad she may have missed her stable life in Paris.

Soon after Joan's release, Charles opened negotiations to marry her to John IV, Duke of Brittany. John IV's second wife, Joan Holland, had died in 1384 and he urgently needed an heir for his duchy. In June 1386 Breton envoys arrived in Navarre to fetch Joan and she sailed for Brittany immediately afterwards, marrying Duke John at Saille on 11 September.[5] Joan must have been apprehensive about her marriage to the middle-aged Duke. However she seems to have consented to the match and it proved to be a happy union. Joan's father promised a generous dowry of 120,000 gold livres, although his early death meant that much of this was never paid. True to his tainted reputation, Charles the Bad suffered a particularly horrifying death in 1387. Suffering from paralysis to his limbs through some ailment, Charles tried to effect a cure by being wrapped from head to toe in bandages. Immobilised in this way, Charles was unable to save himself when a careless servant allowed a candle to ignite the bandages, causing the king to burn to death.[6] Many of Charles's contemporaries probably saw this as divine judgement for Charles's sinister life, although Joan's feelings are not recorded. Joan's time after her marriage was, in any event, taken up with childbearing and, in 1389, she provided an heir to the duchy, as well as bearing six other children during her marriage

John IV had always had strong links with England and he visited the country in April 1398.[7] It is possible that Joan accompanied him on this visit and if so she would have come into contact with Richard II's cousin, Henry Bolingbroke. Joan and Henry certainly met at some point during her first marriage. Henry also spent time in Brittany during his exile in 1399 and is again likely to have spent some time with Joan.[8] No evidence survives of Joan and Henry's meetings with each other but it is likely that there was a mutual attraction. It is unlikely that Joan was ever unfaithful to John but the fact that she and Henry proved so eager to marry suggests something more than just diplomatic relations.

John IV died on 1 November 1399. Joan had been an impeccable wife and he entrusted her with the government of Brittany until their son came of age. Joan ruled Brittany well and arranged an impressive inauguration for her son in 1401, an event which ended her regency.[9] With the end of her regency, Joan may have felt that her role in Brittany was over. She was still only thirty-three and probably desired a second marriage. In 1399 Henry had become King of England and, at some point, he must have contacted Joan with an offer of marriage. Certainly, by March 1402 negotiations had been opened and on 3 April 1402 Joan's emissary and Henry underwent a proxy wedding in England.[10]

Joan had been left wealthy by her first husband and it has often been suggested that Henry's motive in marrying her was to obtain this wealth. However, Joan seems to have kept personal control over her wealth during her second marriage and Henry did not benefit financially from the match. There may have been a political element in the match on both sides. Henry, as a usurper, needed the foreign contacts that Joan could provide and it is likely that Joan wanted to be a queen.[11] The marriage must be considered more than a merely political alliance, however.[12] Henry was clearly partial to Joan and remained faithful to her throughout their marriage so attraction is likely to have played a large part in his proposal of marriage. Joan also gave up her children to marry Henry and it seems inconceivable that, as an independent widow, she would do this if she also was not attracted to Henry.

The marriage negotiations were conducted in secret due to the likely unpopularity of the match in Brittany. When news of the proposed marriage became common knowledge the Breton noblemen reacted in anger, fearing that Henry would obtain custody of their duke. Joan was forced to leave all her children, save her two youngest daughters, behind in Brittany.[13] Joan and her daughters sailed for England on 13 January 1403, enduring a traumatic crossing that was seen by contemporaries as an evil omen:

> As shee crossed the seas for England, her passage was verie dangerous by reason of tempestuous wether, which accident was esteemed ominous in both king Richard's wives [Henry IV's unlucky predecessor as king]. The king received her at Winchester, and there having spent some time in devises of pleasures, upon the viith of Februarie the marriage was solemized between them, and upon the xxvith of the same moneth shee was with all ceremonies of state, crowned at Westminster.[14]

Henry rushed to meet her as soon as he heard that she had landed and Joan must have been pleased at this sign of his affection. She cannot have seen him for over three years and may have worried that neither of them would be as the other expected.

Such worries were in vain. On 8 March 1403 Henry granted Joan a dower of 10,000 marks, the largest dower granted to an English queen up to that time.[15] This was probably both a mark of respect for Joan and intended to demonstrate the wealth and stability of the new Lancastrian dynasty. Coupled with her Breton dower, this grant made Joan exceptionally wealthy. She administered this wealth herself and is known to have held councils and conducted her business at Westminster Palace.[16] Joan was an adept financial manager who excelled in increasing her wealth – although a less pleasant side of her character emerges in stories of her stripping the estates of children in her wardship.[17]

Joan appears to have found happiness in the husband and family she acquired through her second marriage and was quickly on good terms with her stepchildren. In spite of this, she was not popular in England and often found herself censured for her links to Brittany and foreign birth. A parliament in 1404 ordered that all foreigners be removed from the royal households, with the exception of Joan's two daughters.[18] Joan, who appears to have tried to conform, complied with this order and was eventually allowed to keep several Bretons in her household. However, in 1406 parliament once again ordered that foreigners be removed from her household and Joan was compelled to send her daughters back to Brittany.[19] Joan appears to have accepted all of parliament's demands, but the loss of her daughters must have hit her hard. She must have quickly realised that she would always be criticised for her birth and her foreign first marriage but these were not things which could be changed. As Eleanor of Provence and Eleanor of Castile had found before her, the circumstances of a queen's birth could be disadvantageous.

Throughout Joan's time in England, attacks were also made on her for her partiality to foreigners. Joan certainly did seek to promote Bretons who visited England and in February 1404 her son Arthur was granted the earldom of Richmond.[20] It was also at Joan's request in 1405 that Henry IV ordered the release of all Breton prisoners in England without ransom.[21] Joan actively promoted peace between England and Brittany; in 1417 Henry V made a treaty with Brittany at Joan's intercession.[22] Joan's efforts may not always have been treated as pacific in England however and, in 1415, the Bretons were accused of learning state secrets in Joan's household.[23] Once again this was not based in truth but due to her origins people appear to have been ready to believe the worst about her.

Despite being a kind and attentive husband, Henry cannot always have been easy to live with. By around 1408, Henry was suffering from leprosy and pressure appears to have been brought to bear on him to relinquish his crown.[24] Henry seems to have retreated more into his household as his illness progressed and Joan may often have found herself shut away alone with him. It must have been sad for Joan, who had known Henry in the prime of his life, to see him struck down with his disfiguring disease. Henry also appears to have been beset by guilt for his usurpation of the crown. According to John Hayward, his mind was 'perpetuallie perplexed with an endlesse and restlesse chardge, ether of cares, or greifes, or of suspicions and feares'.[25] For Joan, it may, perhaps, have been a relief when Henry died in 1413.[26]

Joan made no attempt to return to either Brittany or Navarre, and, in spite of suspicions raised against her, she was content to stay in England. She was often referred to as Queen Mother in her stepson Henry V's reign and continued to play the public role of queen, taking a prominent place in a procession from St Paul's to Westminster in celebration of Henry V's victory at Agincourt against the French.[27] This must have gone against Joan's own personal feelings about the victory. Her son-in-law, the Duke of Alencon, and her brother Charles of Navarre died fighting for the French and her own son Arthur was captured and brought a prisoner to England.[28] Despite her personal grief, Joan took her duties as Queen of England seriously and took a prominent part in the rejoicing in England. This devotion to duty probably went unnoticed and unappreciated in England.

Henry V's French wars took a harsh toll on his finances and he seems to have begun to look greedily at Joan's immense dower. On 27 September 1419, the English council suddenly made an order depriving Joan of all her possessions and revenues and, four days later, she was arrested on charges of witchcraft at her palace at Havering-atte-Bower.[29] Her arrest would have been an enormous shock to the innocent Joan and she must have been at a loss to explain her situation. The charges stemmed from a confession by her confessor, John Randolf, claiming he had tempted her into using witchcraft to try to kill Henry V.[30] Whilst it is possible that the charges were at first believed, no attempt was made to investigate the matter or bring Joan to trial and it appears that Joan's arrest was a pretext to enable Henry V to take her dower.[31] Certainly, Joan was treated very leniently for someone accused of witchcraft. However, at least at first, she must have been terrified, and a charge of witchcraft was no laughing matter, as the treatment of Joan's stepdaughter-in-law, Eleanor Cobham, Duchess of Gloucester, twenty years later, would indicate.

Like Joan, Eleanor Cobham was also arrested for conspiring to kill the king through sorcery and, according to reports, she and her accomplices produced a wax doll with which to kill the king.[32] Eleanor appears to have dabbled in sorcery for some years before her arrest and a woman known as the Witch of Eye was also arrested at the same time:

> Whose sorcery and witchcraft the same Dame Eleanor had long time used; and by such medicines and drinks as the said witch made, the said Eleanor compelled the aforesaid Duke of Gloucester to love her and to wed her. Wherefore, and also because of relapse, the said witch was burnt at Smithfield.[33]

Eleanor's other accomplice, Roger Bolingbroke, was hanged drawn and quartered for his part in the affair and the duchess herself was also severely punished.[34] After being examined by the king's council, Eleanor was forced to perform a public penance three times by walking bare footed and bare headed through London and carrying a heavy taper.[35] For a woman as proud as Eleanor Cobham, this must have been an ordeal and, following her penance, she was taken away to life imprisonment on the Isle of Man, from which she was never released.[36] Shakespeare, who was clearly fascinated with the story of Eleanor Cobham puts these words into the duchess's mouth as she carried out her penance:

> Ah, Gloucester, teach me to forget myself:
> For whilst I think I am thy married wife,
> And thou a Prince, Protector of this land,
> Methinks I should not thus beled along,
> Mailed up in shame, with papers on my back,
> And followed with a rabble that rejoice
> To see my tears and hear my deep-set groans.[37]

Clearly, a charge of witchcraft was a dangerous and shameful thing and Joan must have been terrified by her arrest.

After her initial terror, however, Joan appears to have settled in easily to her imprisonment and, despite its indignity, managed to maintain a luxurious lifestyle. In the first months of her imprisonment, Joan's accounts show that she had a stable and she was presumably allowed to ride.[38] She was also allowed to keep nineteen grooms and seven pages. Joan's purchases in the first months of her imprisonment also show that she was able to purchase luxuries, such as furs, lace, gold chains and a gold girdle.[39] This was not the usual treatment meted out to an imprisoned witch and demonstrates that the charges were not widely believed.

Joan was also able to stock a large wine cellar and she often entertained. On 1 April 1420, the Archbishop of Canterbury came to dinner. Joan's stepson the Duke of Gloucester also visited on two occasions and the Bishop of Winchester spent the weekend there.[40] Lord Camoys appears to have spent nine months enjoying Joan's hospitality.[41] Joan's treatment shows the absurdity of the charges against her and it is likely that apart from the knowledge that she was a prisoner, Joan was able to lead a comfortable existence in much of her old style. Certainly the visits suggest that she remained a recognised member of the royal family rather than an outcast who had plotted to kill the king through sorcery. She must still have been aware, however, during the period, of the charge that hung over her and, for all the comforts provided for her, she must have longed to be freed.

Joan's innocence can also be seen in Henry V's deathbed remorse at his treatment of her. As he lay dying of dysentery in France, he remembered his stepmother's predicament and ordered that she be immediately released and compensated for the loss of her dower.[42] Joan must have been glad to hear of Henry's remorse although it seems unlikely that she was entirely able to forgive him for his treatment of her. Joan was released soon after Henry's death and much of her dower was returned. In 1422, Joan found herself once again a wealthy and independent widow. Following her release she seems to have led a life of retirement, dying in July 1437.

Joan of Navarre was the only queen of England to be punished for witchcraft and the stigma of this charge still hangs over her reputation. Although there was no substance in the charge, it does illustrate something of the dangers in which royal women could find themselves. Joan of Navarre was never able to win popularity in England due to her foreign birth. She was therefore an easy target when her stepson, Henry V, chose to move against her and his actions helped ensure that she will always have a certain notoriety. Although she was a queen, the charges against her show that, in a hostile England, Joan was also essentially powerless. As a woman, she was already particularly vulnerable to such a charge and as a foreigner she was despised and alone. Joan of Navarre is described as both a witch and as a grasping queen in the sources and, although these charges had little substance, they have clung to her, destroying her reputation. Her notoriety pales in comparison, however, with that of her stepgranddaughter-in-law, Margaret of Anjou, the original She-Wolf of France.

Shakespeare's She-Wolf

Margaret of Anjou

Margaret of Anjou was the first queen of England to be nicknamed the 'She-Wolf of France' and, in spite of losing this name to Isabella of France, she is still remembered as a notorious queen. Portrayals of Margaret over the years show her as a vengeful and ambitious woman who brought war and misery to England and it is in Shakespeare's portrayal of her as an adulteress and warmongerer that she is best remembered. As the leader of the House of Lancaster, Margaret participated in one of the bloodiest civil wars that England has known and her actions certainly helped prolong the war by almost a decade. However her actions, in support of first her husband and then her son, are entirely understandable and without the benefit of hindsight she can never have realised just how futile her actions were. Margaret of Anjou genuinely acted with the best possible motives. She was not a bad woman, in spite of her terrible reputation but, as the wife of an ineffectual and doomed king, she was forced to take on a role that, for a woman, was deemed to be savage. Margaret of Anjou was forced to take the course of action she did but, in the eyes of her contemporaries and many later historians, this did not redeem her.

Margaret of Anjou grew up to be a powerful and dominant woman and she may have learnt the lessons of female power during her childhood. She was born in March 1430 and was the fourth child of Rene of Anjou and Isabel, Duchess of Lorraine.[1] Margaret's childhood was dominated by women following the capture of her father in 1431 at the battle of Bulgneville. On 12 November 1435, Rene's elder brother died and he inherited the county of Anjou as well as the crowns of Jerusalem and Naples. Early the following year, Rene also inherited the kingdom of Sicily.[2] In spite of these grand titles, Rene was only able to exercise authority over Anjou and Lorraine although, as a prisoner, it was his wife Isabel who ruled. Isabel of Lorraine was an indomitable figure and it is likely that Margaret gained much of her idea of queenship from her.

In 1435 Isabel set out with an army to conquer Naples, leaving Margaret in the care of her paternal grandmother, Yolande of Aragon.[3] Yolande was Margaret's second model of a powerful woman. Yolande had ruled Anjou for several years and had also raised the French king, Charles VII, marrying him to her daughter Marie. She could also lay claim to being the most powerful woman in France, something of which Margaret is likely to have taken note.[4] Margaret's mother and Rene (who had been released in 1436) returned to Anjou in 1442, following defeat in Naples, and Margaret passed back into her mother's custody soon after her grandmother's death in that year.

Margaret's childhood must have been overshadowed by the war between England and France. In 1444, a meeting was held at Tours between the French and the English in an attempt to come to peace.[5] It was at this meeting that a marriage between the English king, Henry VI, and a French princess was first suggested and Margaret, as the niece of the Queen of France, was chosen as the most suitable candidate. According to *Hall's Chronicle*, Rene agreed in return for a promise from the English that they would surrender lands in Anjou and Maine to him. Rene was renowned across Europe for his poverty 'callyng himself kyng of Scicile, Naples, and Hierusalem, hauyng onely the name and stile of the same, without any pay profite, or fote of possession'.[6] Henry VI was also eager for the match and asked for a portrait of Margaret to be sent to him.[7] He also agreed to pay for Margaret's journey to England. 'For kyng Reyner her father, for all his long stile, had to short a purse, to sende his doughter honourably, to the kyng her spouse'.[8] To save face, however, Margaret was dowered with the islands of Minorca and Majorca.[9] The only problem with this generous gift was that, as with so many of Rene's 'lands', Henry would have to conquer them if he wanted to assert Margaret's rights there.

Margaret was living with her mother in Angers when the marriage treaty was signed and the two of them set out to meet the English at Tours.[10] On 23 May 1444, Margaret underwent a proxy marriage in St Martin's Cathedral at Tours with the Earl of Suffolk playing the part of Henry VI.[11] Early the following year, Margaret again travelled with her mother and at Nancy she may have undergone another betrothal ceremony. Certainly, her time in Nancy was filled with banquets and entertainments. Margaret then set out for England, accompanied part of the way by both her father and her uncle, Charles VII. She also had an escort of 1,500 people.[12]

Margaret landed in England on 9 April 1445.[13] Henry had been waiting impatiently for Margaret's arrival and, according to one report, determined to visit her in disguise.[14] Henry dressed himself as a squire and took a letter to Margaret. If he intended this to be a romantic meeting, he was to be disappointed. Margaret took the letter from the 'squire' but was so engrossed in reading it that she did not notice Henry and kept him on his knees. It was only later, after Henry had left, that Margaret was told who the squire had been.[15] The couple met officially soon afterwards and were married at Tichfield Abbey on 22 April, before travelling on to London together.[16] Margaret and Henry appear to have got on well with each other from the beginning and Margaret would have been relieved to find her husband congenial. She was crowned in London on 30 April and is recorded as having worn her hair loose under a coronet of pearls and jewels.[17] Margaret probably once again enjoyed being the centre of attention.

Margaret gained a great influence over Henry from early in their marriage.[18] Henry was a gentle and compassionate man and was eager to please his young bride and place her at her ease.[19] Margaret had been conditioned by her family before she left France. On 17 December, for example, she wrote to her uncle, Charles VII to say that she would do all she could to persuade Henry to surrender Maine to France.[20] Her pleas to Henry obviously had their effect and five days later Henry wrote himself to Charles, agreeing to surrender Maine and saying that he did so as a favour to Margaret. Unfortunately, however, whilst Henry's gesture was romantic, it also appears to have been inappropriate and

Henry's ministers refused to surrender the territory until April 1446.[21] Margaret must have been jubilant at her success but it did not augment her popularity in England.

In July 1449 Charles declared war on England once again, ending the truce that Margaret's marriage had ushered in. This also damaged Margaret's image since she was seen as being in league with Henry's hated chief minister, Suffolk. According the *Hall's Chronicle*, it was Margaret and Suffolk who ruled England and the chronicler considered the pair to be lovers, calling Suffolk 'the Quenes dearlynge'.[22] Shakespeare also implies that the pair were lovers and it was a common rumour during Margaret's lifetime.[23] The allegation that Margaret and the much older Suffolk were lovers is untrue and invented to smear the queen. It was Suffolk and his wife who escorted Margaret to England and arranged her marriage and she appears to have looked upon the couple as surrogate parents. Certainly, both she and Henry were close to Suffolk and grieved for him when he was murdered in 1450.[24] Margaret, apparently, refused to eat for three days on hearing the news of Suffolk's death.[25] Touching though her grief is, it did nothing for her reputation which was already shaky, due primarily to the fact of her French birth.

Margaret was also heavily criticised during the early years of her marriage for her failure to conceive. It seems likely that this delay was due more to her youth at the time of her marriage than any failure of Henry to consummate the marriage. Certainly, a delay in childbearing was not unusual in this period and Margaret's contemporary, Cecily Neville, Duchess of York is known to have produced twelve children after a childless decade of marriage.[26] Nonetheless Margaret's childlessness must have caused her considerable worry. Henry had no siblings, uncles or first cousins and the continuation of the House of Lancaster relied on Margaret's ability to produce an heir. It must have been a great relief to Margaret when she finally found that she was pregnant early in 1453. With her pregnancy, Margaret must have finally felt secure in her position as Queen of England, despite the criticism that had been previously levelled at her.

Margaret's joy must have been short-lived, however, and, on 16 July 1453, the English army was decisively defeated in France at the Battle of Castillon, leaving the English in effective control only of Calais.[27] The news of this disaster caused consternation in England which again was unreasonably directed at Margaret as a Frenchwoman. The news of the battle also had a great impact on Henry. On 15 August 1453, he apparently felt very tired and went to bed early.[28] Wheathampstead's Register describes how that night, 'a disease and disorder of such a sort overcame the king that he lost his wits and memory for a time, and nearly all his body was uncoordinated and out of control that he could neither walk, nor hold his head upright, nor easily move from where he sat'.[29] Henry was in a catatonic state, unable to take in anything around him. It seems likely that this condition was hereditary and was inherited from his grandfather, the mad King Charles VI of France. Margaret must have been devastated when she heard of Henry's condition but there was little that she could do and it must have been with a heavy heart that she entered her confinement in London in September.

On 13 October 1453, Margaret gave birth to her only child, Edward of Lancaster, at Westminster.[30] She must have been delighted to have borne a healthy son but this delight would have been tempered with sadness at Henry's continuing incapacity. Edward's birth brought out a fierce maternal instinct in Margaret and from that day onwards her focus was always on his future. Margaret's first concern was to obtain Henry's recognition of his son. This was crucial to Margaret as, according to *Hall's Chronicle*, there were rumours that Edward was not the son of the king, with claims that he was either a changeling or the son of the Duke of Somerset.[31] These rumours again had no basis in fact and Henry himself never doubted Edward's paternity. They may have been stories spread by the rival House of York and throughout her time as queen Margaret, as a prominent member of the House of Lancaster, was a target for Yorkist propaganda. Soon after Edward's birth, the baby was taken to Henry at Windsor in the hope of raising some response in Henry.[32] The Duke of Buckingham presented the prince to Henry, but Henry gave no response:

Natheless the Duke abode stille with the Prince by the Kyng; and what he coude no maner answere have, the Queene come in, and toke the Prince in hir armes and presented hym in like forme as the Duke had done, desiring that he shout blisse it; but alle their labour was in veyne, for they departed thens without any answere or countenaunce saving only that ones he loked on the Prince and caste doune his eyene agen, without any more.[33]

The lack of response from Henry made Margaret determined to protect her son by herself.

Soon after her visit to Henry, in February 1454, Margaret returned to London and presented a bill of five articles to parliament claiming the regency for herself.[34] This was an unprecedented step for a queen of England to take and it is likely that Margaret based her political ambition on the examples of her grandmother, Yolande of Aragon, and her mother, Isabel of Lorraine, both of whom had ruled as regents when their husbands were incapacitated. The political role open to an English queen had diminished since the times of the Angevin and early Plantagenet queens and by the mid-fifteenth century it was unthinkable for a woman to be made regent for any length of time, particularly a Frenchwoman. Henry VI's own mother, Catherine of Valois, had been denied any political position during her son's minority and Margaret's claims to the regency were never countenanced by parliament. On 27 March 1454, the Duke of York, was named Protector of England.[35] Margaret had allied herself with York's enemy, the Duke of Somerset, and this appointment must have horrified her. It seems likely that the investiture of Edward of Lancaster as Prince of Wales in June may have been carried out to appease Margaret. Certainly, she emerged as the leader of the Lancastrian faction during the crisis of Henry's illness.

Margaret joined Henry at Windsor following the declaration of York's Protectorate. She must have been greatly troubled about the future and may have feared that York would take all the power from the crown. It seems likely that during this period she continued to try to wake Henry from his stupor and her efforts appear to have finally become successful in late December 1454, when Henry suddenly recovered:

> The Queen came to him, and brought my lord Prynce with her. And then he askid what the Princes name was, and the Queen told him Edward; and than he hild up his hands and thankid God thereof. And he seid he never knew til that tyme, nor wist not what was seid to him, nor wist where he had be whils he hath be seke til now.[36]

Margaret must have been relieved to finally have Henry's recognition of her son and, soon afterwards, she travelled with Henry to London where he relieved York of his Protectorate and released Somerset from the Tower where he had been imprisoned. Henry's recovery was only partial and Margaret quickly established herself as the real power behind the throne.

Henry's return to power proved to be short-lived and, following his removal from office, York began raising troops. In late May 1455, Henry set out from London to travel to a parliament in Leicester with a number of his important ministers, whilst Margaret remained in London. On 21 May, Henry's men were attacked by an army headed by York at St Albans. This was the first battle of the Wars of the Roses and signified the start of a period of great political instability in England. The Duke of Somerset and other leading Lancastrians were killed and Henry, who was slightly wounded, was taken prisoner by York and escorted back to London.[37] When news reached Margaret of the first Battle of St Albans she withdrew to the Tower with her son. Without an army, however, she was powerless and was forced to accept York's second protectorate, which was declared on 17 November 1455.[38]

Margaret realised that she had little scope for opposition to the Yorkists. On 25 March 1458 she took part in the public 'loveday' reconciliation between the Lancastrians and the Yorkists. The two sides walked in formal procession at St Paul's to symbolise their reconciliation, with Margaret holding York's hand.[39] The loveday was seen as a great symbol of hope but the reconciliation completely fell apart in October 1458, when an attempt was made to assassinate the Duchess of York's nephew, the Earl of Warwick, at Westminster. Warwick fled to Calais where he began raising troops whilst his father, the Earl of Salisbury, raised an army in the north and York began recruiting in Wales. This must have greatly alarmed Margaret and she travelled to Cheshire where she began to raise troops in her son's name.[40]

By 1459, Margaret was the acknowledged military and political leader of the house of Lancaster and she would have known that there was no one else with the capability to protect her son. By October, she had raised a sizeable army and headed to confront the Yorkists in the Welsh marches. Her army greatly outnumbered York's and the Yorkists fled from her, York travelling to Ireland and Salisbury, Warwick and York's son, Edward, Earl of March, to Calais. Margaret must have been jubilant at her victory and, with the Yorkists dispersed, must have been confident that her cause would succeed. In June 1460, however, Warwick and Salisbury returned, defeating a Lancastrian army at Northampton and taking Henry prisoner once again.[41] Margaret and her son must have been waiting near the site of the battle. When they heard of their defeat they fled. During their journey they were robbed of all their possessions and deserted by their guards but made it safely to Harlech Castle.[42] Margaret's determination to remain at large demonstrates that she intended to continue to fight on her son's behalf.

On 10 October 1460, York arrived at parliament in London and sat on the king's throne, formally claiming the crown.[43] When Henry IV usurped the crown from Richard II in 1399 he also ignored the claims of Edmund Mortimer, Richard's acknowledged heir and the great-grandson of Edward III's second son, Lionel of Clarence. York was the son of Edmund Mortimer's sister, Anne Mortimer, and therefore descended from Edward III's second son. Henry VI was only descended from his third. Parliament listened to York's claims and it was decided that, whilst Henry VI should not be unthroned, York would be named as his heir, in preference to Edward of Lancaster.[44]

Margaret was furious when she heard the news of her son's disinheritance and immediately began raising an army again, intent on reasserting her son's rights. According to *Hall's Chronicle*, she marched north with 20,000 men and, on 31 December 1460, met an army commanded by York and Salisbury at Wakefield.[45] The Lancastrians won a decisive victory and York was killed on the field. York's brother-in-law, the Earl of Salisbury, was also captured and executed soon afterwards, without trial. Margaret's men 'came to the place wher the dead corps of the duke of Yorke lay, and caused his head to be stryken of, and set on it a croune of paper, and so fixed it on a pole, and presented it to the Quene'.[46] Margaret must have been jubilant to have the head of her son's greatest enemy before her and she cannot truly be blamed for being pleased at the death of the man who had so threatened her son. She had York and Salisbury's heads set on poles over the gates of York as an act of revenge, before beginning to march south in triumph.

Margaret met a second Yorkist army at St Albans soon after Wakefield and won another decisive victory. Henry VI had been brought from

London as a puppet to lead the Yorkist army and was reunited with his wife and son after the battle. Margaret's feelings on this reunion are unclear. She may have resented Henry's disinheritance of their son and she certainly never seems to have held his interests as paramount after Edward of Lancaster's birth. Nonetheless, Henry was an important political figure and Margaret must have felt that her cause was bolstered by his presence in her army. Following the battle, Margaret marched on London, intending to enter the city. Margaret's army was known for being unruly and, outside the city walls, Margaret received a delegation headed by the Duchesses of Bedford and Buckingham and Lady Scales, who begged her to spare the city and not allow her army to enter, a clear indication of just how unpopular she had become.[47] Margaret agreed to leave and took her army back towards the north. This was probably her greatest mistake and, a few days later, the Yorkists, led by Edward, Earl of March, entered London. On 4 March, Edward was proclaimed King as Edward IV.[48] This proclamation must have come as a shock to Margaret and, on 29 March, her army was decisively defeated at Towton by a force commanded by Edward IV. Margaret, Henry and their son fled to Scotland, hotly pursued by the Yorkists.[49]

For the next two years, Margaret waged a guerrilla campaign in the north against Edward IV. In April 1462 she and her son travelled to France to ask her cousin Louis XI for aid. Louis was not eager to help, but Margaret appealed to his mother, her aunt Marie of Anjou and he finally agreed to help her in exchange for the surrender of Calais.[50] By agreeing to surrender Calais, Margaret obtained important military aid but at the cost of any remaining popularity she had in England. As the last area of English rule in France, Calais held a special place in the hearts of the English and it is clear that Margaret never understood this position.[51] Margaret was given 500 French soldiers and sailed for Scotland in October 1462. She attempted to land at Tynemouth but was repulsed by canon fire, which scattered her fleet. This must have been an arduous journey for Margaret and they finally landed at Berwick, which Margaret used as a base to attack northern England. In May 1464, Edward IV met Margaret in battle on the edge of Hexham Forest. This proved to be a disaster for her and she and her son were forced to flee into the forest where they were attacked by robbers and only survived when one robber took pity on Margaret in her misery.[52] Margaret seems to have given up following her defeat at Hexham Forest. Soon afterwards she and her son sailed again to France, this time not planning an immediate return.

Margaret refused to concede that her cause was lost whilst in France and continued to lobby Louis XI over the years, with little success.[53] She must have spent the lonely years raising her son and attempting to keep his cause alive. The news, in 1465, that Henry VI had been captured hiding in northern England must also have been a blow and she must have considered it unlikely that she would ever see him again once he had been taken to the Tower – and she was correct.

Margaret was something of an embarrassment to Louis XI and it was only in 1470 that she became a useful political figure for him. Relations between Edward IV and his closest ally, the Earl of Warwick, had become increasingly strained during the 1460s and, in 1470, Warwick had fled to France. Louis XI saw an opportunity to attack Edward IV and offered to reconcile Margaret and Warwick so that they could launch a joint invasion of England. Margaret regarded Warwick as her greatest enemy and responsible for all her misery and it took Louis a great deal of effort to persuade her to even see him.[54] Margaret, however, must have recognised the possibilities for the revival of her son's cause and finally agreed to a reconciliation with Warwick. A formal reconciliation was staged on 22 July 1470 and, after keeping Warwick on his knees for quarter of an hour, Margaret formally forgave him.[55] It was agreed that Warwick would restore Henry VI to the throne with French aid. To seal their alliance Margaret's son would be married to Warwick's daughter. Margaret cannot have been happy with this clause but, as a pragmatist, she must have seen it as a small price to pay for the restoration of her son's position.

Warwick sailed to invade England before the marriage but, true to her word, Margaret allowed Edward of Lancaster to marry Warwick's daughter, Anne Neville. Soon after the wedding, news reached her that Warwick had been successful and that Henry VI was restored and Edward IV fled. Margaret must have been jubilant and attempted to sail immediately to England. Bad weather, however, kept her party stranded in France.[56] Finally in April 1471 Margaret and her son and daughter-in-law were able to sail for England, landing on 18 April 1471. Almost immediately upon landing Margaret's hopes would have been dashed. On the day that she set foot once again in England, Warwick had fought a battle with the now returned Edward IV at Barnet and had been heavily defeated and killed and Henry VI had been returned to the Tower.[57] Polydore Vergil writes:

> When she heard these things the miserable woman swooned for fear, she was distraught, dismayed and tormented with sorrow; she lamented the calamity of the time, the adversity of fortune, her own toil and misery; she bewailed the unhappy end of King Henry, which she believed assuredly to be at hand, and, to be short, she behaved as one more desirous to die than live.[58]

This disaster so sudden after Margaret's landing must have dented her confidence but she had spent the last twenty years fighting and she was determined to continue to uphold her son's rights.

Margaret immediately began raising an army in the West Country before marching on to Tewkesbury. There she found Edward IV's army waiting for her and prepared to do battle. According to *Hall's Chronicle*, Margaret and her son rode among the troops encouraging them, although Margaret was not present during the battle.[59] She must have had an anxious wait for news, knowing that her son was fighting and that all his hopes depended on the day. She would have been distraught when news was brought to her that her army was completely destroyed and that her son was among the Lancastrians killed.[60] With the loss of her son, Margaret lost the will to escape and was captured by Edward IV at a religious house near the battlefield.

With her son dead, Margaret was a broken woman with nothing left to fight for. She was taken as a prisoner to London and led through the streets and jeering crowds as the prize captive in Edward IV's victory procession. Margaret was then imprisoned in the Tower, arriving the very night that her husband Henry V was murdered by the victorious Yorkist king. With the death of her husband and son, Margaret was no longer a political force and after a few months in the Tower Edward IV turned her over to the custody of her friend, the Countess of Suffolk at Wallingford.[61] Margaret appears to have borne her imprisonment and may have found some comfort in being lodged with her greatest friend.

In August 1475, Edward IV set out to invade France. At a meeting with Louis XI at Picquigny on 25 August 1475, it was agreed that there would be a nine-year truce between the two countries and that Louis would pay Edward a pension.[62] A further condition of the treaty was that Louis would ransom Margaret for 50,000 crowns. In late January 1476, Margaret sailed for France, landing in Dieppe. Margaret's feelings about her release are unrecorded although it is possible that she was glad to see the back of a country which held such unhappy memories. Margaret travelled to meet Louis's envoys at Rouen where she was made to renounce all her claims to Anjou and Maine as compensation for the ransom Louis had paid for her.[63] Margaret was given a modest pension by her father and was allowed to live in his castle at Reculee. In July 1480, her father died and Margaret found herself entirely dependent on Louis XI. She died in misery and poverty on 25 August 1482 at Dampierre Castle, leaving her few poor possessions to Louis XI.

Margaret of Anjou was forced by necessity to take on an extraordinary role for a medieval queen. Through adverse circumstances, she found herself the leader of a political faction and a military commander. There is no evidence that Margaret ever desired this role; she was motivated by concern for her son throughout. Despite this, Margaret was a hated figure in her own lifetime and has been criticised ever since. There is no doubt that Margaret helped to prolong a war that was already lost and that her actions often did not help her own cause. She was proud, domineering and bloodthirsty at times although much of what made her disliked was forced upon her by the weakness of her husband and his rule. Furthermore there is no doubt that she was the victim of Yorkist propaganda and as she rose to prominence with the growing weakness of Henry VI she was increasingly vilified. To the male propaganda writers, writing to a mostly male audience, Margaret must have made an easy target and as a powerful woman there was no shortage of people prepared to believe the worst of her. However, Margaret never sought the role she was forced to take and all her actions were on behalf of her only child. The Wars of the Roses, like any civil war, forced people into positions that they would not otherwise have taken and Margaret was forced to compromise her reputation for the sake of her child. Margaret of Anjou lived during a difficult period of English history and much of her unpopularity was due to the circumstances in which she found herself. This is very similar to the position of her successor, the first Yorkist queen, Elizabeth Woodville, who was also the victim of propaganda and rumours both from the Lancastrian faction and, more damagingly, the Yorkist side.

The Seductress

Elizabeth Woodville

Elizabeth Woodville is remembered today as the mother of the princes in the Tower. She is often viewed as a tragic figure. Accounts of her life generally bear out the suggestion that she somehow caused her misfortune through her actions – that it was her own greed and ambition which led to the destruction of her family. With the exception of King John's first wife, the ineffectual Isabella of Gloucester, Elizabeth Woodville was the first English queen of the post-conquest period. Her marriage caused a huge stir in England and throughout her lifetime Elizabeth Woodville was dogged by scandal. To many of her contemporaries it was unthinkable that the king would have freely chosen to marry a woman so far beneath him and there were rumours of witchcraft and seduction which marred Elizabeth's reputation both during her lifetime and afterwards. Elizabeth's detractors were simply unable to believe that the couple could have been motivated only by love and this criticism of Elizabeth was something that her greatest enemy, Richard III, was happy to publicise during his reign. Elizabeth Woodville's life was one of great extremes, punctuated by triumph and despair. Her contemporaries believed that she simply overreached herself, causing her position to topple once her protector was dead. In reality, however, as an English queen without a powerful foreign family, when her husband died she was left helpless, an easy target for her political rivals.

Elizabeth Woodville was born in 1437 and was the daughter of Sir John Woodville and his wife, Jacquetta de St Pol, Duchess of Bedford.[1] The marriage of Elizabeth's own parents had caused a great scandal across Europe. Jacquetta was the daughter of the Count of St Pol, one of the greatest noblemen in Luxembourg. She was a descendant of Charlemagne and was married in 1433 to John, Duke of Bedford, the younger brother of Henry V. However the Duke of Bedford did not long survive his wedding, leaving Jacquetta a widow two years later. No one would have seriously thought that the Duchess of Bedford would remain single for long but she stunned all her contemporaries when she married Sir John Woodville, a member of her husband's household and a man vastly beneath her in status. In spite of this, her second marriage appears to have been happy and she bore John thirteen children, of whom Elizabeth Woodville was the eldest.

Little evidence survives pertaining to Elizabeth's childhood, although Thomas Moore claimed that she had been in the service of Margaret of Anjou during her youth.[2] By the mid 1450s, she was married to Sir John Grey. The couple probably lived at Grey's manor at Astley in Warwickshire and had two children, Thomas born around 1455 and Richard in the late 1450s.[3] Grey was an eldest son and a good match for Elizabeth and they may have been happy together. The marriage was destined to be short-lived however and on 17 February 1461, Sir John Grey was killed fighting for the Lancastrians at the second battle of St Albans.[4]

The death of her husband must have been a major blow for Elizabeth and she probably feared for the future. A further blow was dealt a few weeks later when her father and eldest brother were captured by the Yorkists fighting for the Lancastrians at Towton.[5] Following these disasters, Elizabeth returned to her mother at Grafton with her two young sons. The defeat of the Lancastrians at Towton also left Elizabeth in considerable financial straits due to the ensuing confiscation of her Lancastrian family's estates. At some point, following her return home, she devised a way to present a petition to Edward IV whilst he was hunting in the area.[6] According to some reports, she positioned herself under an oak tree with her sons. Elizabeth Woodville was very beautiful and Edward fell in love with her at first sight.

Elizabeth's contemporary, Dominic Mancini wrote that marriage was not the first thing which Edward had on his mind when he fell for the young widow:

> When the king first fell in love with her beauty of person and charm of manner, he could not corrupt her virtue by gifts or menaces. The story runs that when Edward placed a dagger at her throat, to make her submit to his passion, she remained unperturbed and determined to die rather than live unchastely with the king. Whereupon Edward coveted her much the more, and he judged the lady worthy to be a royal spouse, who could not be overcome in her constancy even by an infatuated king.[7]

When he first saw her, Edward wanted Elizabeth to be his mistress. This was a position of honour in medieval England and he must have been surprised at her refusal, perhaps even resorting to threatening rape with a dagger. Elizabeth, however, as the daughter of the Duchess of Bedford, considered the status of royal mistress beneath her own, apparently saying 'that as she wist herself too simple to be his wife, so thought she herself too good to be his concubine'.[8] It seems unlikely that Elizabeth considered marriage a possibility at the beginning of her relationship with Edward but she may have hoped to gain the return of her husband's estates through his infatuation with her. She must have been surprised and flattered when it became clear that Edward wished to marry her.

The exact date and location of Elizabeth's second marriage is unknown, although it may have been on 1 May 1464.[9] It appears to have been an impulsive move and both were forced to keep it secret for some time. Elizabeth was the first English woman to marry the king since the Norman conquest and both Elizabeth and Edward must have realised that it would cause consternation in England. Edward may have not considered the consequences of the marriage properly. It was inappropriate and was later used to bolster accusations of witchcraft against Elizabeth and her mother. Edward had also not seen fit to inform his most powerful magnate, the Earl of Warwick, who was in France arranging a marriage between Edward and the sister-in-law of the King of France.[10] Following Warwick's return, Edward was forced to admit at a council meeting that he was, in fact, already married and had been for some time.

When news of Elizabeth and Edward's marriage was made public, there was universal disapproval. Edward's mother, Cecily Neville, apparently objected that Elizabeth was not good enough for him.[11] She is also supposed to have claimed that he was not the son of her husband, the Duke of York but instead the result of an adulterous affair.[12] Whilst this appears merely to have been an impulsive statement made by the irate duchess, the comment sowed a seed that would bear fruit nearly twenty years later. Edward's brother, George, Duke of Clarence also objected to the marriage, saying that Edward should have married a virgin, rather than a widow with children.[13] By far the most serious opponent to the match was Warwick who was angered at the failure of his marriage negotiations in France. The secret marriage of Edward and Elizabeth caused a rift between Edward and Warwick which eventually resulted in open war between them.

Elizabeth is unlikely to have taken objections to her marriage too seriously. She was already Edward's wife and must have felt that they had presented objectors with a *fait accompli*. Edward also fully supported his wife and made plans for a lavish coronation for her. Attempts were made to stress Elizabeth's grand continental connections. In January 1465 Edward sent envoys to the Duke of Burgundy to arrange for Elizabeth's uncle, Jacques of Luxembourg and a Burgundian entourage to attend Elizabeth's coronation.[14] Elizabeth also adopted a coat of arms incorporating those of St Pol and other maternal connections. Elizabeth's coronation was delayed in order to allow time for her foreign relatives to arrive and she was finally crowned in a glittering ceremony on 26 May 1465.[15] In spite of this, most considered the new queen an upstart. Elizabeth, however, must have felt triumphant and she quickly set about sharing some of her good fortune with her relatives.

Elizabeth has always had a reputation for greed and much of this stems from the series of marriages that she arranged for her siblings once she was queen. Elizabeth's sisters were married in quick succession to the Earls of Essex and Kent, the wealthy Lord Strange and the heir of Lord Herbert. Her youngest sister Catherine also secured one of the most prestigious matches in England when she was married in her infancy to the young Duke of Buckingham.[16] She also arranged rich marriages for her brothers and in February 1467 Elizabeth paid Edward's sister, the Duchess of Exeter, for the marriage of her daughter and heiress to her eldest son Thomas Grey. These marriages were resented by many of the nobility in England as the sheer number of Elizabeth's siblings effectively flooded the aristocratic marriage market. Warwick in particular was angered by Thomas Grey's marriage as the king's niece had previously been betrothed to his nephew, George Neville.[17] Elizabeth's activity on behalf of her siblings and sons severely damaged her reputation amongst the jealous nobility. However, she could not have arranged these marriages without the support of other members of the nobility; Edward's sister, the Duchess of Exeter, could hardly have been forced into treating Elizabeth the way she did on the marriage of her daughter. Elizabeth was fond of her family and it is natural that she would want them to share in her good fortune. The sheer number of her siblings however and the fact that many more established families saw the Woodvilles as upstarts led to an underhand campaign against the queen across much of the nobility.

Elizabeth had already proved herself able to bear healthy children before her marriage to Edward and she quickly conceived by him. Her eldest child by Edward, Elizabeth of York, was born on 11 February 1465 and was quickly followed by two other daughters.[18] The sex of these children must have been a disappointment to their parents but Edward does not seem to have blamed Elizabeth. She was a fond mother who liked to keep her family around her, appointing a number of her relatives to her household staff. Her brother John Woodville was her master of horse and her sister-in-law, Lady Scales was a lady-in-waiting.[19] These appointments caused further resentment but Elizabeth ignored the ill-feeling, perhaps believing that with Edward's protection no ill could befall her. She would have been well aware of the hostility of much of the nobility towards her and it is therefore not surprising that she chose to surround herself with friendly figures, regardless of the fact that this caused further discontent.

Elizabeth quickly took to her role as queen and her marriage with Edward was happy. Nevertheless she must never have been able to forget that Edward was a usurping king and that there were always factions in England working against him. Warwick and Clarence had always opposed her marriage. By 1469 their latent hostility had developed into outright rebellion. Elizabeth was visiting Norwich with her daughters when Warwick and Clarence launched an attack on the king. Events moved quickly and Edward's forces were heavily defeated at the Battle of Edgecote on 26 July.[20] Warwick seized the initiative that this victory afforded and quickly captured Edward IV near Nottingham, taking him as a prisoner to his castle at Middleham. This must have been a blow for Elizabeth and she was probably terrified about what would befall her husband. An even greater blow was dealt when news reached Elizabeth at Norwich that her father and brother John Woodville had been captured by Warwick's forces near Coventry and executed without trial. Elizabeth must have plunged into mourning and she would have despaired for the future.

There can have been no doubt in anyone that Warwick and Clarence's attacks were aimed against the Woodvilles. Soon after Elizabeth's return to London, her mother was publicly charged with witchcraft.[21] As the fate of Jacquetta's own sister-in-law Eleanor Cobham had shown, such a charge could be disastrous and Elizabeth would have been aware of the dissent around London against both her and her mother. Some of the claims were of enchantments that Jacquetta used to persuade the king to marry her daughter, again highlighting Elizabeth's extreme unpopularity and the suggestion that she was unworthy to be a queen. Elizabeth and Jacquetta must have spent a tense time until, finally, they heard that Warwick had been forced to release Edward. Elizabeth must have been glad to be reunited with her husband and to have his protection again. Any sense of triumph would have been short-lived. Following a brief exile, Warwick and Clarence returned to England allied with the Lancastrians in September 1470, with an army, and intent on deposing Edward IV.

Edward quickly realised that the Lancastrians were too strong and fled to Burgundy from Kings Lynn, abandoning his family. Elizabeth was in London when news reached her of Warwick's invasion and it must have been with a sinking heart that she realised that Edward was once again unable to protect her. Unwilling to simply surrender, Elizabeth began to provision the Tower to withstand a siege.[22] Warwick was too strong and by early October Elizabeth, her mother and daughters had entered the sanctuary at Westminster Abbey.[23] Soon afterwards, Warwick entered the city and removed Henry VI from the prison in the Tower to the rooms Elizabeth had prepared in the same fortress for her own confinement. From inside the sanctuary, Elizabeth and her mother must have heard the commotion that the restoration of Henry VI entailed with despair. Elizabeth probably feared that she would be forcibly removed from the sanctuary at any time and must have been relieved to discover that the new regime had decided to leave her untouched. As a queen without strong foreign connections, there was little Elizabeth could do but wait and see what direction events took.

Elizabeth had been in sanctuary for several weeks when she gave birth to her first son by Edward.[24] A small christening was arranged for the infant in Westminster Abbey with the Abbot and Prior of the Abbey standing as godfathers and Lady Scrope as godmother. These sponsors were a far cry from the foreign royalty the eldest son of a king could usually expect for his godparents. Elizabeth and Jacquetta appear to have made the best of their time in sanctuary and it is likely that Elizabeth relied on her mother considerably. The sanctuary was small and it must have been uncomfortable for the women sharing a space with three young girls and a newborn baby. They would have pinned all their hopes on Edward obtaining sufficient support abroad to try to win back his crown, or at the very least rescue his family.

Edward had been working hard to gain support on the continent and eventually on 11 March 1471 he sailed for England with an army. He made swift progress through England. On 11 April, he was admitted to London by the townspeople.[25] Henry VI was quickly returned to the Tower and Elizabeth, her mother and children emerged from sanctuary. The meeting between Edward and Elizabeth must have been emotional, with Elizabeth proud to show Edward their baby son. She was probably relieved to be able to move freely around London for the first time in months and to assume her role as queen again. Despite her optimism, however, Elizabeth would have been aware that Edward had not yet won the country back. After capturing Henry VI and releasing Elizabeth, he again marched out of London at the head of an army, this time to confront Warwick at Barnet. Elizabeth must have had an anxious wait for news on the day of the battle and must have been relieved to hear of Edward's victory. This was followed on 4 May 1471 by the defeat of Margaret of Anjou at Tewkesbury, leaving Edward secure once more on his throne.

Elizabeth appears to have quickly settled back into her role as queen. As before, she played a major role in the upbringing of her children and in 1473 she accompanied her son Edward to Ludlow so that he could rule as Prince of Wales.[26] Edward was still only two years old and it was Elizabeth who effectively ruled the principality. She also appointed the Prince's council while she was there, filling the leading positions with her brother, Earl Rivers, and son, Richard Grey. Elizabeth was back with her son in London in summer 1475 when Edward IV assembled an army to invade France. It is a mark of his confidence in her abilities that he appointed her as the effective ruler of England in his absence by placing their son, the nominal regent, in her care. Edward's campaign in France proved to be brief, but Elizabeth must have been glad of the trust Edward placed in her.

Edward IV was a notorious womaniser and took numerous mistresses throughout his marriage which Elizabeth deliberately ignored. Elizabeth was five years older than Edward and it is a mark of her personal qualities and attractions that she was able to retain his love until his death. Elizabeth bore her youngest child, Bridget, in November 1480, when she was 43, demonstrating that she and Edward still enjoyed a close and loving marriage. It is possible that Edward enjoyed the happy family atmosphere that Elizabeth brought him when his own brothers were often at odds. By Christmas 1482 Edward's health was deteriorating and it is likely that Elizabeth quickly became concerned about him. He died on 9 April 1483, a death hastened by his overindulgence in food and drink.[27]

Elizabeth must have been grief-stricken at Edward's death yet realising that there was a great deal to be done to ensure the smooth succession of her son. According to the *Crowland Continuations*, Edward IV's council attended Elizabeth at Westminster soon after Edward's death in order to arrange Edward V's journey to London.[28] The Woodvilles were still perceived with suspicion in England. The council feared that Edward V would be brought to London with a large force in order to enforce the Woodville's rule. This was put to Elizabeth at the council meeting and she agreed to write to Edward to instruct him to bring no more than 2,000 men.[29] Elizabeth probably later came to regret her willingness to allay the council's fears, but in April 1483 she had nothing to fear. Edward V's accession had been uncontested and Elizabeth was content to wait in London for her son to arrive.

Edward V set out for London soon after news of his father's death reached him in Wales. He made steady progress and on arriving in Stony Stratford his escorts heard that his uncle, Richard, Duke of Gloucester and the Duke of Buckingham had arrived at Northampton.[30] Elizabeth's brother Earl Rivers with Elizabeth's son

Sir Richard Grey rode out to meet the two dukes and the four spent a pleasant evening together, feasting and drinking.[31] They agreed to spend the night at the dukes' camp and in the morning were horrified to find that they had been placed under arrest in the night. With Rivers and Grey imprisoned, Gloucester and Buckingham rode to intercept the king at Stony Stratford. They told the young king that they had arrested his uncle and half-brother because they and his elder half-brother, Thomas Grey, Marquis of Dorset had planned to rule the country through him.[32] The young king protested their innocence but there was little the boy could do. Gloucester and Buckingham took control of his progress to London.[33]

Elizabeth Woodville heard the news of Gloucester's coup just after midnight the following day.[34] She and Dorset immediately:

> Began collecting an army, to defend themselves and to set free the young
> king from the clutches of the dukes. But when they exhorted certain
> nobles who had come to the city, and others, to take up arms, they per-
> ceived that men's minds were not only irresolute, but altogether hostile
> to themselves.[35]

It must have been a shock to Elizabeth to realise just how unpopular she had become and she may have realised, perhaps for the first time, just how vulnerable Edward's death had left her. Certainly, without the support of the people of London, there was little Elizabeth could do except gather her children and flee into sanctuary at Westminster. Elizabeth must have been appalled to find herself once again in need of the church's sanctuary and conditions, which this time with two sons and near-adult daughters, must have been very uncomfortable. She must have felt alone and her contemporaries seem to have believed she was acting unreasonably. The following day, for example, the Chancellor visited her in sanctuary and gave her the great seal, to demonstrate that there was no threat to her position.[36] This may have been some comfort to her, but soon afterwards the Chancellor came to her again. He had been sent by Gloucester to obtain the surrender of her youngest son, Richard, Duke of York.[37]

The Chancellor tried to persuade Elizabeth to acquiesce by arguing that Edward V needed his brother's company. She replied that it would be better for both boys to be with their mother then attacked Gloucester verbally for keeping her son away from her. The Chancellor, clearly believing that Richard meant the children no harm, offered Elizabeth a pledge for her youngest son's safety. According to Thomas Moore, Elizabeth replied that 'each of these children is the other's defence while they be asunder, and each of their lives lie in the other's body. Keep one safe and both be sure, and nothing for them both more perilous than to be both in one place'.[38] Elizabeth feared that Gloucester meant to gain control over her sons and kill them. The sanctuary had already been surrounded by soldiers, however, and Elizabeth must have feared that Gloucester would forcibly enter the sanctuary to remove them all. She therefore kissed her youngest son and, weeping, handed him over to the Chancellor.[39] For a fond mother like Elizabeth, this must have been the most traumatic event of her life.

Events moved quickly following the surrender of the Duke of York. Six days later on 22 June, a sermon was preached at Paul's Cross calling Edward IV a bastard and claiming that he and Elizabeth had never actually been married.[40] Gloucester claimed that Edward had been pre-contracted to Eleanor Butler before his marriage to Elizabeth and that his marriage had never been valid.[41] This claim never seems to have been widely believed and Elizabeth is likely to have been incredulous at the suggestion. Most people in England seem to have seen it for the pretext it was, allowing Gloucester to remove his young nephew and claim the throne as Richard III. Soon after Richard III's accession, Edward V and his brother Richard, Duke of York disappeared into the Tower and were never seen again. It was widely believed that Richard ordered their murders soon after his coronation and Elizabeth is also likely to have believed that he murdered her sons. It is very likely that he followed the precedent set by all other English usurping kings and murdered his predecessor.

Elizabeth must have been horrified at her predicament, having gone from being Queen of England to merely Dame Elizabeth Grey over the course of a few weeks. However she was not beaten but quickly began plotting against the new king. At a council meeting a few days before his accession, Richard III had accused Elizabeth of using sorcery against him together with Edward IV's mistress, Jane Shore.[42] This was not the first accusation of sorcery against Elizabeth and it would have further damaged her already poor reputation, something of which Richard III would have been very much aware. Whilst it seems unlikely that Elizabeth and Jane Shore were using witchcraft to injure Richard, she did begin plotting with Lady Margaret Beaufort soon after her son's deposition. Lady Margaret Beaufort was a descendant of John of Gaunt, the third son of Edward III. Her only child, Henry Tudor, was the leading Lancastrian claimant and had been in exile on the continent for a number of years. Elizabeth and Margaret shared a physician and he carried messages between the two women who both had good reason to despise Richard III.[43] Margaret, with the consent of her son, promised that he would marry Elizabeth's eldest daughter Elizabeth of York if Elizabeth Woodville would support Henry's bid for the throne. Excited by the prospect of a throne for her daughter, Elizabeth agreed.

Elizabeth and her son, Dorset, were heavily involved in the rebellion which broke out in October 1483, aimed at deposing Richard III. The rebellion involved uprisings throughout England and an invasion by Henry Tudor from Brittany. Elizabeth must have been eager for news in her sanctuary and would have been distraught to learn of Richard's decisive action to confront the rebels. Henry Tudor's fleet was scattered by storms and returned, beaten, to Brittany. Elizabeth must have felt that her last hope of removing Richard from the throne had passed.

Elizabeth was more than ten years older than Richard and she must have considered it unlikely that she would live to see another king on the throne. At some point Elizabeth accepted that for her daughters' future, as well as her own, she had to make terms with Richard III and leave sanctuary. After obtaining promises from Richard that he would do her and her daughters no harm, Elizabeth left sanctuary. Throughout her life, Elizabeth was very resourceful and it is likely that she accepted this situation as the best that she could hope for. At some point, she is known to have written to Dorset in France to recommend that he abandon Henry Tudor and return home to England.[44] Elizabeth probably lived quietly, visiting court on state and family occasions. It seems likely that she knew and approved of Richard's scheme to marry her daughter, Elizabeth of York. However, again, her hopes of a crown for her daughter were dashed and Elizabeth must have resigned herself to living out her life in obscurity.

Elizabeth Woodville's fortunes changed again in August 1485. She was living in London when Henry Tudor launched a second invasion of England, having sworn before he left to marry Elizabeth of York. Elizabeth must have watched his progress with interest and, in spite of her reconciliation with Richard III, she must have been pleased to hear of his death in battle. Richard had been responsible for the deaths of three of her four sons, as well as her brother; even after making terms with him she cannot have been sorry to hear of his death. Soon after Henry VII's accession, the Act invalidating Elizabeth's marriage was repealed by parliament – a satisfying vindication for Elizabeth.

After the marriage of Elizabeth of York and Henry VII, Elizabeth Woodville appeared to settle down into life as queen dowager. As the mother of the queen and not the king, however, Elizabeth appears to have resented being given less prominence in Henry's regime than his own mother, Margaret Beaufort and it has been suggested that she began to conspire against him. The early years of Henry's reign were plagued by pretenders to his crown and one of the most dangerous was Lambert Simmnel. He was a boy who had been taught to impersonate first Richard, Duke of York and then Clarence's son, the Earl of Warwick. He was a particularly convincing pretender and, according to Francis Bacon:

> So that it cannot be, but that some great person that knew particularly and familiarly Edward Plantagenet [Warwick], had a hand in the business, from whom the priest might take his aim. That which is most probable, out of precedent and subsequent acts, is, that it was the Queen Dowager, from whom this action had the principle source and motion. For certain it is, she was a busy negotiating woman, and in her withdrawing-chamber had the fortunate conspiracy for the king against King Richard the third been hatched; which the king knew, and remembered perhaps but too well; and was at this time extremely discontent with the king, thinking her daughter, as the king handled the matter, not advanced but displeased: and none could hold the book so well to prompt and instruct this stage-play as she could.[45]

In this account, Elizabeth is portrayed as a conniving woman and there is no doubt that throughout her life Elizabeth was implicated in conspiracies and other underhand political dealings. As the facts of her life show, however, without the protection of a powerful foreign family she was forced to plot in order to ensure the security of herself and her family. There were rumours that Henry VII did not treat his wife, who had after all been the heiress of England, exactly as he should have. Elizabeth as a fond mother may well have been anxious to ensure her daughter's position. Elizabeth Woodville herself had also suffered attacks on her position during Richard III's reign and it is therefore not surprising that she was fearful of a loss of influence during the reign of his successor. Elizabeth Woodville never had enough political influence to enable her to change her situation openly and she was therefore forced into conspiracies throughout her widowhood.

As soon as the plot became known to Henry he seized Elizabeth's property and sent her to the convent at Bermondsey, officially claiming it as punishment for her delivering her daughters into Richard III's custody.[46] The rebellion was soon destroyed by Henry but he does not seem to have forgiven Elizabeth and she lived quietly for the rest of her life, dying at Bermondsey on 8 June 1492 at the age of fifty-five.[47] She was given a quiet funeral, attended by Dorset and some of her daughters, and was buried beside her second husband, Edward IV.

Elizabeth Woodville had one of the most eventful lives of any medieval queen, marked by great highs and lows. Certainly, much of this turmoil was caused by the era in which she lived and her contemporary, Margaret of Anjou, cannot be said to have been much happier. Elizabeth was attacked during her lifetime for her marriage; in this and the marriages that she arranged for her family she was seen as greedy and grasping. During the tumultuous events of 1483, Elizabeth appears as a wailing Cassandra, foreseeing all too clearly what would occur and unable to make herself believed. She was also criticised for her decision to make terms with Richard III and then for her plot against Henry VII. However, it is difficult to see how any of this was really Elizabeth's fault and it appears almost as if Elizabeth's contemporaries, in seeking to see her as the architect in her own ruin, were trying to distance themselves from their own parts in the acceptance of Richard III and deposition of Edward V. Elizabeth Woodville did not set out to marry Edward IV but it is hard to blame her for accepting such a glittering marriage when it was offered to her. She and Edward also appear to have been happy and mere ambition is unlikely to have driven Elizabeth's actions. She was also envied and disparaged from the start of her queenship and it is therefore easy to see why she sought to raise her relatives to positions where they could keep her company. It is also clear that, for all the criticism of Elizabeth, there was a time during Edward IV's reign when a Woodville marriage was desirable and it is hardly Elizabeth's fault that, in a time of high infant mortality, so many of her siblings survived to adulthood. As an Englishwoman, Elizabeth was easy to attack. Her parents could not threaten an invasion or lobby the Pope in her support as the families of foreign-born queens could. Ultimately she was an easy target for bullying and neutralisation, as both Richard III and Henry VII discovered. That Elizabeth still sought to improve her position and that of her children in the face of this treatment is hardly unacceptable, even if she did sometimes employ underhand methods. No one could have predicted the life Elizabeth Woodville would lead at her birth. Edward IV's marriage, as the first to an English commoner since the Norman conquest, set a precedent that would be followed enthusiastically by the couple's grandson, Henry VIII.

Anne Boleyn

Anne Boleyn is the most controversial woman ever to wear the crown of England. Like Elizabeth Woodville, she rose from humble origins to marry the king but her king was already married. By deciding to marry, Anne Boleyn and Henry VIII set in motion a divorce which dragged on for over six years and dramatically changed the course of English history. Anne Boleyn had a huge impact on religion in England and helped to shape the course England would take into the early modern period. In spite of this, however, she was never popular and Anne's security was ultimately based on maintaining the king's love. One of the most studied of her generation, Anne Boleyn's life held moments of great triumph and calamity. She is also one of the most vilified, though Henry should bear most of the blame, as he held the power in their relationship. Anne ended up an unfortunate victim, just like Henry's first wife, Catherine of Aragon.

Anne Boleyn was probably born in 1500 at Blickling Hall in Norfolk.[1] Anne's father was Sir Thomas Boleyn whose family had married well, over a number of generations. Thomas had continued his family's policy of good marriages, marrying Elizabeth Howard, sister of the Duke of Norfolk. The Howards were one of the premier families in England and Anne would have been aware of the advantages of her connection to the family from an early age. Both of Anne's parents also had strong connections with the court and her mother had been one of Catherine of Aragon's ladies.[2] In 1512 Sir Thomas Boleyn was sent as ambassador to Margaret of Austria in Brussels and the two got on well.[3] It is likely that Margaret offered to take one of his daughters into her household during his stay in Brussels and Thomas, perhaps viewing his younger daughter as more promising than his elder Mary, sent Anne.

Margaret of Austria's court was renowned throughout Europe as a centre of learning and Anne appears to have quickly absorbed its culture. Anne was famous throughout her life for her intelligence and she learnt French easily, as a language in which she was noted for being fluent. Anne probably enjoyed the status of being one of Margaret's maids of honour but she did not stay there long. In August 1514, England switched its allegiance from the Empire to France and Thomas was obliged to write to Margaret for the release of his daughter.[4] Anne's French skills were probably required and at some point in late 1514 she travelled to Paris to join the household of Mary Tudor, Henry VIII's sister and the new Queen of France. Anne was probably sorry to leave Margaret of Austria but she flourished in France where her sister was also one of the queen's ladies. Mary Tudor returned to England in April 1515 and was accompanied by Mary Boleyn, who had already disgraced herself by becoming the mistress of the French king. Anne, however, passed into the household of the new Queen of France, Claude.

Anne Boleyn's life in France is not recorded in any sources but she was young and probably quickly became French in all but birth. It is likely that she took part in Claude's coronation at St Denis in 1516 and other ceremonial events at the French court. Anne clearly received an excellent education in France and she is known to have been able to play the lute and sing and dance well. She would probably have been happy to remain in France. In 1515, however, Anne's great-grandfather, the Earl of Ormonde, died. The earl had expressed a wish that he be succeeded by his grandson, Sir Thomas Boleyn, but, soon after his death, the earldom was seized by his cousin, Piers Butler. Thomas appealed for the title to the king and the dispute dragged on for several years. In 1522, Cardinal Wolsey brokered a solution, that Piers Butler would keep the title and his eldest son, James Butler, would marry Thomas's only unmarried daughter, Anne Boleyn.

The solution suited the king and Anne was duly sent for, arriving at the English court in 1522. Anne quickly made a stir. According to George

Wyatt, 'in beauty she was to manie inferior, but for behaviour manners, attire and tonge she excelled them all. For she had bene brought up in France'.[5] Anne Boleyn was never called a beauty and did not conform to contemporary ideals of beauty. She had a dark complexion with dark eyes and dark hair. It is also possible that she had a rudimentary sixth finger on one hand which she disguised with hanging sleeves, something which might have been taken as a sign of witchcraft.[6] Her French upbringing had taught Anne grace and an ability to make the most of herself. She stood out as exotic amongst the Englishwomen of the court. In March 1522, she was one of the seven ladies chosen to take part in a masque before the court.[7] The seven ladies stood in a wooden castle and were each given a virtue to represent, the king's sister taking 'Beauty' and Anne, appropriately as it turned out, playing 'Perseverance'. The seven ladies wore white satin and bonnets of gold and jewels and defended their castle with rose petals against a company of knights, led by the king. Anne must have greatly enjoyed herself and her place in the masque demonstrates just how highly she was held amongst the ladies of the court.

Anne is little documented between 1522 and 1526 but she appears to have quickly established herself as one of Catherine of Aragon's ladies. Negotiations for her marriage to James Butler dragged on but it soon became clear that they would come to nothing, perhaps due to her father's unwillingness to abandon his hopes of a title. Anne enjoyed court life and it is likely that she would also have been unwilling to marry her Irish cousin and leave court for his estates. Some time after her arrival at court she also became involved with another, more eligible, suitor. According to Cavendish's *Life of Wolsey*, Henry Percy, who was heir to the earldom of Northumberland, often spent time in the queen's chambers and would flirt with her ladies there.[8] It quickly became apparent that he preferred Anne Boleyn to all the other ladies:

> There grew such a secret love between them that at length they were engaged together, intending to marry. This came to the king's knowledge, who was then much offended. Wherefore he could no longer hide his secret affection, but revealed his secret intention unto my lord Cardinal in that behalf; and consulted with him to break the engagement.[9]

It is unlikely that the king had any romantic feelings for Anne at that time but he probably still hoped that the Butler marriage would occur and was angry that Anne and Percy should have gone against his wishes. Henry may well have felt that Anne was too far beneath Percy socially to ever be a credible wife for him.

Following the king's intervention, Henry Percy was summoned to Wolsey and rebuked by the Cardinal for attaching himself to a woman who was beneath him.[10] Percy wept and tried to defend Anne, saying that she was the woman he loved most and pointing out her noble descent. This was fruitless and Wolsey sent for Percy's father who took him back to Northumberland and married him swiftly to the Earl of Shrewsbury's daughter. It is unclear whether Anne returned Henry Percy's affection, but she may have done. Certainly, she blamed Cardinal Wolsey for the loss of such a grand marriage and later became his greatest enemy. There was certainly a secret engagement between Anne and Henry Percy, although both attempted to suppress the knowledge of this once she became queen. Anne's affair with Henry Percy clearly shows her appeal and ability to breach convention and arrange a marriage for herself. It also shows clearly, for the first time, the great ambition which the daughter of Sir Thomas Boleyn could harbour.

Henry Percy was not the only person with whom Anne became romantically involved during her first years at court. She also attracted the attentions of the married poet, Sir Thomas Wyatt. The exact nature of Anne and Wyatt's relationship is unclear and Anne, who was trying to arrange an advantageous marriage, may have seen the relationship as merely harmless flirtation. Wyatt was clearly interested in Anne and in one poem refers to his love for 'Brunet'.[11] This Brunet is obviously Anne Boleyn and Wyatt's original final line for this poem refers to 'Her that did set our country in a rore'. There is no doubt that this refers to Anne. The exact nature of Anne and Wyatt's relationship is perhaps summed up in another poem by Wyatt:

> Whose list to hunt: I know where is an hind
> But as for me, alas I may no more
> The vain trevail hath wearied me so sore,
> I am of them that farthest come behind
> Yet may I by no means be wearied mind

Draw from the deer, but as she fleeth afore
Fainting I follow. I leave off therefore,
Sithens in a net I seek to hold the wind
Who list her hunt, I put him out of doubt,
As well as I may spend his time in vain,
And graven with diamonds in letters plain
There is written her fair neck round about
'Noli me tangere, for Caesar's I am,
And wild for to hold, though I seem tame'.[12]

From the evidence of this poem it seems likely that Wyatt pursued Anne, hoping that she would become his mistress but that this affair was never consummated and Anne considered him the least of her suitors. Anne knew the value of marriage and would not have thrown away her propects for a mere flirtation. Nevertheless the liaison did prove useful to her since Wyatt's interest in Anne seems to have triggered the king's own interest in her.

The exact date of the king's interest in Anne Boleyn is unclear but there is no doubt that she was present at court for some time before she came to his attention. Her sister, Mary Boleyn, had been the king's mistress during the early 1520s and it is likely that initially Henry expected Anne to fulfil a similar role to that of her sister. A number of love letters written by Henry to Anne survive and it seems that he first sought to offer her the position of his official mistress. Anne, perhaps remembering how her own sister had been cast aside by the king once he had tired of her, refused Henry's offer and instead retreated to her family home of Hever. Henry did not, however, forget about Anne and wrote to her begging her to return to court.[13]

By around 1526, Henry was apparently completely confused about Anne's conduct towards him. In his fourth surviving letter to Anne he begged to know her feelings towards him:

I beseech you now with all my heart definitely to let me know your whole mind as to the love between us; for necessity compels me to plague you for a reply, having been for more than a year now struck by the dart of love, and being uncertain either of failure or of finding a place in your heart and affection.[14]

The fact that Anne was unavailable caused what had begun as a flirtation to become an obsession. By the time of this letter, Henry was desperate to win Anne and undertones in the letter suggest that he would even be prepared to offer her marriage. On receiving the letter, Anne must have realised that she was now being offered something more than merely being Henry's mistress. Although her reply does not survive, Henry's next letter refers to her submission to him and a present that she commissioned representing a maiden in a storm-tossed ship.[15] Henry signed this letter with a drawing of a heart and it is clear that this was the moment that their relationship became a serious commitment for them both.

Anne made it clear to Henry from the start that only marriage would suffice. She may well have based her stance on that taken by Elizabeth Woodville and from this would have known the heights a woman who stood out against the king could reach. Henry had been married to Catherine of Aragon for almost twenty years by the time he began his relationship with Anne but his passion for Anne meant that he was eager to be rid of Catherine. Although Henry always claimed that it was his conscience that compelled him to leave an ungodly marriage with Catherine, who had been the wife of his elder brother, there is no doubt that in 1527 his instigation of divorce proceedings was due to his desire to marry Anne. Anne Boleyn was at first kept separate from the divorce but as time went by she was given more prominence at Henry's court.

In December 1527, she moved to court permanently and kept a queenly state, despite the presence of her rival, Catherine.[16] In 1527, Anne must have felt triumphant and she and Henry probably believed that their marriage was imminent. However, as the divorce dragged on, both became increasingly frustrated and Anne was able to direct Henry's frustration towards her long-term enemy, Cardinal Wolsey. Anne appears to have been willing to work with Wolsey whilst she thought that he could procure the divorce for her. When it became apparent that he could not achieve this, she became hostile towards him, perhaps believing that he was deliberately procrastinating.

Wolsey knew of Anne's attitude towards him and attempted to gain her favour through providing feasts and entertainments for her and the king.[17] This did not help him however, and she built up an anti-Wolsey faction at court whilst he was absent on a diplomatic mission to France.

She also spoke against Wolsey to Henry and took great pains to keep the two apart. One day when Wolsey had an appointment with Henry in the early morning, he arrived to find Henry ready to ride on a hunting expedition arranged by Anne.[18] Anne provided a picnic so that Henry would not need to return all day and Wolsey spent a fruitless day waiting for Henry to return before returning home without seeing him. Wolsey was unable to compete with the influence of Anne Boleyn and he was arrested for treason, primarily due to his inability to obtain Henry's divorce. Wolsey died on 29 November 1530 on his way to prison.[19]

In spite of the delay in Henry's divorce, Anne had gradually taken on more of a queenly role. On 8 December 1529, Sir Thomas Boleyn was made Earl of Wiltshire and Ormonde. Anne took the place of the queen at the celebrations the next day.[20] On 1 September 1532, Anne was also created Marquis of Pembroke in her own right and given £1,000 worth of land.[21] On 11 October 1532, Henry and the new Lady Marquis sailed to Calais for a meeting with the French king.[22] Anne must have been glad to return to France for a visit and she may have speculated just how much her status had changed in the decade since her return to England. Francis I of France certainly remembered Anne. On one occasion Anne and Francis dined together and then sat and talked privately. The recognition of Anne's position by the King of France gave Anne and Henry confidence in French support for their marriage. They slept together for the first time in Calais and Anne must finally have been certain that her marriage would occur soon. Events were, in any event, forced to move quickly after the French visit and Anne became pregnant early in 1533.

By early 1533 it was clear to everyone that the Pope would never grant Henry his divorce. Catherine of Aragon was the aunt of the Emperor Charles V who was currently holding the Pope as a virtual prisoner and would never allow his aunt to be disgraced. After years of fruitless waiting, by 1533 both Henry and Anne had begun to look around for alternative solutions but it was Anne that took the initiative. At some point in the early 1530s, Anne acquired a copy of *The Obedience of a Christian Man and How Christian Rulers Ought to Govern*, which had been published by the religious reformer, William Tyndale.[23] This book suggested an answer to Henry's problem and Anne marked out passages for Henry to read, including arguments that the king's law was God's law and not the law of the Pope. Henry was very taken with the idea and with the death of the elderly Archbishop of Canterbury, was able to put these ideas into reality. Henry appointed Anne's chaplain, Thomas Cranmer, to the vacancy and with his archbishop's compliance, declared himself Head of the Church of England, denying the Pope's authority in England.

Anne was very interested in religious reform and must have approved of Henry's actions towards the Church. According to her chaplain, William Latymer, Anne believed that her elevation to the queenship was the work of God.[24] Whilst Latymer wished to provide a flattering picture of Anne in his biography of her it is possible that Anne saw herself as appointed by God to spread reform. During her time as queen, she was certainly very interested in Protestantism. She is known to have patronised Protestants who had been persecuted on the continent, welcoming a Nicholas Borbonius who had been imprisoned in France for speaking against the Pope.[25] Anne also used her influence with Henry to have reforming churchmen appointed to prominent Church positions and tried actively to turn people away from the Pope. Whilst Anne was visiting Winchcombe during her marriage, she sent commissioners to investigate the relic of the blood of Christ that was housed at nearby Hailes Abbey.[26] The blood was found to be either that of a duck or red wax and Anne had Henry remove it from the abbey. Anne was clearly committed to reform in England and she is known to have kept a copy of the English Bible in her chamber so that anyone who wished to read it could do so. It certainly must have pleased Anne that her marriage led to the break with Rome and the English Reformation.

The date of Anne and Henry's marriage was not recorded and it was deliberately kept secret whilst Henry's divorce was finalised. They were probably married around 25 January 1533, around the time that Anne would have begun to suspect that she was pregnant.[27] Although the marriage remained secret for several months, Anne was jubilant and dropped hints to members of the court, claiming that her craving for apples meant that she was pregnant.[28] Anne finally appeared publicly as queen at Easter 1533.[29] Henry wanted his second marriage to appear completely legitimate and arranged a grand coronation for Anne, intending to demonstrate the finality of what he had done for her. On 20 May 1533, Anne made a ceremonial entry into London and was given a gun salute from the Tower and the guns on the ships in the

Thames.[30] She spent the night before her coronation in the royal apartments at the Tower and then, on 31 May set out for Westminster Abbey in a rich chariot, covered in cloth of silver and followed by an escort of ladies in gowns of crimson velvet. Anne must have been exhausted by her coronation, but also triumphant. Only the hostility of the crowds that flocked to see her procession must have marred the day for her and they reportedly taunted her with cries of 'Ha! Ha!' in a mocking salute to the entwined initials of Henry and Anne that appeared on banners around the city.

Anne Boleyn made many enemies during her rise to the queenship. She is known to have become estranged from her aunt, the Duchess of Norfolk, early in Henry's courtship of her. The duchess was one of Catherine of Aragon's most enthusiastic supporters.[31] Several reports state how, secure in the hold she had over the king, Anne became proud and haughty and she alienated many of her supporters. She also quarrelled with both her father and her uncle the Duke of Norfolk so her relations with Norfolk during her reign were always uneasy.[32] It is likely that, in an apparently unassailable position after her marriage, Anne no longer needed the support of her family as she had once done, believing that Henry would protect her. Anne was also disliked by the majority of people of England. Catherine of Aragon and her daughter Mary were very popular in England and Anne Boleyn was seen as beligerent and Henry's concubine. Anne must have known of the hostility towards her but it is likely that she did not believe it posed her any threat. Anne adopted as her motto, 'the most happy', and must have felt secure in her new position as queen in 1533.

Both Henry and Anne eagerly anticipated the birth of their child and Anne entered her confinement at Greenwich in early autumn. On 7 September 1533, she gave birth to a daughter, who was named Elizabeth, in honour of Henry's mother.[33] The sex of their child must have been a huge blow to both parents and it is clear that both were confidently expecting a son. The child was perfect, however, resembling her father, and the couple appear to have tried to make the best of the situation.[34] After her initial disappointment evaporated, Anne probably believed that she would quickly bear another child. She was an attentive mother to Elizabeth. The child was fostered out at Hertford when she was just three months old, but she was brought to visit court often and Anne visited her regularly.[35] Anne took a great interest in her upbringing and welfare, regularly ordering clothes and presents for her daughter. She was also ambitious for Elizabeth and wished her to have the opportunity to learn Latin, a language of which Anne herself was ignorant.[36] She also wished Elizabeth to be taught Hebrew, Greek, Italian, Spanish and French. Despite her fondness for Elizabeth, Anne cannot have believed that she would remain Henry's heir for long. She became pregnant within four months of Elizabeth's birth and must have hoped that this would produce the son Henry required.[37] It would have been a blow to both her and Henry when she miscarried in July 1534. There is no evidence that she conceived again before late 1535.

Henry had been attracted by Anne's confidence and her willingness to stand up to him and argue with him.[38] Whilst these were qualities that he admired in a mistress, he expected submission from his wife. In summer 1534, Anne discovered that Henry was having an affair with one of her ladies.[39] She remonstrated with him as she had many times before during their relationship but Anne must have been horrified by Henry's reaction this time. Henry told her bluntly that it was not her place to criticise him and that she should remember where she came from. He also told her that he would not raise her again if he had the chance to. This exchange must have shocked Anne, concerned that she was losing her hold over Henry. However they appear to have been reconciled and in December 1534 it was Henry himself who informed her gently of the death of her pet dog.[40] In the summer and autumn of 1535, Anne and Henry went on progress together. This was a success and Anne became pregnant in October 1535, soon after their return.[41] Nonetheless by late 1535 Anne must have been aware that she had lost much of her influence over Henry and that she needed a son to safeguard her position as queen.

Anne must have been jubilant and hopeful of a happy future in January 1536 when she heard of Catherine of Aragon's death that month. The event meant that Anne was the sole Queen of England and she must have felt as though a burden had been lifted from her. She is recorded as having celebrated the death with Henry by wearing yellow.[42] She must have eagerly anticipated the birth of the child that she believed would ensure her own safety. On 24 January, however, Henry suffered a bad fall from his horse and was unconscious for several hours.[43] Anne was informed of the accident and was terrified. On 29 January 1536, the day of Catherine of Aragon's funeral, Anne miscarried a male child.[44] Anne blamed her terror at Henry's fall but the miscarriage caused a rift between Henry and Anne and at that point Henry may have begun to believe that Anne, like Catherine of Aragon before her, would not be able to bear him a living male child.

Despite her miscarriage, Anne's position was still fairly strong in early 1536 and Henry does not seem to have been contemplating removing her. However in the spring of 1536 Anne's fiery temper once again got the better of her and she fell out with Thomas Cromwell, the king's first minister and her greatest supporter.[45] This quarrel ultimately proved fatal to Anne. Cromwell, probably fearing that she would attempt to bring him down, transferred his allegiance to her rival for Henry's affections, her own lady-in-waiting, Jane Seymour. Anne probably did not realise just how dangerous her rift with Cromwell was and her fall was unexpected.

On 1 May 1536, Henry and Anne sat together to watch jousting at Greenwich.[46] Anne must have been perturbed when Henry rose suddenly during the jousting and left without saying a word. The next day Anne's brother Viscount Rochford and a courtier, Henry Norris, both of whom had taken part in the tournament, were arrested and taken to the Tower.[47] It is unclear whether Anne heard of this before her own arrest that evening. She must have been surprised and frightened by her arrest and before entering the Tower she fell to her knees and begged God to help her, saying she was guilty of no crime.[48] She was taken inside the Tower and lodged in the same apartments in which she had stayed the night before her coronation, an irony that did not fail to escape Anne. She must have been horrified when she heard that she was accused of incest with her brother and adultery with the noblemen Henry Norris, Francis Weston and William Brereton and her musician, Mark Smeaton.[49] A woman as intelligent as Anne Boleyn would never have acted in such a foolhardy way and it is clear that these charges were a pretext to allow the king to be rid of his wife. Anne was tried within the Tower on 15 May and the result was a foregone conclusion. Anne's uncle, Norfolk, presided over a court that sentenced her to be either burnt or beheaded, according to the king's pleasure.

Anne and her brother defended themselves eloquently at their trials but for Anne her trial may have been the moment when she realised that Henry meant to kill her. She may previously have hoped that Henry would merely divorce her, but his problems with Catherine of Aragon meant that Henry did not want another ex-wife. Anne spent her final few days preparing herself for death. On 17 May 1536, Anne's supposed lovers were taken out to Tower Hill and executed.[50] Anne must have known of these deaths and would have then considered her death a virtual certainty. She was probably also informed that on that same afternoon, Archbishop Cranmer held a church court at Lambeth and annulled her marriage due to her precontract with Henry Percy.[51] Anne is known to have had a wry sense of humour and it may have touched her that she was being executed for adultery against a man to whom she had now officially never actually been married.

Anne Boleyn was led out onto Tower Green early the next day. As a concession to her, Henry had sent to France for a swordsman to cut off her head and it is possible that Anne herself requested this.[52] She was probably consoled somewhat by the knowledge that she was to be dispatched by an expert and that it would be quicker than death by axe. Anne was dressed entirely in black and carried a book of psalms on her way to the scaffold.[53] It was customary for a condemned person to make a final speech on the scaffold. Anne's speech appears remarkably conciliatory towards a husband who had condemned her to death and she may have feared for Elizabeth's safety. Her speech went as follows:

> Good Christian people, I am come hether to dye, for according to the lawe and by the lawe I am iudged to dye, and therefore I wyll speake nothing against it. I am come hether to accuse no man, nor to speake any thyng of that wherof I am accused and condemned to dye, but I pray God save the king and send him long to reign over you, for a gentler nor a more mercyfull prince was there neuer: and to me he was ever a good, a gentle, and sovereign lorde. And if any persone will medle of my cause, I require them to iudge the best. And thus I take my leave of the worlde and of you all, and I heartely desire you all to pray for me.[54]

With these words, Anne, former Queen of England, knelt down and prayed, before being decapitated with one stroke of the sword.

The life and death of Anne Boleyn shocked Europe. She had been a controversial figure even in her own lifetime. She was an intelligent, ambitious woman and her life was one of great extremes. Anne was innocent of the charges of adultery and incest laid against her; most people in England would have seen them as a pretext to allow Henry to remarry. However as an Englishwoman Anne was as vulnerable as her predecessor, Elizabeth Woodville, had been when the protection of the king was withdrawn. Henry was free to execute her to rid himself of her, something that had not been possible in the case of his foreign-born wives. Anne Boleyn was a proud and aspiring woman and these facets of her character, so important in securing the throne for her, ultimately also led her to her death, as she quickly proved not to be the kind of wife that Henry wanted. This was not Anne's fault and she never appears to have understood that what Henry admired in a mistress was not what he required in a wife. Although she could not have known it at the time, Anne Boleyn was the second wife of England's most married monarch and her story was unnervingly echoed in that of her first cousin, Catherine Howard, who was destined to become Henry's fifth queen.

Treachery & Misjudgement

Catherine Howard

Catherine Howard was the second of Henry VIII's wives to be beheaded for adultery but unlike her cousin Anne Boleyn, Catherine was guilty. Catherine may have been as young as fifteen when she caught the eye of the king and she was completely ill-equipped to deal with the demands of queenship. At a time when queens were expected to be chaste and virginial at marriage, Catherine had already enjoyed affairs with two lovers. She then preceded to commit adultery with a third, possibly with the intention of producing a son for the ageing king. Catherine Howard loved the trappings of power that queenship brought her but she was unable to see the danger that also accompanied the position. Catherine's sudden arrest and execution caused shock across Europe but the picture of her conduct that emerged from Henry's investigations meant that there was little sympathy for her. There is no doubt however that Catherine Howard was completely unsuited for the position of queen. Further to this, although she was disloyal, her relatives and her husband must also bear some of the blame for her downfall, since it was they who initially placed her in such an inappropriate position.

Catherine Howard's date of birth is not recorded but she was probably born between 1521 and 1525. Since Catherine was not listed in her step-grandfather's will of 1524 but was in his wife's of 1527, it is entirely possible that she was born around 1525.[1] She would therefore have been only around fifteen at the time of her marriage, an unusually early age even for the Tudor period. Catherine's mother Joyce Culpeper was a widow when she married Lord Edmund Howard and it is likely her wealth attracted him to her. Certainly Joyce Culpeper's stepfather and mother were suspicious of Edmund and entailed Joyce's inheritance on her children.[2] Edmund was also to marry two more wealthy widows following Joyce's death when Catherine was still very young.

Lord Edmund Howard was a younger son of the Duke of Norfolk and as such a member of the most prominent noble family in England. However he was ineffectual, never finding favour at court or lasting employment. The only evidence of his character also suggests that he was henpecked by his wives. In a letter to Lady Lisle, Edmund wrote:

> Madame, so it is I have this night after midnight taken your medicine, for the which I heartily thank you, for it hath done me much good and hath caused the stone to break, so that now I void much gravel. But for all that, your said medicine hath done me little honesty, for it made me piss my bed this night, for the which my wife hath sore beaten me, and saying it is children's parts to bepiss their bed.[3]

Edmund Howard was constantly short of money and from August 1537 until just before his death in 1539, he was absent from England in his capacity as Mayor of Calais.[4] Catherine probably had little contact with either of her parents. At some point during her childhood she was sent to join the household of her father's stepmother, the Dowager Duchess of Norfolk at her home in Horsham.

It was not unusual for noble girls to be boarded out in the households of wealthy relatives and Catherine's parents probably hoped that she would receive a good education at her grandmother's house. Catherine would have been educated with the other noble girls in the duchess's household and she was taught to read and write although it is unlikely that her education extended much beyond this. The duchess, however, also wanted Catherine to be musical and appointed a neighbour, Henry Manox, to teach her the virginals.[5]

Socially Henry Manox was far beneath Catherine. However he and Catherine quickly began a relationship. Manox himself spoke about how 'he fell in love with her and she with him, but the duchess found them alone together one day and gave Mrs Katharine two or three blows, and charged them never to be alone together'.[6] Catherine must have been very young when she and Manox first began their affair and it is likely that he initiated it, perhaps hoping to marry a Howard bride. Catherine was probably flattered by the attentions of an older man and may have been encouraged by the other girls in the household to reciprocate. There was little privacy in the duchess's household and Catherine would have known about the love affairs of the other members of the household.

Manox always denied that he and Catherine consummated their relationship and Catherine's extreme youth and inexperience probably played a part in this. They do appear to have lain naked together, however, and it was later claimed that Manox knew of secret marks on Catherine's body.[7] Manox was dismissed when the duchess discovered him and Catherine meeting secretly in the duchess's chapel chamber.[8] For Catherine, this probably marked the end of the affair; she may never have taken the relationship very seriously, instead seeing Manox as an amusement. Manox was not deterred, however, and followed the household when it moved to the duchess's house at Lambeth. Catherine was probably irritated by the appearance of her former lover because by this time she had found a new lover.

Catherine met Francis Dereham when the household moved to Lambeth. He was of a much higher status than Henry Manox. He was also young, handsome and attractive to women, becoming a favourite of Catherine's grandmother, the Duchess of Norfolk. Catherine was one of many young girls in the duchess's household and the line between servants and noblewomen was blurred. Catherine shared a dormitory with both girls of her own rank and the duchess's female servants and there would have been very little privacy. Catherine would have learnt from an early age that it was possible to take a lover with impunity and she may have imitated the older girls. Catherine's youthful activities with Henry Manox were probably almost a game to her and an attempt at playing at being grown up. By around 1537, however, Catherine was ready to embark on a more mature affair. The girls' dormitory would be locked at night but the key was easily stolen from the duchess.[9] Once the door was unlocked the young men of the household would come to visit the girls, bringing food for midnight picnics.[10] Catherine probably enjoyed the danger of these secret meetings and the chance to flirt with the young men. Soon, however, she and Dereham were known to favour each other over any others.

Catherine Howard and Francis Dereham certainly consummated their relationship.[11] This would have seemed like a normal practice to Catherine growing up in the easy atmosphere of the girls' dormitory and she later admitted that she had been taught about contraception and knew how to stop herself from conceiving a child.[12] Catherine always denied that she and Francis Dereham had entered into any engagement with each other but Dereham claimed that he considered himself betrothed to her.[13] As with Catherine's affair with Manox, it seems likely that Catherine saw her action as harmless fun with a man who was her social inferior. Dereham probably hoped to marry Catherine and so ally himself with her powerful family and the couple addressed each other as husband and wife and talked of a marriage.[14] They also exchanged love tokens, Dereham giving Catherine velvet and satin for a gown and also lending her £100 when he left for Ireland. Catherine, who would not have had money for these luxuries herself, was probably pleased to play the role of Dereham's wife whilst they were in Lambeth together.

Catherine and Dereham's relationship was soon common knowledge around the duchess's household. Henry Manox had followed the household to Lambeth and quickly became jealous of Catherine's new relationship. Hoping to have Dereham sent away, Manox wrote an anonymous letter to the duchess, informing her of the midnight picnics in the dormitory and of Catherine and Dereham's affair.[15] He then left the letter on her pew in the chapel. According to Manox, Catherine found the letter and showed it to Dereham. Catherine was probably furious with Manox, believing her connection with him to be historic and she instructed her new lover to warn Manox off. Armed with the letter, Dereham turned on Manox, abusing him for attempting to betray Catherine. It seems likely that the duchess already knew about her granddaughter's love affair. The duchess appears to have been happy to ignore the evidence of love affairs in her household, providing that they were carried out discretely. According to the account of Katherine Tylney, one of the girls in the household, once the duchess:

found Dereham embracing Mrs Katherine Howard in his arms and kiss-
ing her, and thereat was much offended and gave Dereham a blow, and
also beat the Queen [Catherine Howard] and gave Joan Bowmar a blow
because she was present. When Dereham was wanted the duchess would
say, 'I warrant you if you seek him in Katherine Howard's chamber you
shall find him there'.[16]

The duchess probably reasoned that as long as the affair did not disturb
her peace, it was harmless. She did however ask her son, Catherine's
uncle, to speak to Catherine about what was expected of her as a
Howard.

Catherine probably never seriously considered the prospect of marrying Dereham, expecting the affair to simply dwindle out when they
parted in the autumn of 1539.[17] In late 1539, Henry VIII's marriage to
his fourth wife, Anne of Cleves, was announced and over sixty ladies
were appointed to serve the new queen, one of whom was Catherine
Howard. Catherine must have been thrilled to hear that she was to visit
court for the first time. It seems likely that this appointment marked the
end of her affair with Dereham in her eyes and she probably expected
to find a high-status husband at court. This is certainly what her uncle,
the Duke of Norfolk, and grandmother would have had in mind when
putting Catherine forward for the appointment. Catherine would have
been provided with fine new clothes for her position at court and probably felt proud of her new situation.

Catherine Howard has been called the most beautiful of all Henry
VIII's wives and it is possible that this was why she was selected above
her cousins and sisters to represent the Howard family at court. She
was described by the French ambassador as 'a lady of great beauty'[18],
although he later qualified this by saying she was more graceful than
beautiful and very short.[19] Even if Catherine Howard was not a beauty,
she certainly stood out at court, probably due to her liveliness and her
youth. It is likely that she gained many admirers and it quickly became
apparent that one of these admirers was the king. Catherine was a first
cousin of Anne Boleyn and her relatives had first-hand experience of
how to attract and keep Henry's interest. Catherine was tutored by her
family on how to behave and she presented an air of youthful purity.[20]
For Henry, Catherine appeared the exact opposite of his hated wife,

Anne of Cleves and, by mid-1540, it was clear to the court that he wished to free himself of his current wife so that he could marry Catherine. Catherine cannot have found the aged and bloated king attractive, but she probably revelled in the presents and status that his affection gave her. According to the French ambassador, 'the king is so amorous of her that he cannot treat her well enough and caresses her more than he did the others'.[21] Catherine's youth made Henry feel youthful again and the couple were married quietly on 28 July 1540.

Catherine was probably aged only around fifteen or sixteen at the time of her marriage and appears to have been determined to enjoy herself. Henry adored her and caressed her publicly, pandering to her every desire. Catherine loved dancing and spent much of her time as queen enjoying the pursuit, even dancing with her husband's ex-wife, Anne of Cleves. Catherine also loved presents and Henry showered her with gifts. Over Christmas and New Year 1540–1541, Catherine received a number of rich presents from Henry, including a square containing twenty-seven table diamonds and twenty-six clusters of pearls.[22] Catherine probably also loved the ceremony that went with being a queen. She had her own private barge, a huge household and probably enjoyed the status that her role as queen conferred on her. Catherine was probably thrilled when on her first ceremonial entry to London she was saluted by the guns from the Tower as she passed by barge down the river.[23] For Catherine, being queen must have seemed beyond her wildest dreams and she was determined to make the most of the opportunities that her role opened up for her.

Henry's marriage to Catherine rejuvenated him and he appeared almost young throughout the second half of 1540.[24] Henry was nearly fifty, however, and this transformation could not last forever. In March 1541, Henry's leg ulcer, which had given him trouble for several years, dramatically closed causing his life to be in danger. Probably not wishing his pretty young wife to see him in such a way, Henry barred Catherine from his presence. After his recovery, Henry remained depressed and this was the first sign of trouble in their marriage. Catherine must have been alarmed at Henry's moods and may have sought consolation elsewhere. In May 1541 Catherine also seems to have become somewhat depressed.[25] When Henry anxiously asked her why, she said that she had heard a rumour that he intended to take Anne of Cleves back. Henry immediately sought to console her, saying that he would never take Anne back, even if he were free. Catherine may not have been entirely reassured, however, as Henry does not seem to have ruled out the possibility of exchanging her for someone else. Despite these troubles, Catherine was still in high favour when she and Henry set out on a northern progress in the summer of 1541.

Henry had reigned for over thirty years in 1541 but had never visited the northern part of his kingdom. He had long planned, and put off, a progress to the north but finally, in the summer of 1541 was ready to set out. Henry and Catherine left London on 30 June with a great company of people and provisions.[26] Henry had designed his progress to be a show of strength to the rebellious north. Catherine must have been excited at the prospect of travelling as queen although they were hampered from the start by bad weather and she may have rapidly begun to lose patience with the muddy, dilapidated roads. Nonetheless Catherine appears to have performed the public role of queen to perfection on the progress. She wore crimson velvet when she and Henry rode into Lincoln where they retired to their tent outside the city to change their clothes.[27] The royal couple then emerged, Henry dressed in cloth of gold and Catherine in cloth of silver, and were ceremonially welcomed to Lincoln. Catherine must have been bored by the speeches and pageants that accompanied these visits, but there were no complaints made about her conduct. After Lincoln, the progress moved on, reaching Pontefract on 23 August and York on 16 September.[28]

Catherine's public conduct as queen was immaculate but her private conduct left a great deal to be desired. She probably became acquainted with Thomas Culpeper soon after arriving at court to wait on Anne of Cleves. Culpeper was a distant cousin of Catherine's mother and presented a very different proposition to either Henry Manox or Francis Dereham. When he and Catherine met he was already a member of Henry's privy chamber, in high favour with the king. He was also young and handsome, no doubt attracting Catherine's attention early on. He must have been an enormous contrast to Catherine's sickly and elderly husband. Catherine and Culpeper probably became lovers early in her marriage and Catherine's maids certainly noticed the queen's suspicious conduct, giving Culpeper loving glances from the window and barring her maids from entry to her bedchamber unless they were summoned.[29] Catherine was so much in Henry's favour, however, that no one dared to go to the king with their suspicions. Catherine was infatuated with Culpeper and gave him a velvet cap decorated with a jewelled brooch, warning him to hide it so no one would guess where he had got such a rich item.[30]

Catherine knew that her affair with Culpeper was wrong but showed an almost childlike naivety in her conduct. She appears to have considered her husband to be an almost God-like figure and warned Culpeper not to mention their relationship in the confessional as Henry, as Head of the Church, would surely hear what he said.[31] Catherine also committed details of her affair to writing, a dangerous practice in Henry's suspicious court, and her only surviving letter is a love letter to Culpeper. Catherine wrote this letter around April 1541, before the progress:

> Master Culpeper, I heartily recommend me unto you, praying you to send me word how that you do. It was showed me that you was sick, the which thing troubled me very much till such time that I hear from you praying you to send me word how that you do, for I never longed so much for [a] thing as I do to see you and to speak with you, the which I trust shall be shortly now. The which doth comfortly me very much when I think of it, and when I think again that you shall depart from me again it makes my heart to die to think what fortune I have that I cannot be always in your company. It my trust is always in you that you will be as you have promised me, and in that hope I trust upon still, praying that you will come when my Lady Rochford is here for then I shall be best at leisure to be at your commandment, thanking you for that you have promised me to be so good unto that poor fellow my man which is one of the griefs that I do feel to depart from him for then I do know no one that I dare trust to send to you, and therefore I pray you take him to be with you that I may sometime hear from you one thing. I pray you to give me a horse for my man for I had much ado to get one and therefore I pray send me one by him and in so doing I am as I said afor, and thus I take my leave of you, trusting to see you shortly again and I would you was with me now that you might see what pain I take in writing to you. Yours as long as life endures, Katheryn.[32]

Catherine's letter demonstrates the love she felt for Culpeper and the pains she took in writing to him. She was unwise to record her feelings and it is possible that Culpeper kept this letter as evidence against her should her ever need it. Throughout her brief time as queen, Catherine showed a disregard for personal safety. She underestimated the potential dangers incurred by her actions. She also showed naivety in August 1541 by appointing Francis Dereham as her private secretary.[33] Catherine simply does not seem to have realised that as queen she was constantly watched, her activities scrutinised. She continued her affair with Culpeper during the northern progress.

Catherine confided her affair to her kinswoman, Lady Rochford, who was also one of her ladies. Lady Rochford was the widow of George Boleyn, Viscount Rochford, and had given evidence against her husband in the allegations of incest against him and his sister, Anne Boleyn. She was therefore well used to court intrigues and perfectly suited to organising meetings between Catherine and Culpeper. Catherine kept her other ladies barred from her bedchamber and, according to *Hall's Chronicle* she had Culpeper:

> brought to her chamber at Lyncolne, in August laste, in the Progresse tyme, by the lady of Rocheforde, and were there together alone, from a leven of the clocke at nighte, till foure of the clocke in the morning, and to hym she gave a chayne, and a riche cap.[34]

Throughout the progress, Catherine would wait until her household were in bed and then send Lady Rochford to let Culpeper into her chamber by the most private entrances. They would then spend part of the night together with only Lady Rochford there as any type of chaperone. Catherine met Culpeper like this throughout the journey and her servants came to suspect that something was amiss. A medieval queen had to be above suspicion of sexual impropriety to ensure the legitimacy of her children, and Catherine was playing a dangerous game. She had not become pregnant in over a year of marriage and it is possible that she reasoned that Henry could not give her a child. It is certainly possible that Catherine and Culpeper wished to conceive a royal heir themselves and so secure both of their positions at court.[35]

Catherine remained oblivious to any danger when the progress returned to Windsor on 26 October 1541.[36] She was probably looking forward to returning to her life of pleasure in London and it is likely that she intended her affair with Culpeper to continue. As a Catholic queen, however, Catherine had many enemies. Soon after Henry and Catherine's return from their progress, Archbishop Cranmer was approached by John Lassells, a religious reformer. Lassells' sister, Mary Hall, had been raised with Catherine in the duchess's household and reported to her brother that the queen had been 'light of living' and had had sexual relationships with both Francis Dereham and Henry Manox.[37] Cranmer was shocked at what he heard and, on 2 November, handed a letter containing Lassells's revelations to Henry. Henry reacted with disbelief as he had no reason to doubt Catherine's honesty and ordered an investigation to protect her reputation. He said nothing of the matter to Catherine, believing it to be entirely false, and he and Catherine continued for a week in the high spirits with which they had returned from their progress. Henry's peace of mind was shattered, however, when both John Lassells and Mary Hall stood by their stories. Under pressure, Henry Manox also confessed to having caressed Catherine and Dereham to having known her carnally. Faced with this evidence, Henry was devastated, and burst into a fit of weeping, demanding a sword to slay her himself.[38] He was completely disillusioned with his seemingly pure young wife.

On 4 November 1541, guards burst into Catherine's room at Hampton Court when she was practising her dance steps. Catherine would have been shocked and confused by this unexpected occurrence and her first though must have been that Henry had discovered about Culpeper. According to the French ambassador, 'she was taken no kind of pastime but kept in her chamber, whereas, before, she did nothing but dance and rejoice, and now when the musicians come they are told that it is no more time to dance'.[39] For a girl as joyous and active as Catherine, the change from queen to prisoner must have been hard to bear and her thoughts probably turned quickly to her cousin, Anne Boleyn. There is a legend at Hampton Court that Catherine slipped her guard and ran down the corridor from her rooms to the palace chapel where Henry was hearing mass.[40] As she reached the door, she was grabbed by her guards and dragged screaming back to her rooms, ignored by her husband. If this ever occurred, it must have been on 6 November as Henry left the palace quietly that evening, never to be near her again. Catherine's escape is part of the tragic legend that surrounds Catherine Howard and her ghost reputedly re-enacts her escape in the haunted gallery.

On 7 November Cranmer and Norfolk, Catherine's uncle, came to interrogate her in her rooms.[41] They found her hysterical and were unable to make any progress with her. The next day, Cranmer returned to her alone, later describing her state as pitiable.[42] Cranmer explained to her that Henry knew of her relationships with Manox and Dereham and Catherine must have been greatly relieved that Culpeper's name was not mentioned. In tears, she confessed to Cranmer of her relationships with Dereham and Manox although she denied any marriage contract with Dereham. Henry appears to have been planning nothing worse than divorce for Catherine at this time and Catherine's grandmother, the duchess, also stated that she was not worried about her, pointing out that she could not be executed for her conduct before her marriage.[43] The duchess predicted that Catherine's marriage would be annulled and her granddaughter sent back to her in disgrace. At that time the worst that could be proved against Catherine was that she had not been a virgin at the time of her wedding. Only Catherine, Culpepper and Lady Rochford knew that Catherine had committed a far worse crime against the king.

On 11 November, it was decided that Catherine would be taken to Syon House where she would be lodged modestly without any of the state of a queen.[44] On 13 November, Catherine's household was officially discharged and the next day Catherine was taken to Syon with only four gentlewomen and two chamberers to serve her and keep her company.[45] The change in status must have been dramatic for Catherine and she always refused to admit that she was no longer queen. Her jewels were also confiscated and she was allowed only a modest wardrobe, including six French hoods with gold trim, but no jewels.[46] She probably thought that this would be the worst that would happen to her and envisaged her future as one of long and dull retirement.

However by 11 November, Thomas Culpeper's name had begun to be mentioned in the investigations surrounding Catherine. A charge of adultery was a much more serious offence than that of pre-marital unchastity and Catherine must have been concerned that the king would find out about Culpeper in his investigations. Catherine was questioned regarding Culpeper and under pressure admitted that they had met and that she had given him presents but denied that they had consummated their relationship.[47] She placed the blame on Lady Rochford for encouraging her to meet with Culpeper. Lady Rochford, however, claimed that Catherine and Culpeper had committed adultery and blamed Catherine for forcing her to become involved. Culpeper also denied his guilt, claiming that 'it was the queen who, through Lady Rochford, solicited him to meet her in private in Lincolnshire, when she herself told him that she was dying for his love'.[48] Catherine, Lady Rochford and Culpeper each blamed the others, hoping to save themselves and this suggests that Catherine and Culpeper's relationship was not genuinely romantic.

Culpeper and Lady Rochford were quickly arrested and Lady Rochford reputedly went mad in prison.[49] Dereham and Culpeper were tried together in early December and, despite both denying their guilt, were condemned to death. The two men were executed at Tyburn on 10 December 1541. Culpeper's sentence was commuted to beheading by a king who probably retained some vestige of affection for him. Dereham, however, suffered the full traitor's death of being hanged drawn and quartered.[50] It seems likely that Henry retained an especial hatred for Dereham, seeing him as the corrupter of his pretty young bride.[51] Catherine's feelings at these executions are not recorded. She may have been horrified at the deaths of these two men that she had loved. Equally, however, she may have blamed them as the cause of her own misfortunes. Soon after the executions, Catherine's grandmother and uncle, Lord William Howard, were taken to the Tower for their complicity in Catherine's youthful conduct.[52] Despite the deaths of Dereham and Culpeper, Catherine probably still hoped that she would escape with her life. By early 1542, it was rumoured that Henry intended to divorce Catherine and condemn her to life imprisonment.[53]

Catherine's hope was misplaced, however. On 16 January 1542, parliament opened in London and they condemned Catherine and Lady Rochford to death without trial.[54] On 10 February 1542, Catherine was taken from Syon by water to the Tower.[55] Catherine's barge would have passed under the heads of Dereham and Culpeper on London Bridge and she must have shuddered at this sight of her lovers.[56] Catherine was terrified. Once inside the Tower, she gave herself up to weeping and tormenting herself.[57] On the evening of 12 February, she was told that she would die the next day.[58] Catherine calmed herself somewhat when she heard this news and asked for the block to be brought to her so that she could practice for the next morning.[59] Early on 13 February, Catherine and Lady Rochford were led out of the Tower together. Catherine was to be executed first. She was so weak that she could hardly speak and had to be helped up to the scaffold.[60] She does not appear to have made a long speech due to her extreme terror but confessed that she deserved to die before kneeling and placing her head on the block. Catherine was then beheaded with an axe, being followed by her accomplice, Lady Rochford, a few minutes later.

Catherine Howard was almost certainly under twenty when she died and may have been as young as sixteen or seventeen. Her life was short and extreme, just like that of her cousin and predecessor, Anne Boleyn. Catherine Howard was plucked out of obscurity by her marriage to the king and was completely unsuitable for her role as queen. Although she was certainly guilty of adultery and pre-marital misconduct, blame for her conduct lay at least in part with her family and the king for placing her in a situation for which she was quite unsuitable. Catherine Howard lived only a short life and left little legacy, her only lasting contribution being a law that made it illegal for a non-virgin to marry the king. However she was not the only Tudor queen to die as a teenager on the executioner's block and her husband's great-niece, Lady Jane Grey, also suffered the same fate primarily due to the ambitions of her family.

Aspiring to the Crown

Lady Jane Grey

Lady Jane Grey is often portrayed as an innocent victim and martyr to her family's ambition. To a large extent this is true and Jane failed to fully assert her independence during her short reign of nine days. However, there was more to Lady Jane Grey than passive acceptance. Jane certainly did not see herself as a mere passive figure in the events surrounding her usurpation of the throne. When faced with the temptation of the crown, Jane was unable to stop herself from accepting it and quickly became accustomed to ruling, even sending out troops against the rightful heir, Mary Tudor. Lady Jane Grey certainly recognised that she was guilty of treason and this was also the viewpoint taken by her contemporaries. Jane was very young and placed in a difficult, if not impossible situation. However, she was not without free will and the way in which she exercised this led her down a treasonous and ultimately fatal path. Nevertheless she should be considered more tragic than evil – it was her royal blood together with the actions of others that led to her downfall at the executioner's block.

In October 1537, the only remaining male descendants of Henry VII were Henry VIII and his nephew, James V of Scotland. This was significant for Frances Brandon and her husband, Henry Grey, Marquis of Dorset. That month they were preparing for the birth of their eldest child and would have been aware that should the child prove to be a boy, he would have high hopes of inheriting the crown of England. Frances Brandon was the eldest daughter of Mary Tudor, Queen of France and thus the niece of Henry VIII and she was already high in the line of succession. It must have been a disappointment, therefore, when, early in the month, the Marchioness gave birth to a girl at her estate at Bradgate.[1] The baby's birth would have been further overshadowed when in that same month the queen, Jane Seymour, finally provided Henry VIII with his longed for son, Edward. The Dorsets' daughter was quickly baptised Jane, after the queen, before her father hurried to London to attend the prince's more significant christening. Left with her daughter at Bradgate, Frances Brandon must have been disappointed and this feeling would have increased with the births of two further daughters.

Lady Jane Grey spent her earliest years with her parents at Bradgate. As the niece of the king, Frances Brandon expected to live in some style and she raised her daughters like princesses.[2] To satisfy her mother's ambitions, Jane was subjected to a rigorous formal education from the age of three or four with tutors engaged to teach her Greek, Latin, modern languages, music and Bible studies, as well as the more traditional female pursuit of needlework.[3] By the mid-sixteenth century the education of women had become fashionable and Jane thrived on her studies. She appears to have been something of a child prodigy, as the scholar, Roger Ascham found when he visited her in 1551. Ascham found Jane reading Plato in Greek and, when he questioned her as to why she was not out hunting with the rest of the household, she informed him that:

One of the greatest benefits that ever God gave me, is that he sent me so sharp and severe parents, and so gentle a schoolmaster, for when I am in the presence either of father and mother, whether I speak, keep silence, sit, stand, or go, eat, drink, be merry, or sad, be sewing, playing, dancing, or doing anything else, I must do it as it were in such weight, measure, or number, even so perfectly as God made the world; or else I am so sharply taunted, yea, presently sometimes with pinches, nips, bobs, and other ways which I will not name for the honour I bear them; so without measure disordered, that I think myself in hell till the time come that I must go to Mr Elmer, who teacheth me so gently, so pleasantly, with such fair allurements to learning, that I think all the time nothing, whilst I am with him; and when I am called from him I fall on weeping because whatsoever I do else but learning in full of great trouble, fear, and whole misliking unto me.[4]

Jane Grey had an unhappy childhood with her parents and used learning as a refuge. Jane's conversation with Ascham, who was a near-stranger to her, also shows that she had no time for the faults that she perceived in her parents and in others.

Jane did not have an easy relationship with her parents and she may have been glad of any excuse to leave their household. It was common for young girls to be boarded out in the households of ladies of higher status and since Jane was the great-niece of the king, the only suitable household was that of the queen. By late March 1547, Jane is recorded as a member of the Queen Dowager, Catherine Parr's household at Chelsea.[5] She was probably sent there soon after Henry VIII's death and must have welcomed the chance to be away from her bullying parents for the first time. Catherine Parr was fond of Jane and she flourished in the queen's household. It was probably in Catherine Parr's household that Jane became exposed to the radical Protestantism that would shape her later life and lead eventually her to her death.

Soon after Jane joined Catherine Parr's household, the queen married Thomas Seymour, the uncle of the new king, Edward VI. Seymour was an unscrupulous figure and quickly saw the advantage to his wife's possession of Jane, approaching the Dorsets and offering to arrange a marriage for Jane to the king.[6] In reality, Edward's marriage was never in Seymour's hands and the king himself had already made it clear that he wished to marry a foreign princess. However, the Dorsets, unaware of the emptiness of Seymour's words and excited at the prospect of their daughter marrying the king, agreed to sell Jane's wardship and marriage to Thomas Seymour for money. Jane was probably also interested in the possibility of becoming a queen and certainly relished in the flattery that rumours of her engagement to the king brought. She engaged in a correspondence with the European religious reformer Henry Bullinger, who wrote to her as though she were a future queen.[7] Jane was probably flattered by the sudden interest in her and it must have been a disappointment to her when these schemes came to nothing. Jane remained in Seymour's household following the death of the queen in September 1548 and was still there when, on 17 January 1549, Seymour was arrested for treason.[8] When the Dorsets heard of this they whisked Jane back to Bradgate away from the scandal. It is unlikely that Jane was glad to be back with her parents.

As she grew older, Jane was expected to play more of a public role. By the terms of Henry VIII's will, Jane was fourth in line to the throne, after Edward VI's two sisters and her own mother, and her family was in high favour at court.[9] On 4 October 1551 Jane's father was created Duke of Suffolk and she accompanied her parents to court later that month for a visit from the Scottish queen, Mary of Guise.[10] Frances Brandon was also very friendly with her cousin, Mary Tudor, and Jane is known to have gone with her mother to visit the heir to the throne on at least two occasions.

By the early 1550s, Jane had become a radical Protestant and was extremely critical of Catholic Mary's way of life. On a visit to Mary's house at Newhall in summer 1552, Jane offended Mary by openly criticising one of Mary's ladies for following the Catholic habit of curt-seying to the altar in church.[11] On another occasion, Mary who was fond of children gave Jane some tinsel cloth of gold and Jane refused to wear it, saying she preferred the sombre black of Protestantism.[12] These incidents show Jane's precocity and intelligence but they also highlight a less congenial side to her character, showing religious bigotry and a complete disregard for the feelings of a woman who had been kind to her. Lady Jane Grey seems to have become a religious fanatic incapable of seeing such matters from alternative points of view.

However Mary's Catholicism was not only a cause of concern to Lady Jane Grey and by 1552 it had become an important matter of state. In March 1552, Edward VI fell ill and although he seemed to make a good recovery, he fell ill again that summer. Like Jane, Edward had been raised to be a radical Protestant and was deeply troubled by the thought that his Catholic half-sister would succeed him. Early in 1553 he wrote, apparently of his own initiative and in his own hand, his device for the succession, disinheriting both his half-sisters due to their supposed ille-gitimacy.[13] Edward's will for the succession left the throne to any sons of Frances Brandon and failing that, the sons first of Lady Jane Grey and then the sons of her younger sisters. It is probable that, in early 1553, Jane was completely unaware of her increasing political importance.

Edward's protector, the Duke of Northumberland was also concerned about the prospect of Mary succeeding. He had publicly attacked her religion and knew that she would not look kindly on him after her accession. Northumberland, therefore, also cast around looking for a way to debar her from the throne. In late April or early May he wrote to Suffolk asking that he persuade either his wife, Frances Brandon, or his daughter, Jane, to accept the crown.[14] It is unlikely that Northumberland ever contemplated making Frances Brandon queen. According to the *Vita Mariae Angliae Reginae*, Northumberland secretly manipulated Edward VI so that he left the crown to Lady Jane Grey.[15] Edward VI was probably easy to persuade and he altered his will with his own hand, leaving the crown to Jane and her heirs male.

Northumberland's price for supporting Jane was that she marry his youngest and only unmarried son Guildford Dudley. The Suffolks willingly accepted this match, seeing it as Jane's best chance of a crown and her betrothal was announced in late April or early May.[16] Jane tried to reject Guildford, showing that same independence of spirit which she showed throughout her life. Nonetheless, she was forced to comply with both physical and verbal abuse from her parents.[17] It is possible that Jane had a personal dislike for the spoilt Guildford Dudley and she never seems to have been very well disposed towards him. Jane's feelings were of no consequence, however, and they were married in a magnificent ceremony at Northumberland's London residence on 25 May 1553.[18] The French ambassador and most of the English nobility were present, although the king was too ill to attend. Jane's hair was decorated with pearls and she wore finery borrowed from the royal stores. Despite the glamour of the ceremony, Jane must have been thoroughly miserable at having to marry a man she detested.

Jane disliked Guildford and appears to have been frightened of his family. Despite her obvious dislike of her own parents, Jane begged to be allowed to remain with them after the wedding but was forced to stay with her husband's family. She stayed only a few days in Northumberland's house, however, before falling ill and was sent to Chelsea to rest.[19] Jane apparently believed that Northumberland was trying to poison her, a surprising belief given how important she was to him. Jane probably enjoyed the quiet of Chelsea and the chance to be alone with her books. She was there on 9 July when Guildford's sister, Mary Sidney came to take her to Syon House in London.[20]

Edward VI died on the evening of 6 July.[21] The next day, Northumberland kept his death secret but began secretly to fortify the Tower. On 8 July, he summoned the Lord Mayor of London and six aldermen and informed them that Edward VI had died and had named Jane as his successor. On 9 July, the Council joined Northumberland and the Suffolks at Syon House and bowed low before Jane when she was brought into the room. Jane must have been terrified when she entered the room to find the royal council together with her parents, husband and parents-in-law bowing to her and she fell to the ground weeping.[22] According to one report, Jane then tried to refuse the crown:

> That the laws of the kingdom, and natural right, standing for the king's sister, she would beware of burdening her weak conscience with a yoke, which did belong to them; that she understood the infamy of those, who had permitted the violation of right to gain a sceptre, that it were to mock God, and deride justice, to scruple at the stealing of a shilling, and not at the usurpation of a crown.[23]

Lady Jane Grey clearly knew that to accept the crown was to do wrong. However, from where she lay, weeping on the floor, she was also tempted. According to her own account, Jane 'humbly prayed and besought Him that he would make it so that what had just been given to me was rightfully and legitimately mine'.[24] Jane apparently expected a sign from God if he was displeased by her and receiving none took it as a sign of God's wish that she should accept the crown. From that moment, Lady Jane Grey agreed willingly to usurp the crown of England.

In the afternoon of 10 July, Jane was conveyed by water to the Tower, where she was received as Queen.[25] Jane may have felt a certain satisfaction that it was her mother who had to hold her train in the procession to the Tower and she wore platform shoes in order to appear taller to the watching crowd.[26] According to Jane herself in a letter to Mary she:

> was brought to the Tower and the Marquis of Winchester, the great treasurer, gave me the jewels and together with them, he also brought the crown. It so happened that, without my asking him or others asking him

in my name, he wanted me to put the crown on my head, to see if it fitted or not. I refused to do it, resorting to a number of excuses, but he added that I should be brave and take it, and also that he would make another to crown my husband. I listened to these words with a discomforted and reluctant spirit; and an infinitely displeased heart.[27]

Jane was overwhelmed and frightened by her sudden elevation but even then showed an independent spirit that suggests she was no passive victim. On hearing that another crown would be prepared for Guildford, Jane refused point blank to crown him, saying that she would make him a duke and nothing more.[28] Guildford, who was present, rushed to complain to his mother. The Duchess of Northumberland came storming into Jane's presence shouting that her son would not stay another night with such an ungrateful wife. She and Guildford then tried to leave the Tower but Jane sent the Earls of Arundel and Pembroke to stop them from leaving, anxious to prevent the public slight that Guildford's leaving would be to her. This incident, although almost farcical, indicates that Jane might not have proved to be quite the compliant puppet queen that Northumberland had hoped. She was certainly prepared to stand up to the bullying of her husband and his mother once she was queen.

Jane must have felt in a more stable position once she was established in the Tower and it is likely that she believed the council when they said her accession was secure. It was therefore a blow to everyone in the Tower when, on 12 July, a letter was delivered from Mary, in which she claimed the crown. Northumberland had attempted to capture Mary before Edward VI's death but she had escaped him, travelling to her manor at Kenninghall where she quickly began to attract supporters. Mary's letter caused consternation in the Tower and Jane must also have been concerned for her position. When it was suggested that Suffolk should lead a force against Mary, he was 'cleane dissolved by the speciall meanes of the lady Jane his daughter, who, taking the matter heavily, with weeping teares made request to the whole councell that her father might tarry at home in her company'.[29] Jane must have been gratified to see that, once again, the assembled lords were forced to obey her and it was decided that Northumberland would be sent instead.

The next morning, Northumberland began to recruit an army. After dinner, he went to Jane and she gave him his commission to lead her army and leave to depart. He set out the next morning with 600 men but was clearly uncomfortable with the reception he received from the hostile populace, pointing out to one of his men that, 'the people prece to se us, but not one sayeth God spede us'.[30] Mary had always been popular with the people in England whereas Jane was unfamiliar and simply could not command public support. By the time Northumberland left, word had already been brought to Jane that Mary had been proclaimed in Buckinghamshire and Norwich. A further blow came when word reached the Tower that six royal ships that had been sent to Yarmouth to capture Mary had deserted Jane for Mary, the crews mutinying and threatening to throw their captains in the sea if they would not agree.[31]

Jane must have been glad to see Northumberland leave the Tower, as it is clear that she hated him. She must have been worried by the threat of Mary, however, especially when it was realised that with Northumberland gone, many of the council were actively trying to leave the Tower. On 16 July, the treasurer, the Marquis of Winchester, was found to have left the Tower secretly.[32] Jane acted decisively when she heard this and, at 7pm, ordered that the gates of the Tower be locked and the keys brought up to her. It was officially announced that a seal had been stolen but everyone in the Tower knew the truth. At midnight that same night, the Treasurer was found in his London house and taken back to the Tower by Jane's guards.

By 18 July, however, most of the council had managed to escape and on the evening of 19 July, they proclaimed Mary at Cheapside.[33] By 18 July Northumberland had also come to realise that his cause was lost. Knowing that reinforcements would never come, he left Bury St Edmunds to return to Cambridge.[34] During the night of 19 July he heard that Mary had been proclaimed in London. The next morning he proclaimed her himself at Cambridge before being arrested. Jane probably first realised that her cause was lost when her father came to her on the 19th as she was eating dinner and tore down the cloth of estate above her head with his own hands. He then went out onto Tower Hill and proclaimed Mary himself before fleeing to his London house.[35] The loss of her crown cannot have been entirely unexpected for Jane and the sound of rejoicing at Mary's accession could be heard from the Tower.[36] When Lady Throckmorton returned to the royal apartments that evening from standing proxy for Jane at a christening, she found them deserted and was told that Jane was now a prisoner in the Deputy Lieutenant's house in the Tower.[37]

Jane must have been frightened to find herself deserted by everyone and a prisoner in the Tower. Her father had been arrested soon after Mary's accession but was quickly released after Frances Brandon interceded for him with Mary.[38] She does not seem to have interceded for her daughter, however. Mary had always been fond of Jane and did not believe that she was responsible for her actions. It appears that she privately told Jane she would be released once events surrounding her attempted coup had calmed down. Jane must have been relieved to hear this and quickly settled into life at the Tower. She may have gained some satisfaction when Northumberland was also brought to the Tower as a prisoner and was disgusted when he converted to Catholicism in an attempt to save himself from execution. Jane is reported to have watched Northumberland going to church before his execution from her window and it is likely that she felt a certain satisfaction that the man who brought her so low was going to die. His conversion did not save him and he was beheaded at the Tower on 21 August 1553.[39]

Jane kept in good spirits during her imprisonment and the author of the *Chronicle of Queen Jane* dined with her on 29 August 1553 at the house of Partrige, the Lieutenant of the Tower. According to his account, she was anxious for news of London:

'The Quenes majesty is a mercyfull princes; I beseech God she may long contynue, and sende his bonntefull grace upon her'. After that, we fell in matters of religion, and she axed what he was that preached at Polles on Sonday before; and so it was tolde hir to be one [blank in original]. 'I praie you,' quod she, 'have they masse in London?' 'Yay for suthe', quod I, 'in some places'. 'Yt may so be,' quod she, 'yt is not so strange as the sodden convertyon of the late duke [Northumberland]; for who wolde have thought' saide she, 'he would have so don?' Yt was answered her, 'Perchance he thereby hoped to have had his pardon'. 'Pardon?' quod she, 'we worthe him! He hath brought me and our stocke in most miserable callamyty and mysery by his exceeding ambicion.'[40]

Jane had not forgiven Northumberland and ranted for some time over the meal about his wickedness.

Despite her anger at Northumberland, Jane was probably comfortably housed in the Tower and may even have been relieved to be spared her parents' company. Although she had an assurance from Mary that she would be spared, it was necessary that she and the other conspirators be put to trial and on 13 November 1553 Jane, Guildford, his brothers Henry and Ambrose, and Thomas Cranmer the Archbishop of Canterbury were led out of the Tower to the Guildhall for their trials.[41] They walked in procession behind a headsman carrying an axe turned away from them and Jane must have looked striking dressed in black with a black velvet book hanging from her dress and another in her hand. The verdict of the trial was predictable. All of the accused were sentenced to death, being returned to the Tower with the headsman's axe facing towards them. Despite the verdict, Jane must have felt certain that she would be released and on 28 December she was given the liberty of the Tower and the freedom to walk in its gardens.

No doubt Mary meant to release Jane once memory of the coup had faded. However, on 25 January, the council heard that a rebellion, led by Thomas Wyatt, had flared up in Kent.[42] That same day it was also discovered that the Duke of Suffolk had mysteriously vanished from his London residence. The rebellions were aimed at Mary's proposed marriage to Philip of Spain and quickly gained public support. By 30 January, Wyatt's army was camped at Blackheath and Greenwich.[43] Mary's own quick thinking saved the situation and she was able to rally the people of London to her cause, crushing the rebellion. With the defeat of Wyatt, attention then turned to Suffolk who had ridden north trying to stir up the people against the Spanish marriage.[44] He gained little support and eventually fled to his manor at Astley where he was found hiding in a hollow tree. Suffolk was quickly arrested and brought to the Tower. Although she played no part in these activities his actions signed Jane's death warrant. Jane understood this and wrote to him soon after his arrest, writing 'Father, although it hath pleased God to hasten my death by you, by whom my life should rather have been lengthened, yet I can so patiently take it, that I yield God more hearty thanks for shortening my woeful days.[45]

Suffolk's actions and Wyatt's rebellion illustrated to Mary and her council the danger of allowing Jane to live. On 12 February, Guildford

Dudley was led out to a scaffold on Tower Hill and beheaded.[46] Despite ordering her death, Mary still appears to have remembered Jane fondly and sent the Dean of St Paul's to her in an attempt to save her soul through conversion to Catholicism.[47] Jane received him politely and the pair debated for some time, probably keeping Jane's mind off her approaching death. Nevertheless she remained staunch in her evangelical Protestantism until the end.

On 12 February 1554, the sixteen-year-old Lady Jane Grey was led out to a scaffold on Tower Green.[48] She wore the same dress that she had worn to her trial and carried a book, praying all the way to the scaffold. Jane then mounted the scaffold and gave a dignified speech, admitting that she had acted unlawfully but denying that the guilt was hers. She then recited a psalm and it was only then that her nerves and her youth began to show:

> Forthwith she untied her gown. The hangman went to her to help her of therewith; then she desired him to let her alone, turning towards her two gentlewomen, who helped her off therwith, and also with her frose past and neckerchief, giving to her a fayre handkercher to knytte about her eyes.

> Then the hangman kneeled downe, and asked her forgeveness whome she forgave most willingly. Then he willed her to stand upon the strawe; which doing, she sawe the block. Then she sayd, 'I pray you dispatch me quickly'. Then she kneeled down, saying, 'Will you take it of before I lay me downe?' and the hangman answered her, 'No, madame'. She tyed the kercher about her eyes; then feeling for the blocke, saide, 'What shall I do? Where is it?' One of the standers-by guyding her thereunto, she layde her heade down upon the block, and stretched forth her body and said; 'Lorde, into thy hands I commende my spirite!' And so she ended.[49]

No one in England saw the execution of Lady Jane Grey as anything other than judicial murder and her death clouded Mary's reputation. However, in spite of the popular disapproval which Jane's execution generated, she was never popular in England and her death incurred no outpouring of public grief. Lady Jane Grey was used as a pawn by her relatives and even though she allowed herself to be used and appears to have relished the chance to wear the crown she was still an innocent victim of the actions of others. Lady Jane Grey was not born to be a queen but her royal blood placed her close enough to be in danger, a fact that was entirely out of her control. Opinionated and bigoted, Jane often appears in an unattractive light but it was she who won the posthumous popularity battle with Mary Tudor and she is remembered as a tragic victim of the Catholic queen. However, during their lifetimes when the two were pitted against each other, it was Mary who proved overwhelmingly the more loved. It was only later, during her own disastrous reign that Mary Tudor's own reputation became notorious.

Bloody Mary

Mary I

Mary I was the first effective queen regnant of England and she swept to power on a wave of popular support. She died just five years later universally hated, with bonfires lit in the street to celebrate her death. Today she is remembered as 'Bloody Mary', a bigoted Catholic so secure in her convictions that she burnt her own subjects in an attempt to purge England of Protestantism. Mary Tudor had a difficult life and although personally kind and likeable, she was used as a model of an evil queen by her half-sister, Elizabeth I. Mary's ideas were still essentially medieval and it is appropriate that her medieval attitude caused much of her unpopularity. Mary Tudor was never able to see that England had changed dramatically from the time of her childhood. In her essential attitude she was the last medieval Queen of England.

Mary Tudor was the only surviving child of Henry VIII and his first wife, Catherine of Aragon, being born on 18 February 1516.[1] As their only child, Mary was adored by both her parents during her childhood and her father loved to display her to visitors to his court.[2] Mary was a pretty child and grew up to resemble her father. According to a description of her given by the French ambassador in 1541, Mary was 'of middle stature, and is in face like her father, especially about the mouth, but has a voice more manlike, for a woman, than he has for a man'.[3] For Henry, Mary was a useful diplomatic tool and her earliest childhood was dominated by various betrothals to European royalty. Henry also saw Mary's birth as a promise that he and Catherine would soon have living sons. Although Mary's sex was, of course, a disappointment to her father, the fact that here at last was a healthy child, outweighed any other disadvantage.

Mary would have known from her earliest childhood that her destiny was to marry a foreign prince. However, as she grew older she must have become increasingly aware of her position as her father's heiress. Catherine of Aragon's last pregnancy occurred in 1518 and by the early 1520s it must have been clear to both Henry and Catherine that they would have no further children together. Catherine of Aragon, herself the daughter of a female monarch, accepted this early and arranged for Mary to have an education suitable for a future ruler. In her adulthood, Mary could read and write in English and Latin, speak French and understand Spanish.[4] She was also musical, being able to sing, dance and ride. Henry considered Mary his heir. In 1525 she was sent to Ludlow to govern as Princess of Wales, the only female ever to hold this title in her own right.[5] Mary stayed in Ludlow for eighteen months, returning to London in 1527.[6]

Mary returned to a court very different to the one she had left in 1525. By 1527, Henry had met Anne Boleyn and had instigated his divorce proceedings against Catherine of Aragon. Mary probably first heard of her parents' divorce from gossip in her household. She must have been shocked and probably did not believe it at first. Mary always supported Catherine and remained loyal to her mother until her own death. She was with her mother at Windsor when Henry rode away from Catherine for the final time, to never see her again.[7] The close relationship between Mary and Catherine frightened Henry. In May 1533 he forbade them to communicate with each other. Their correspondence continued secretly, but they were never to see each other again and Mary felt the separation from her mother keenly. In April 1533 Mary was informed of Henry's second marriage and her own illegitimacy. The loss of her status and title hit Mary hard and worse was to follow when she was sent to serve her infant half-sister, Elizabeth, in December 1533.

Mary had been stripped of her status as Henry's heiress when he divorced her mother. The birth of Elizabeth in September 1533 gave

Henry a new heiress. Elizabeth was given her own household at Hatfield House and Mary was forced to join her. Mary did not prove as malleable as Henry and Anne Boleyn hoped and she refused to cooperate once in Elizabeth's household. In March 1534 Mary had to be carried struggling into her litter when she refused to move with Elizabeth's household from Hatfield.[8] That proved to be a humiliating experience for Mary and the next time the household moved, she entered her litter without force. However once inside, Mary had her litter bearers run so that she arrived at her destination an hour before Elizabeth and therefore occupied the chief place on arrival. This must have given Mary a measure of personal satisfaction but in reality she was powerless to alter her situation. In spring 1534, Mary was locked in her room with a guard at the door when she refused to take the oath of succession that bastardised her and denied her parents' marriage.[9] Mary apparently felt desperate and secretly petitioned her cousin Emperor Charles V to smuggle her out of England.[10] Nonetheless she was closely guarded and any chance of escape was missed.

The death of her mother in January 1536 was a further blow for Mary and she must have felt totally isolated. She still held out against Anne Boleyn's efforts to befriend her and after Anne's death Mary wrote to her father's first minister, Thomas Cromwell, to ask for his help in reconciling her with her father.[11] Mary believed that Anne Boleyn was the sole cause of her mistreatment and she must have hoped that with Anne gone, Henry would welcome her again as his legitimate daughter. Mary's illusions about her father were shattered when, following her approach to Cromwell, a commission was sent to her at Hunsdon to extract the oath of succession from her. Mary once again stood out against Henry's agents but eventually without her mother's influence she gave in, signing a document that acknowledged that her parents had never been married and her own illegitimacy.[12] Mary never forgave herself for betraying her mother and this single act contributed to much of the unhappiness she experienced in her later life. Her father's harsh treatment of her in the summer of 1536 also shattered any illusions she had about him. In her later life, Mary spoke of Henry with respect, but never with any trace of admiration or affection.[13] Rumours later accredited Mary with having Henry's body exhumed and his heart burnt.[14] It is unlikely that this ever occurred but, certainly, Mary saw

Henry as the man who had destroyed both her happiness and that of her beloved mother.

Mary's capitulation pleased Henry and she was invited back to court and given her own household again. However she was not legitimised and lost any status she had as heir apparent with the birth of her half-brother Edward in October 1537. Mary remained in her father's favour for the rest of his life and acted as his court hostess from the death of Catherine Howard until his marriage to Catherine Parr in 1543.[15] In 1544, Mary was restored to the succession by an act of parliament but even this triumph must have rankled, as she remained illegitimate.[16] Despite her illegitimacy, Mary remained of interest to the European powers and received several offers of marriage. It is probable that she wished to marry and have children, but her father would never allow her to leave the country. The report of a French ambassador relates how Mary greatly desired to have children.[17] The death of Henry VIII in January 1547 left Mary as a wealthy independent landowner and heir presumptive to England but changed little in her personal situation.

Mary had always been a devout Catholic and this orthodoxy brought her into conflict with Edward VI's council. Edward VI's council was made up of religious reformers and England was quickly moved in a more Protestant direction. Mary always made it clear that she disapproved of this religious change and as the heir apparent, this was a major threat to the council. During 1549 Mary was visited by two members of Edward's council who came to examine her over her adherence to the new religious laws. Mary must have presented a formidable figure to the councillors and replied that 'she would have the old service until the king came of age, and would not obey the Protector's laws because he was no king'.[18] This attitude displeased Edward's protector, the Duke of Somerset, and pressure was put on Mary to conform. As the cousin of the emperor, however, Mary had a powerful supporter and she appealed to Charles V for help. Charles V immediately sent his ambassadors to the Duke of Somerset. He demanded that Mary be given an assurance that she could use her own services regardless of what the law said in England.[19] Faced with threats from the emperor, Somerset capitulated and gave Mary a verbal assurance that she could follow the Roman Catholic faith in her own household. Mary must have been glad of this victory and she made a point of allowing anyone who wished to hear her mass.

Whilst Mary had an assurance from Somerset, she soon found that this was worthless. In 1549, John Dudley, Earl of Warwick engineered a coup against Somerset, appointing himself Protector and creating himself Duke of Northumberland. Northumberland was not prepared to turn a blind eye to Mary's Catholicism and sent commissioners to Mary at Kenninghall.[20] Mary was no longer a girl of seventeen and she stood up to the commissioners imperiously answering them that she was not subject to the council and so did not have to follow their religion. The pressure on her was not relieved, however, and members of Mary's household were arrested for attending her church services. By May 1550 Mary had had enough of the council's harassment and asked the Spanish ambassador for the emperor's help in escaping to the continent.[21] Edward VI was twelve years old and in good health; Mary must have foreseen years of pressure from the king and his council. In June 1550 two imperial ships landed at Harwich. They then moved on to Woodham Water near one of Mary's manors, pretending to sell corn. When the captain of one of the ships landed and went to Mary, he found her still unpacked and refusing to leave. This was Mary's last chance of escape to her family in Spain and it marked a turning point for her, finally committing herself to life in England. Soon after the ships had left, the council heard of the escape plan and Mary was forced to move inland.

In spite of her decision to remain in England, Mary's troubles were not over. Late in 1550, Mary was summoned before the council to account for her religion.[22] Mary, perhaps with new resolution following her decision to remain in England, remained stubborn in her religion in spite of being berated by Northumberland. She must have been relieved during her stay at court when a message arrived from Charles V threatening war if Mary was not permitted to hear mass. The council were forced to relent in the face of threats of war and Mary was allowed to return to her house at Newhall. Northumberland and the council were still concerned with Mary's status as heir to the throne, however, and it is likely that, in spite of her victory, Mary knew that they were working against her. In late 1552 she must have heard reports that Edward VI was ill and probably followed them closely. On 4 July 1553, both Mary and Elizabeth received summonses to visit Edward at court at Greenwich. Mary was unsure of what action to take and began to move hesitantly towards London. She was at Hoddesdon on 6 July 1553 when she received word that Edward had already died and that her summons was a trap. Mary acted decisively and she and eight followers fled during the night to her house at Kenninghall.[23]

Mary had always been very popular in England and rumours of her rebellion against Northumberland spread through East Anglia.[24] In Mary's absence, Northumberland proclaimed Lady Jane Grey as queen and Mary immediately wrote to the council in London claiming the throne for herself. By taking this action, Mary realised that Northumberland would send an army against her. Recognising that Kenninghall could not withstand an attack, she moved her forces to her castle at Framlingham, the strongest fortification in Suffolk. Without even having to muster troops, people flocked to Mary to fight for her and she must have been glad of this show of loyalty towards her. It is likely that Mary gradually grew in confidence as she received reports that towns across England were declaring for her rather than Jane. On 20 July, Mary was finally ready to meet Northumberland and she mustered and inspected her army at Framlingham. Mary was completely unaccustomed to war and rode her usual horse to review her troops:

> While her majesty was approaching, the white horse which she was riding became rather more frisky at the unaccustomed sight of such an army drawn up in formation than her womanly hesitancy was prepared to risk, so she ordered her foot-soldiers, active and dutiful men, to lift up their hands and help their sovereign until she was ready to get down.[25]

Mary's review of the troops shows just how unusual a situation this unmarried woman of 37 found herself in. She acquitted herself well, however, surveying the troops on foot, speaking and approaching her men, gaining her soldiers' love. Mary must have been pleased at what she saw of her troops although she was probably apprehensive at her coming military campaign against Northumberland. When Mary returned to the castle later that day she was informed that Northumberland's army had deserted and that she had been proclaimed queen throughout England.[26] Mary was jubilant and always considered her victory over Northumberland to be a miracle from God.

Mary spent the next few days discharging her army before setting out in triumph to London where she was met by celebrations.[27] One of Mary's first acts as queen was to repeal her parent's divorce and to declare herself legitimate, something which probably gave her a great deal of personal satisfaction.[28] She then turned her attention towards religion. Mary, who was so staunch in her own beliefs, never realised the extent to which Protestantism had been adopted in England and she never understood that Protestants could be as convinced of their own justification as she was of hers. Before the end of July 1553, Mary had written to the Pope to request that England return to his authority.[29] Mary did not envisage too many problems with the implementation of this policy but as her reign progressed, she became increasingly vicious in her attempts to stamp out Protestantism in England.

Mary was the first queen regnant of England to be crowned and she arranged a magnificent ceremony. On 30 September 1553, Mary rode in an open carriage magnificently dressed.[30] Mary's headdress alone was so decked in precious stones that the weight required Mary to hold her head up with her hands.[31] Mary must have felt triumphant and probably still believed that her triumph was God's work and that he favoured her and her work. On 1 October, Mary, dressed in a long scarlet robe, was escorted by the same company to Westminster Abbey. In the Abbey she was crowned and anointed as England's first queen regnant to assert a lasting authority over England. At that moment, Mary must have felt that the unhappiness of her earlier life was washed away and she was even content to give a prominent position to her much younger sister, Elizabeth, the daughter of her greatest enemy, Anne Boleyn. Mary probably felt secure in her position and did not yet see Elizabeth as a rival. Mary also probably saw her coronation as a single female as an oddity and it was expected by all, including Mary, that she would quickly marry and provide England with a king.

Mary had always relied on her cousin Charles V for advice and, soon after her accession, she declared to Simon Renard, the Imperial ambassador that she would follow Charles's advice over her choice of a husband.[32] This was an opportunity Charles had been waiting for and he offered his son and heir, Philip of Spain. Philip was twenty-six and already a widower with a son.[33] He was also renowned across Europe for being sombre, dull and dedicated to his work. Mary first protested at this offer, arguing that, at thirty-seven, she was too old for Philip. There is no doubt, however, that Philip was the bridegroom that Mary wanted. Despite her protestations she quickly consented. Mary had always felt a closeness with her mother's Spanish family and it probably pleased her to strengthen her ties with Charles V. Despite Mary's happiness with her choice it was widely disapproved of in England. News of the proposed Spanish marriage spread fear amongst the xenophobic English and there was widespread opposition to Mary's choice.

Soon after Mary's marriage treaty was concluded in early 1554, she received word that a rebellion had broken out in Kent, led by Sir Thomas Wyatt.[34] Mary was in London when she heard the news and immediately showed the same spirit that had won her the throne of England. According to the *Vita Mariae Angliae Reginae*:

> The Queen left the palace and came to the City Guildhall, riding through the streets preceded by her council and followed by a company of ladies, addressing the people as she went with wonderful good nature and uncommon courtesy, and all the time exhibiting a cheerful countenance, worthy of such a princess. Dismounting, she entered the Guildhall and delivered a splendid speech to her citizens; the good princess, an incomparable oratrix, could command such eloquence that with her gentle and pleasant speech she completely calmed the Londoners, who were in such tumult over the Spanish marriage.[35]

Mary's speech saved the situation. The following day on 5 February, when Wyatt and his rebels arrived at Southwark, they found the Bridge closed and the Londoners refused to open it for them. On 6 February, Wyatt attempted to seize Kingston Bridge but again found it defended and was forced to camp at Brentford whilst he formulated a new plan. The next day he managed to cross the Thames into London but was quickly arrested whilst his men either fled or were killed. Mary must have been relieved that the rebellion was over, but she had been badly frightened and her reaction, which would have been considered normal in a king, was considered savage in a queen.

Wyatt was tried for treason on 15 March 1554 and implicated Mary's half-sister, Elizabeth, claiming that he wrote to her declaring his plans to rebel.[36] Mary had already begun to suspect that her sister was involved and on 18 March Elizabeth was taken as a prisoner to the Tower. Wyatt was executed on 11 April and died proclaiming that Elizabeth was innocent of complicity in his rebellion. Mary remained unconvinced. Although Elizabeth was released from the Tower, she was placed under house arrest at Woodstock where she remained for several months.[37] Mary was unable to prove that Elizabeth had been involved in the rebellion but she never trusted her sister again. Mary had been fond of Elizabeth whilst she was a child but as Elizabeth grew older, Mary came to see in her an unnerving resemblance to Anne Boleyn. Mary was fond of declaring that Elizabeth was not her sister at all and looked like Mark Smeaton, one of Anne Boleyn's supposed lovers.[38] The thought of Elizabeth succeeding her filled Mary with dread and she was desperate to marry quickly and bear a child.

Despite Wyatt's rebellion, plans for Mary's wedding continued unaffected. On 19 July 1554 Philip landed at Southampton.[39] Mary travelled to Winchester to meet him and she and Philip talked privately for over an hour on their first meeting.[40] Mary, who had already fallen half in love with Philip's portrait, was very impressed with her bridegroom. Philip was less impressed and the Spaniards in his train declared privately that Mary looked older than had been expected and was badly dressed. Philip knew where his duty lay, however, and was nothing but courteous to Mary during their early meetings. On 25 July 1554, Mary and Philip were married in Winchester Cathedral by the Bishop of Winchester. Before the service, the Bishop declared that Charles V had abdicated the thrones of Naples and Jerusalem to his son so that Mary would not have to marry a mere prince.[41] This probably appealed to the romantic in Mary who had been waiting for a husband to come for her all her adult life. Mary clearly had a romanticised idea of marriage and wanted the ceremony to fit with her own romantic ideas. According to one report, 'the queens marriage ring was a plain hoope of gold without any stone in it: for that was as it is said her pleasure, because maydens were so married in olde tymes'.[42] Mary always expected Philip to become King of England and on 5 May 1554 he was granted the crown matrimonial for the duration of her lifetime.[43]

Mary believed that her accession to the crown was a miracle and that God would also give her a child to continue her work when she was gone.[44] She was therefore pleased to be told by her doctors in September 1554 that she was expecting a child.[45] Mary confidently expected that she would give birth to a healthy prince and she showed all the signs of pregnancy. At Easter 1555, Mary went into confinement at Hampton Court for a child that was expected in May. On 30 April 1555, the news broke throughout England that Mary had given birth to a healthy prince and bonfires were lit and church bells rung.[46] By 2 May, this news had also reached the imperial court at Antwerp and Charles V ordered immediate rejoicing for the birth of his grandson.[47] Mary must have been embarrassed by this celebration since it quickly became clear to everyone that the news was nothing but an unfounded rumour and no child had yet been born.

Mary waited through the whole of May for a birth that did not occur and her doctors hurriedly began to recalculate, first saying June and then July. By late May, however, Mary's stomach had begun to decrease in size and it began to dawn on those around her that there would be no child.[48] Only Mary refused to believe that she had been mistaken and she spent her time weeping and praying whilst she continued to wait. Philip was impatient to leave for the continent, having stayed in England only to await the birth of his child. Finally in early August, the court abruptly moved to Oatlands, signalling to the world that Mary's confinement had ended.[49] Mary must have been devastated by the failure of her 'pregnancy' and her grief was confounded on 29 August when Philip sailed to Flanders. Mary wrote to him fondly every day but Philip's replies quickly became fewer and fewer and Mary realised that he had deserted her.

With the failure of her marriage and dashed hopes of a child, Mary threw herself into her religion. She came to believe that she had earned God's displeasure with her failure to punish Protestants enough and that this was why He had not given her a child. Mary had begun to burn Protestants in February 1555 but these dramatically increased following Philip's departure, in Mary's bid to please God and so earn His favour again. Thousands of Protestants were burned during Mary's reign and she earned the nickname, 'Bloody Mary' for this policy. Mary burned a number of high profile Protestants as well as many ordinary men and women. Bishops Ridley and Latimer were burned at Oxford on 16 October 1555.[50] Mary probably also gained some personal satisfaction from the burning of Thomas Cranmer, Archbishop of Canterbury. Mary refused to pardon Cranmer even after he recanted of his heresy and returned to the Roman Catholic Church and it is likely that this was at least in part due to the old grudge she bore against him for the divorce of her mother.[51] It was Cranmer who had pronounced Henry VIII's headship of the Church of England and the divorce of Catherine of Aragon and Mary probably always held him to be one of the men to blame for her mother's unhappiness. Heretics were burnt during the reigns of Mary's brother and her father but it is Mary who is remembered as the most cruel. This is to a large extent due to the fact that Protestantism ultimately triumphed. It is John Foxe's view of Mary that endures to this day:

> Before her was never read in history of any king or queen of England since the beginning of the kingdom, under whom, in time of peace, by hanging, heading, burning, and prisoning, so many Englishmen's lives, were spilled within this realm, as Queen Mary, for the space of four years.[52]

Mary's burnings damaged both her reputation and what remained of her popularity within England.

Charles V abdicated in early 1556 and Philip wrote to Mary informing her that she was now Queen of Spain.[53] As King of Spain, Philip found himself quickly embroiled in a war with France and he wanted English support. Mary refused to cooperate without seeing Philip in person and so Philip, realising reconciliation was necessary, sailed to England, landing at Dover on 18 March 1557.[54] Mary was overjoyed that her husband had returned to her and quickly forgave him his neglect of her. She agreed to Philip's demands that England declare war on France and was devastated when he left to fight his wars on 6 July 1557. Mary travelled with him to Dover and saw him onto his ship. She never saw him again. The war proved a disaster to England and, once again, Mary's Spanish marriage was blamed for English troubles. On 7 January 1558 Calais, the last English possession in France fell to the French. Mary is remembered as the monarch who lost the last vestige of the great Angevin empire. Mary fully understood the significance of this loss, reportedly saying 'when I am dead and opened, you shall find Calais lying in my heart'.[55] It was almost the last failure of her reign.

Soon after Philip left England for the last time, Mary came to believe that she was pregnant once again.[56] Mary, remembering her previous humiliation, delayed announcing her pregnancy until she was certain, although Philip and most of the people of England remained sceptical. Mary was as convinced by this pregnancy as she was by the last. In March 1558 she made a will leaving everything to the child she would bear. Once again, she was disappointed and by late May, well over nine months since Philip's departure, even Mary had to admit that she was mistaken. It is probable that Mary's second 'pregnancy' was in fact a symptom of cancer. After the failure of her second 'pregnancy', Mary retreated into her ill health and disappointment. In November 1558 Philip's ambassador, the Count of Feria found Mary dying when he arrived in England. According to his dispatch to Philip, 'she was happy to see me, since I brought her news of your majesty, and to receive the letter, although she was unable to read it'.[57] Even to the last, Mary deluded herself that her husband loved her and Feria reported to Philip that she had kept all the letters that Philip had sent her.[58] Mary had been reluctant to name her hated sister Elizabeth as her successor but under pressure from both Philip and her council she relented, agreeing to accept her as her heir.[59] As she lay dying, members of Mary's court flocked to her successor at Hatfield. Mary died on 17 November 1558 aged forty-two. She died a disappointed and unhappy woman and bonfires were lit and church bells rung in London to celebrate her death and the accession of Elizabeth.[60]

Mary Tudor's reign is remembered as an dark time for England and her reign is overshadowed by the glory of Elizabeth's. Although a good woman, Mary was a failure as a queen and she lost her reputation and popularity in her misguided policies and marriage. As the first effective queen regnant of England, Mary Tudor was a novelty and she did not have the imagination to invent a new role for herself, instead relying on medieval ideas of what a queen should be. It was only with the reign of Elizabeth that queenship was able to move in a different direction, something which Mary had failed to achieve. Mary Tudor will always be remembered as Bloody Mary. Although personally she appears to have been kindly and humane, she was also fanatical in her beliefs and she allowed great cruelty to be carried out in order to further these policies. There is no doubt that Mary thought she was fulfilling God's will and that the burnings were for the country's own good, but this viewpoint was not shared with most of her contemporaries or posterity. Mary's accession to the throne was one of the most popular in English history and the English wanted to love her. Nevertheless by the end she was universally despised. Even Mary's beloved husband, Philip, professed himself only mildly regretful at his wife's death and Mary Tudor died as she had lived, unloved and ultimately a failure.

Conclusion

Medieval and Tudor England had many queens, whose numbers far exceeded that of kings. The fact that there were over fifty in all makes it unsurprising that many are remembered in stereotypical ways. Some are remembered as good queens, some remain in obscurity and others are notorious. As the stories of their lives show, the bad queens were numerous and diverse but they all failed to live up to the requirements of what a good queen should be which damned them to failure. As these examples demonstrate, higher standards were often expected of queens simply because they were women and many were censured for acts that would not even have been criticised in kings. As women, they were also often seen as a threat to the male elite. Male chroniclers and church-men recorded events but often drew negative conclusions. Women were simply not expected to lead political lives during the medieval period and, even today, political queens, such as Margaret of Anjou or Emma of Normandy, are remembered unfavourably compared to their political male contemporaries. In the medieval period, a man could carry out damning acts and still not be damned for it. However for a woman even insignificant acts could be seen as blameworthy. Once a medieval queen lost her reputation, it was gone forever.

Although the women described here all fall into one category of notorious queens, the actual facts behind their notoriety were very varied and, throughout the period, a number of patterns can be seen.

This demonstrates clearly the stereotypical way in which many of the women are remembered; the idea of a notorious queen, for all its apparent diversity, is as stereotyped as that of a good queen.

Eadburh's life is remembered as a cautionary tale about just what made a truly bad queen. According to the stories, Eadburh acted politically for her own benefit and was also unfaithful and greedy. Worst of all, she is remembered as a woman who murdered her husband. Few queens in the medieval period even came close to Eadburh's alleged wickedness, although Aelfthryth and Isabella of France are arguably as notorious. These three women represent the very worst category of medieval queens and few chronicles have a good word to say about them. According to the sources, all three were apparently happy to resort to murder for their own political benefit and are still remembered as She-Wolves today. Each woman is reputed to have murdered her husband, a major sin in anyone's eyes. Whether they were guilty of these crimes or not (and the evidence is particularly dubious in the case of Eadburh) all three women are recorded as murderers and adulterers. This record survived to make them notorious to the present day. It is not taken into account that none of these women had a voice to tell their own story and that all that survives is the judgement of men plainly hostile to them. Once criticised in this way it was nearly impossible for the women to redeem themselves.

The next category of notorious queens that can be identified are the women who took on a man's role and who can be said to have been politically active for their own benefit. This category includes Emma of Normandy, Aelfgifu of Northampton, Empress Matilda, Margaret of Anjou and Mary I. Some of these women nominally acted for their sons and other male kinsmen and queens such as Emma of Normandy and Aelfgifu of Northampton upheld the pretence of acting on behalf of their sons. Not all of these women had a male kinsman behind which to hide their actions. The Empress Matilda and Mary I both encountered difficulties in ruling as a queen regnant in medieval England. All the political queens mentioned above are remembered in a negative light. Their actions are seen as unwomanly and very far from what a good queen should be. However most of them had little choice. Once again, this is an example of the negative way that female political power was perceived, even when, in actual fact, the women's actions were entirely justified.

The next category of notorious queens must be those who committed adultery. Queens were expected to be fertile and provide their husbands with an heir. Consequently faithlessness in a queen was heavily punished, in spite of the double standard which allowed kings to openly keep mistresses. Queens accused of this crime include the highly notorious queens, Eadburh, Aelfthryth, Isabella of France and Margaret of Anjou. However others such as Eleanor of Aquitaine, Isabella of Angouleme, Anne Boleyn and Catherine Howard are more specifically remembered as adulteresses and it is this act of betrayal (or, in the case of some, supposed betrayal) which has seen the queens remembered, over the centuries, as notorious. Not all of these women were guilty of adultery – Anne Boleyn and Margaret of Anjou certainly were not. However, infidelity was a much more serious crime for a woman than a man and the suggestion of it could destroy a reputation. Even Catherine Howard, who was certainly guilty of cuckoldry does not appear entirely blameworthy but rather as a woman entirely unsuited for the position in which she found herself. To accuse a queen of adultery was to ruin her and the case of Anne Boleyn shows just how clearly the enemies of particular queens realised this.

Incest in queens was seen in a similar way, being taken as a manifestation of the sexual immorality of many of England's wicked queens. Judith of France, Aelfgifu of the House of Wessex, Eleanor of Aquitaine and Anne Boleyn were all accused of this crime. Their actions were also strongly associated with ambition and greed, major sins for queens to commit – Edith Godwine, Eleanor of Provence, Eleanor of Castile, Joan of Navarre and Lady Jane Grey all experienced misfortune as a result of allegations of avariciousness. Again, however, ambition was something that was entirely acceptable in a man. In a woman however it was a vice and something to be criticised. This was particularly the case when the queen so accused also had the misfortune to be of foreign birth. Foreign queens received extra criticism, in spite of the fact that their marriages were generally arranged for them.

By breaking down the notorious queens into categories, it is possible to demonstrate some of the vices which were taken to denote a delinquent queen and then used as a means of attack. A bad queen was a woman willing to commit murder or was at least associated with rumours of murder. A bad queen was also one who acted politically for her own benefit, often at the cost of the best interests of her own husband or son. A bad queen might also be an adulteress, or commit incest to further her ambitions and a bad queen was also greedy and ambitious. These vices make up the definition of just what was considered an unpricipled queen and can be opposed to ideas of a good queen. A good queen was chaste, passive and devoted to her family, with no political will save that of her husband. These ideals had developed even by the reign of Eadburh in the late eighth century.

The queens discussed here were all, for a variety of reasons, portrayed as She-Wolves. It would be naïve to assert that all the queens were innocent of the crimes of which they are accused. There is no doubt that some were, indeed, guilty as charged. Judith of France, for example, did marry her stepson. Aelfthryth murdered her stepson. The Empress Matilda was the leader of a faction in a civil war and sought power in her own right. Eleanor of Aquitane rebelled against her husband. Isabella of France deposed and murdered her husband. Catherine Howard committed adultery and Mary I burned heretics at the stake. That all of these women carried out these actions is not in doubt. However, when the facts of their lives are discussed it is difficult to see how they can always be considered entirely blameworthy. Empress Matilda, for example, was the leader of a civil war faction because her crown was usurped. The action she took would be expected of a king but, as she found, it was a very different position for a queen. Eleanor of Aquitaine's husband was repeatedly unfaithful and a king would certainly be expected to imprison, or even kill an unfaithful wife, as Henry VIII did to Catherine Howard. Again, why should it be so different for a woman? Finally, Isabella of France endured years of harsh treatment from her indifferent and, ultimately, cruel husband. Again she cannot be blamed for wanting to improve her life.

Until very recently, history has almost exclusively been written by men with their own male point of view. Generally the women described here were not passive or retiring and, as a result of this, they were seen as a threat to the established male order and targets ripe for attack. Women were simply not expected to have political power and, as a result, many queens found an inherent contradiction in their role which was, after all, a political and public one. Some queens managed to negotiate this successfully and others less so, however for women under the constant scrutiny of chroniclers it was easy to be considered a failure. The role of queen was developing throughout the medieval period and the women described here were often the most proactive agents in this process. Their circumstances and actions pushed them into the public eye and this was considered unacceptable to their more conservative contemporaries. To many people in the medieval period, the role of queen was really only that of king's wife and for women who sought to be queens there was often a tightrope to walk to secure the preservation of their reputations. The women described here failed to walk the tightrope for one reason or another and as a result they were attacked. To be a She-Wolf is to be remembered as notorious, whatever the facts of the individual queen's life and, once the chronicles had been written, the true facts of the lives were often forgotten.

Endnotes

Chapter 2: Pre-Conquest Queens

1 Asser, chapter 13 (in Keynes and Lapidge 2004:72)
2 Stafford 1997:56
3 Stafford 1983:2
4 Charter LVI (in Pierquin 1912:417)
5 Asser, chapter 2 (in Keynes and Lapidge 2004:68)
6 Asser, chapter 23 (in Keynes and Lapidge 2004:75)
7 William of Malmesbury (in Preest 2002:124)
8 William of Malmesbury (in Preest 2002:124)
9 William of Malmesbury (in Preest 2002:127)
10 Asser, chapter 2 (in Keynes and Lapidge 2004:68)
11 Florence of Worcester (in Stevenson 1987:214 and 234)
12 Encomium Emmae Reginae (in Campbell 1998:33)
13 Regularis Concordia (in Symons 1953:2)
14 Aelfric's Life of St Aethelwold (in Whitelock 1979:905)
15 Life of King Edward who Rests at Westminster (in Barlow 1962:41)
16 Life of King Edward who Rests at Westminster (in Barlow 1962:41)
17 Cnut practised polygamy, maintaining both Emma of Normandy and Aelfgifu of Northampton as his queens

Chapter 3: Incestuous Queens

1 Nelson 1992:136
2 William of Malmesbury (in Stephenson 1989:88)
3 Simeon of Durham (in Stevenson 1987:53)
4 Florence of Worcester (in Stevenson 1853:209)

5 Asser chapter 13 (in Keynes and Lapidge 2004:72)

6 Annals of St Bertin's (in Whitelock 1979:343)

7 Annals of St Bertin's (in Whitelock 1979:343)

8 Kirby 2000:165

9 Stafford 1990a:146

10 William of Malmesbury (in Stephenson 1989:94)

11 Asser chapter 12 (in Keynes and Lapidge 2004:70)

12 William of Malmesbury (in Stephenson 1989:95)

13 Asser chapter 13 (in Keynes and Lapidge 2004:71)

14 Anglo-Saxon Chronicle A for 855 (in Swanton 2000:66)

15 William of Malmesbury (in Stephenson 1989:95)

16 Bede II.5 (in Shirley-Price 1990:112)

17 Asser chapter 17 (in Keynes and Lapidge 2004:73)

18 William of Malmesbury (in Stephenson 1989:97)

19 Asser chapter 12 (in Keynes and Lapidge 2004:70)

20 Kirby 2000:167

21 A grant by Aethelbald of land at Teffont (Charter 3 in Kelly 1996:16-17)

22 Simeon of Durham (in Stevenson 1987:54)

23 Nelson 1992:203

24 Stafford 1998:87

25 Nelson 1992:203

26 Chronicle of Aethelweard (in Campbell 1962:55)

27 Life of St Dunstan (in Whitelock 1979:901)

28 Life of St Dunstan (in Whitelock 1979:90)

29 Stafford 1990b:61

30 Stafford 1990b:61

31 William of Malmesbury (in Preest 2002:275)

32 William of Malmesbury (in Stephenson 1989:128)

33 Stafford 1989:48

34 Yorke 1997:77

35 S1292 (in Sawyer 1968:373)

36 Yorke 1997:78

37 Florence of Worcester (in Stevenson 1853:944) and Simeon of Durham (in Stevenson 1987:91) for example

38 Anglo-Saxon Chronicle D for 958 (in Swanton 2000:113)

39 Simeon of Durham (in Stevenson 1987:91)

40 William of Malmesbury (in Preest 2002:17)

41 William of Malmesbury (in Stephenson 1989:129)

Chapter 4: Murder & Adultery in the Anglo-Saxon Court

1 Simeon of Durham for 802 (in Stevenson 1987:50)

2 Simeon of Durham for 802 (in Stevenson 1987:50)

3 Anglo-Saxon Chronicle A for 787 (actually 789) (in Swanton 2000:54)

4 Anglo-Saxon Chronicle A for 836 (actually 839) (in Swanton 2000:62)

5 Asser chapter 13 (in Keynes and Lapidge 2004:72)

6 Asser chapter 15 (in Keynes and Lapidge 2004:72)

7 Asser chapter 15 (in Keynes and Lapidge 2004:72)

8 Asser chapter 15 (in Keynes and Lapidge 2004:72)

9 Asser chapter 13 (in Keynes and Lapidge 2004:71)

10 Stafford 2001:259

11 Anglo-Saxon Chronicle E for 1043 (actually 1045) (in Swanton 2000:165)

12 William of Malmesbury (in Stephenson 1989:185-6)

13 William of Malmesbury (in Stephenson 1989:186)

14 Florence of Worcester (in Douglas and Greenaway 1981:221)

15 Florence of Worcester (in Douglas and Greenaway 1981:221)

16 Life of King Edward who Rests at Westminster (in Barlow 1962:23)

17 Life of King Edward who Rests at Westminster (in Barlow 1962:31)

18 Simeon of Durham (in Stevenson 1987:130)

19 Stafford 2001:271

20 William of Malmesbury (in Stephenson 1989:191)

21 Life of King Edward who Rests at Westminster (in Barlow 1962:54)

22 Anglo-Saxon Chronicle E for 1075 (in Swanton 2000:212)

23 Gaimar line 3601 (in Hardy and Martin 1888, discussed in Wright 1939:148)

24 William of Malmesbury (in Stephenson 1989:139)

25 Gaimar line 3731 (in Hardy and Martin 1888, discussed in Wright 1939)

26 William of Malmesbury (in Stephenson 1989:140)

27 William of Malmesbury (in Stephenson 1989:140)

28 William of Malmesbury (in Stephenson 1989:140)

29 Historia Eliensis, quoted and translated in Wright 1939:158-9

30 Historia Eliensis, quoted and translated in Wright 1939:159

31 Historia Eliensis, quoted and translated in Wright 1939:160

32 William of Malmesbury (in Stephenson 1989:141)

33 In the New Minster Charter of 966, Edmund witness above Edward and he is described as the king's legitimate son, as opposed to Edward, who is simply the king's son (in Miller 2001:103)

34 Anglo-Saxon Chronicle E for 970 (in Swanton 2000:119)

35 Anglo-Saxon Chronicle D for 975 (in Swanton 2000:121)

36 Life of St Oswald by Byrhtferth of Ramsey (in Whitelock 1979:912)

37 Life of St Oswald by Byrhtferth of Ramsey (in Whitelock 1979:914)

38 Life of St Oswald by Byrhtferth of Ramsey (in Whitelock 1979:914)

39 William of Malmesbury (in Stephenson 1989:143)

40 William of Malmesbury (in Stephenson 1989:145)

41 Florence of Worcester (in Stephenson 1853:87)

42 William of Malmesbury (in Stephenson 1989:140)

43 William of Malmesbury (in Stephenson 1989:144)

Chapter 5: Female Power Struggles

1 Letter of Pope John XV to all the faithful, concerning the reconciliation of Ethelred, King of England, and Richard, Duke of Normandy (in Whitelock 1979:894-5)

2 Anglo-Saxon Chronicle E for 1000 (in Swanton 2000:133)

3 Anglo-Saxon Chronicle E for 1002 (in Swanton 2000:134)

4 Anglo-Saxon Chronicle F for 1003 (in Swanton 2000:134)

5 Anglo-Saxon Chronicle E for 1013 (in Swanton 2000:143)

6 Anglo-Saxon Chronicle E for 1013 (in Swanton 2000:143)

7 Anglo-Saxon Chronicle E for 1013 (in Swanton 2000:144)

8 Anglo-Saxon Chronicle E for 1013 (in Swanton 2000:144)

9 Anglo-Saxon Chronicle E for 1014 (in Swanton 2000:144)

10 William of Malmesbury (in Stephenson 1989:164)

11 William of Malmesbury (in Stephenson 1989:164)

12 Anglo-Saxon Chronicle E for 1016 (in Swanton 2000:146)

13 Life of King Edward who Rests at Westminster (in Barlow 1962:8)

14 Anglo-Saxon Chronicle E for 1016 (in Swanton 2000:148)

15 Anglo-Saxon Chronicle E for 1016 (in Swanton 2000:153)

16 Encomium Emmae Reginae Book II chapter 16 (in Campbell 1998:33)

17 Encomium Emmae Reginae Book II chapter 16 (in Campbell 1998:33)

18 Anglo-Saxon Chronicle E for 1017 (in Swanton 2000:155)

19 Encomium Emmae Reginae Book II chapter 16 (in Campbell 1998:35)

20 Campbell 1971:69

21 Campbell 1971:69

22 Stafford 1997:226

23 Stafford 1997:229

24 For example, she is described as a queen in a grant by Cnut of lands at Landrake and Tinnel in 1018 (in Whitelock 1979:597-599) and as Cnut's consort in a charter recording the restoration of lands to the New Minster at Winchester in 1019 (in Whitelock 1979:599-601)

25 Stafford 1997:233

26 Old English Letter of Wulfstan, Archbishop of York, informing King Cnut and Queen Aelfgifu that he has consecrated the Archbishop of Canterbury (in Whitelock 1979:601-2)

27 Strachan 2004:106

28 Stenton 1971:405

29 Campbell 1971:74

30 Campbell 1971:74

31 St Olaf's Saga (in Hollander 2002:525)

32 St Olaf's Saga (in Hollander 2002:525)

33 Campbell 1971:74

34 St Olaf's Saga (in Hollander 2002:528)

35 St Olaf's Saga (in Hollander 2002:528-30)

36 Campbell 1971:75

37 Anglo-Saxon Chronicle E for 1036 (actually 1035) (in Swanton 2000:159)

38 Encomium Emmae Reginae, Book III chapter 1 (in Campbell 1998:41)

39 Anglo-Saxon Chronicle E for 1036 (actually 1035) (in Swanton 2000:159)

40 Florence of Worcester (in Whitelock 1979:315)

41 Florence of Worcester (in Whitelock 1979:315)

42 Encomium Emmae Reginae Book III chapter 1 (in Campbell 1998:41)

43 Stafford 1997:239

44 Encomium Emmae Reginae Book III chapter 2 (in Campbell 1998:41)

45 Encomium Emmae Reginae Book III chapter 3 (in Campbell 1998:43)

46 Simeon of Durham (in Stevenson 1987:115)

47 Anglo-Saxon Chronicle A for 1037 (in Swanton 2000:160)

48 Encomium Emmae Reginae Book III chapter 8 (in Campbell 1998:49)

49 Campbell 1971:78

50 Encomium Emmae Reginae Book III chapter 14 (in Campbell 1998:53)

51 Anglo-Saxon Chronicle C for 1043 (in Swanton 2000:162)

52 Anglo-Saxon Chronicle D for 1052 (Swanton 2000:176)

Chapter 6: Post-Conquest Queens

1 Matilda was the only child of Count Eustace of Boulogne and, on her marriage, her father abdicated in favour of Stephen (in the Gesta Stephani, chapter 2 in Potter 1976:5). Eleanor of Aquitaine was the eldest of the two daughters of William X, Duke of Aquitaine.

2 Mitchell 1986:30

3 Patterson 1973:5

4 Warren 1997:66

5 Orderic Vitalis (in Chibnall 1968:211)

6 Orderic Vitalis (in Chibnall 1968:223)

7 Honeycutt 2003:91

8 William of Malmesbury (in Mynors 1998:757)

9 Honeycutt 2002:122

10 For example, Matilda of Boulogne led an army to besiege Dover in the name of her husband (Tanner 2002:140)

Chapter 7: Arrogance & Pride

1 Chibnall 1991:9

2 Henry of Huntingdon, iii.27 (in Greenaway 2002:52)

3 Anglo-Saxon Chronicle E for 1110 (in Swanton 2000:242)

4 Henry of Huntingdon, iii.27 (in Greenaway 2002:52)

5 John of Worcester (in McGurk 1998:135)

6 Pain 1978:15

7 Henry of Huntingdon, iii.36 (in Greenaway 2002:58)

8 Pain 1978:17

9 William of Malmesbury (in King and Potter 1998:7)

10 William of Malmesbury (in King and Potter 1998:7)

11 William of Malmesbury (in King and Potter 1998:7)

12 William of Malmesbury (in King and Potter 1998:19)

13 Pain 1978:26

14 Pain 1978:26

15 Chibnall 1991:60

16 Chibnall 1994:277

17 Henry of Huntingdon, iii.41 (in Greenway 2002:63)

18 Pain 1978:28

19 Chibnall 1991:70

20 Henry of Huntingdon, iii.43 (in Greenway 2002:63)

21 Henry of Huntingdon, iii.43 (in Greenway 2002:64)

22 William of Malmesbury (in King and Potter 1998:25)

23 William of Malmesbury (in King and Potter 1998:27)

24 Gesta Stephani, chapter 2 (in Potter 1976:5)

25 Chibnall 1991:198

26 John of Worcester (in McGurk 1998:253)

27 John of Worcester (in McGurk 1998:269)

28 John of Worcester (in McGurk 1998:269)

29 John of Worcester (in McGurk 1998:271)

30 John of Worcester (in McGurk 1998:293)

31 William of Malmesbury (in King and Potter 1998:87)

32 Gesta Stephani, chapter 58 (in Potter 1976:119)

33 Gesta Stephani, chapter 58 (in Potter 1976:121)

34 Gesta Stephani, chapter 61 (in Potter 1976:123)

35 Gesta Stephani, chapter 61 (in Potter 1976:123)

36 Gesta Stephani (in Potter 1976:121)

37 Gesta Stephani (in Potter 1976:121)

38 Gesta Stephani (in Potter 1976:121)

39 Gesta Stephani, chapter 60 (in Potter 1976:123)

40 Gesta Stephani, chapter 60 (in Potter 1976:123)

41 Gesta Stephani (in Potter 1976:125)

42 Gesta Stephani (in Potter 1976:127)

43 Gesta Stephani (in Potter 1976:125)

44 Gesta Stephani (in Potter 1976:127)

45 Henry of Huntingdon (in Greenway 2002:81)

46 Gesta Stephani (in Potter 1976:129)

47 Gesta Stephani (in Potter 1976:133)

48 Anglo-Saxon Chronicle E for 1141 (in Swanton 2000:266)

49 John of Worcester (in McGurk 1998:305)

50 Pain 1978:126

51 Gesta Stephani (in Potter 1976:143)

52 Pain 1978:126

53 Chibnall 1991:151

54 Chibnall 1991:160

55 Henry of Huntingdon (in Douglas and Greenaway 1981:334)

Chapter 8: Rebellion & Infidelity

1 Meade 1977:19

2 Meade 1977:19

3 Meade 1977:32

4 Meade 1977:37

5 Boyd 2004:15

6 Boyd 2004:13

7 Meade 1977:47

8 Weir 1999:18

9 Meade 1977:51

10 Meade 1977:51
11 Meade 1977:63
12 Boyd 2004:55
13 Boyd 2004:56
14 Weir 1999:42
15 Weir 1999:42
16 Weir 1999:43
17 Boyd 2004:45
18 Weir 1999:45-6
19 Odo of Deuil, Book I (in Berry 1948:9)
20 Weir 1999:51
21 William of Newburgh, chapter 20(1) (in Walsh and Kennedy 1988:93)
22 William of Newburgh, chapter 31(1) (in Walsh and Kennedy 1988:129)
23 William of Newburgh, chapter 20(1) (in Walsh and Kennedy 1988:93)
24 Odo of Deuil, Book IV (in Berry 1948:67)
25 Meade 1977:116
26 Odo of Deuil, Book VI (in Berry 1948:117)
27 Odo of Deuil, Book VI (in Berry 1948:119)
28 Strickland 1851:247
29 Odo of Deuil, Book VII (in Berry 1948:131)
30 Meade 1977:124
31 Meade 1977:124
32 John of Salisbury, XXIII (in Chibnall 1986:53)
33 John of Salisbury, XXIII (in Chibnall 1986:53)
34 Meade 1977:144
35 Meade 1977:153
36 Meade 1977:156
37 Gerald of Wales (in Douglas and Greenaway 1987:415)
38 William of Newburgh, chapter 31(2) (in Walsh and Kennedy 1988:129)
39 William of Newburgh, chapter 31(2) (in Walsh and Kennedy 1988:129)
40 Gerald of Wales (in Douglas and Greenaway 1987:411)
41 Capgrave (in Hingeston 1858:140)
42 Meade 1977:180
43 Meade 1977:181
44 Weir 1999:99
45 Weir 1999:94
46 Meade 1977:197
47 Meade 1977:198
48 Meade 1977:207
49 Meade 1977:219
50 Boyd 2004:154
51 Kelly 1950:109
52 Meade 1977:222
53 Boyd 2004:154
54 William of Newburgh (in Douglas and Greenaway 1981:363)
55 Weir 1999:173
56 Meade 1977:288
57 Boyd 2004:205

58 Meade 1977:336
59 Kelly 1950:190
60 Kelly 1950:226
61 Meade 1977:366
62 Weir 1999:255
63 Matthew Paris (in Richard 1874:347)
64 Martindale 2003:143
65 Boyd 2004:241
66 Richard of Devizes (in Appleby 1963:14)
67 Richard of Devizes (in Appleby 1963:14)
68 Richard of Devizes (in Appleby 1963:49)
69 Richard of Devizes (in Appleby 1963:61)
70 Kelly 1950:303
71 Boyd 2004:273
72 Meade 1977:392
73 Crawford 2002:36
74 Crawford 2002:40
75 Boyd 2004:280
76 Boyd 2004:298
77 Kelly 1950:360
78 Warren 1997:77
79 Warren 1997:79
80 Warren 1997:83
81 Meade 1977:434

Chapter 9: 'More Jezebel than Isabel'

1   Vincent 2003:174
2   Vincent 2003:175
3   Warren 1997:67
4   Cazel and Painter 1948:82
5   Cazel and Painter 1948:82
6   Weir 1999:336
7   Boyd 2004:313
8   Strickland 1851:332
9   Boyd 2004:312
10 Boyd 2004:313
11 Weir 1999:336
12 Weir 1999:337
13 Strickland 1851:332
14 Boyd 2004:314
15 Richardson 1946:296
16 Warren 1997:75
17 Warren 1997:84
18 Strickland 1851:335
19 Warren 1997:86
20 Warren 1997:93

21 Warren 1997:95

22 Vincent 2003:183

23 Warren 1997:169

24 Vincent 2003:193

25 Strickland 1851:344

26 Vincent 2003:193

27 Matthew Paris (in Richardson 1874:563)

28 Vincent 2003:203

29 Strickland 1851:340

30 Vincent 2003:198

31 Vincent 2003:198

32 Snellgrove 1950:13

33 Vincent 2003:195

34 Vincent 2003:195

35 Matthew Paris (in Richardson 1874:647

36 Matthew Paris (in Richardson 1874:653-633)

37 Matthew Paris (in Richardson 1874:668)

38 Strickland 1851:347

39 Warren 1997:236

40 A papal letter of February 1215 instructs the Bishops of Chichester, Bath and Exeter to restrain those interfering with Isabella's property (in Snellgrove 1950:11)

41 Vincent 1950:206

42 Crawford 2002:53

43 Snellgrove 1950:14

44 Snellgrove 1950:15

45 Vincent 2003:209

46 Vincent 2003:209

47 Vincent 2003:210

48 Snellgrove 1950:17

49 Vincent 2003:211

50 Snellgrove 1950:17

51 Strickland 1851:354

52 Snellgrove 1950:20

53 Strickland 1851:554

54 Matthew Paris (in Vaughan 1984:109)

55 According to Mathew Paris, three half-brothers and a half-sister of Henry III arrived in England in 1247, for example (in Vaughan 1984:109)

Chapter 10: Nepotism & Greed

1 Biles 1983:113

2 Strickland 1844:22

3 Biles 1983:113

4 Biles 1983:114

5 Howell 1998:23

6 Biles 1983:114

7 Strickland 1844:80

8 Howell 1998:27

9 Howell 1998:27

10 Letter CCCCXCVII Henry III to Alexander III of Scots, 2 July 1253 (in Shirley 1866:99)

11 Howell 1998:101

12 Howell 1998:102

13 Howell 1998:130

14 Howell 1998:132

15 Ridgeway 1989:591

16 Ridgeway 1989:592

17 Ridgeway 1989:592

18 Howell 1998:33

19 Howell 1998:54

20 Matthew Paris (in Rothwell 1975:127)

21 Biles 1983:114

22 Howell 1998:116

23 Prestwich 1997:9

24 Parsons 1998:12

25 Capgrave (in Hingeston 1858:157)

26 Parsons 1977:7

27 Parsons 1998:18

28 Prestwich 1997:22

29 Biles 1983:121

30 Biles 1983:123

31 The Annals of Dunstable (in Rothwell 1975:201)

32 Annals of Dunstable (in Rothwell 1975:201)

33 Annals of Dunstable (in Rothwell 1975:201)

34 Annals of Dunstable (in Rothwell 1975:202)

35 Annals of Dunstable (in Rothwell 1975:202)

36 Annals of Dunstable (in Rothwell 1975:203)

37 Annals of Dunstable (in Rothwell 1975:205)

38 Annals of Dunstable (in Rothwell 1975:207)

39 Parsons 1998:24

40 Annales Londonienses (in Stubbs 1858:64)

41 Annals of Dunstable (in Rothwell 1975:207)

42 Annals of Dunstable (in Rothwell 1975:207)

43 Biles 1983:127

44 Annales Londonienses (in Stubbs 1882:68)

45 Biles 1983:128

46 Annales Londoniensis (in Stubbs 1882:71)

47 Parsons 1998:25

48 Strickland 1844:155

49 For example, Capgrave says Joan of Acre was born during the crusade(in Hingeston 1858:168)

50 Capgrave (in Hingeston 1858:162)

51 Camden (in Piggott 1971:321)

52 Prestwich 1997:78

53 Powrie 1990:9

54 Powrie 1990:9
55 Prestwich 1997:126
56 Prestwich 1997:126
57 Parsons 1977:7
58 Prestwich 1997:126
59 Crawford 2002:60
60 Parsons 1998:37
61 Biles 1983:129
62 Crawford 2002:73
63 Prestwich 1997:124
64 Prestwich 1997:125
65 Prestwich 1997:104
66 Parsons 1998:78
67 Parsons 1998:124
68 Prestwich 1997:124
69 Parsons 1998:113
70 Prestwich 1997:43
71 Parsons 1998:44
72 Parsons 1998:44
73 Camden (in Piggott 1971:285)
74 Camden (in Piggott 1971:321)
75 Parsons 1991:23
76 Howell 1998:309

Chapter II: The She-Wolf of France

1   The Chronicle of Lanercost (in Maxwell 1913:180)
2   Weir 2005:6
3   Froissart (in Johnes 1901:2)
4   Doherty 2003:43
5   Chronicle of Lanercost (in Maxwell 1913:186)
6   Annales Paulini (in Stubbs 1882:258)
7   Weir 2005:19
8   Weir 2005:20
9   Strickland 1844:214
10 Annales Paulini (in Stubbs 1882:262)
11 Capgrave (in Hingeston 1858:74)
12 Weir 2005:36
13 Weir 2005:31
14 The Chronicle of Lanercost (in Maxwell 1913:186)
15 The Chronicle of Lanercost (in Maxwell 1913:187)
16 Weir 2005:49
17 Strickland 1844:218
18 The Chronicle of Lanercost (in Maxwell 1913:196)
19 Strickland 1844:223
20 The Chronicle of Lanercost (in Maxwell 1913:198)
21 Menache 1984:108

22 Weir 2005:71
23 Capgrave (in Hingeston 1858:179)
24 Menache 1984:108
25 Menache 1984:108
26 Conway Davies 1967:105
27 Conway Davies 1967:106
28 Weir 2005:92
29 Weir 2005:96
30 Weir 2005:100
31 Annales Paulini (in Stubbs 1882:279 and 291)
32 Doherty 2003:62
33 Doherty 2003:66
34 Weir 2005:131
35 Capgrave (in Hingeston 1858:188)
36 Capgrave (in Hingeston 1858:188)
37 Fryde 1979:18
38 Annales Paulini (in Stubbs 1882:307)
39 Weir 2005:160
40 Chronicle of Lanercost (in Maxwell 1913:249)
41 Annales Paulini (in Stubbs 1882:308)
42 Chronicle of Lanercost (in Maxwell 1913:249)
43 Froissart (in Johnes 1901:3)
44 Chronicle of Lanercost (in Maxwell 1913:249)
45 Chronicle of Lanercost (in Maxwell 1913:250)
46 Chronicle of Lanercost (in Maxwell 1913:250)
47 Mortimer 2003:147
48 Chronicle of Lanercost (in Maxwell 1913:251)
49 Crawford 2002:88
50 Menache 1984:111
51 Crawford 2002:89
52 Annales Paulini (in Stubbs 1882:316)
53 Chronicle of Lanercost (in Maxwell 1913:251)
54 Weir 2005:236
55 Chronicle of Lanercost (in Maxwell 1913:253)
56 Annales Paulini (in Stubbs 1882:319)
57 Pipewell Chronicle (in Rothwell 1975:287)
58 Chronicle of Lanercost (in Maxwell 1913:287)
59 Weir 2005:255
60 Capgrave (in Hingeston 1858:198)
61 Capgrave (in Hingeston 1858:198)
62 Capgrave (in Hingeston 1858:198)
63 Capgrave (in Hingeston 1858:198)
64 Chronicle of Lanercost (in Maxwell 1913:260)
65 Chronicon Galfridi le Baker de Swynbroke (in Myers 1969:50)
66 Chronicon Galfridi le Baker de Swynbroke (in Myers 1969:50)
67 Geoffrey Le Baker, Chronicle (in Myers 1969:52)
68 Geoffrey Le Baker, Chronicle (in Myers 1969:53)
69 Chronicle of Lanercost (in Maxwell 1913:266)

70 Bond 1853:454
71 Bond 1853:455
72 Bond 1853:462
73 Doherty 2003:179
74 Thomas Grey (in Starr and Hendrickson 1966:20)

Chapter 12: Later Medieval & Tudor Queens

1 Hall's Chronicle (Johnson, et al, 1809:477)
2 Hall's Chronicle (Johnson, et al, 1809:477)
3 Foxe 1965:559
4 Foxe 1965:559
5 Catherine of Aragon was appointed as regent in 1513 when Henry VIII invaded France (Hall's Chronicle in Johnson, et al, 1809:548) and Catherine Parr when Henry VIII invaded France in 1544 (Fraser 1992:372)
6 Most people in England apparently accepted that Elizabeth's claim to the throne, as the eldest daughter of Edward IV, was stronger than that of her husband, Henry VII (Francis Bacon in Lumby 1885:8)
7 Francis Bacon in Lumby 1885:8

Chapter 13: Witchcraft

1 Howitt p158
2 Jones 2000:2
3 Strickland 1844:46
4 Strickland 1844:47
5 Jones 2000:4
6 Howitt p161
7 Jones 2000:6
8 Strickland 1844:162
9 Jones 2000:8
10 Strohm 1998:155
11 John Hayward (in Manning 1991:180)
12 Kirby 1970:135
13 Jones 2000:11
14 John Hayward (in Manning 1991:180)
15 Strohm 1998:157
16 Strohm 1998:157
17 Jones 2000:14
18 Strickland 1844:85
19 Strickland 1844:89
20 Strickland 1844:83
21 Strickland 1844:84
22 Howitt p167
23 Strohm 1998:165
24 Eulogium Historiarum (in Myers 1969:205)

25 John Hayward (in Manning 1991:197)

26 Eulogium Historiarum (in Myers 1969:205)

27 Howitt p166

28 Howitt p166

29 Myers 1985:94

30 Myers 1985:94

31 Myers 1985:101

32 Hole 1990:119

33 The Condemnation of Eleanor Cobham for Witchcraft, 1441 (in Myers 1969:870)

34 The Trial of Eleanor Cobham (in Wilkinson 1964:59)

35 The Condemnation of Eleanor Cobham for Witchcraft, 1441 (in Myers 1969:870)

36 Hole 1990:121

37 Henry VI part II (Act II Scene 3) (Shakespeare, in Wells and Taylor 1994:68)

38 Myers 1985:96

39 Myers 1985:97

40 Myers 1985:98

41 Myers 1985:98

42 Myers 1985:102

Chapter 14: Shakespeare's She-Wolf

1 Erlanger 1970:35

2 Erlanger 1970:50

3 Erlanger 1970:52

4 Haswell 1975:19

5 Hall's Chronicle (Johnson, et al, 1809:203)

6 Hall's Chronicle (Johnson, et al, 1809:204)

7 Strickland 1844:186

8 Hall's Chronicle (Johnson, et al. 1809:205)

9 Haswell 1975:40

10 Erlanger 1970:66

11 Hall's Chronicle (Johnson, et al, 1809:205)

12 Erlanger 1970:73

13 Maurer 2003:20

14 Haswell 1975:53

15 Milanese State Papers: Report to Bianca Maria Visconti, Duchess of Milan, 24 October 1458 (in Dockray 2000:15)

16 Bagley p45

17 Brut Chronicle (in Dockray 2000:13)

18 Erlanger 1970:88

19 Griffiths 1998:249

20 Bagley p49

21 Bagley p49

22 Hall's Chronicle (Johnson, et al, 1809:219)

23 Haswell 1975:57

24 Bagley p67

25 Erlanger 1970:116

26 Maurer 2003:41

27 Erlanger 1970:145

28 Erlanger 1970:145

29 Whethamsted's Register (in Dockray 2000:6)

30 Paston Letter 195 (in Gairdner 1896:263)

31 Hall's Chronicle (Johnson, et al, 1809:230)

32 Paston Letter 195 (in Gairdner 1896:263)

33 Paston Letter 195 (in Gairdner 1896:263-264)

34 Paston Letter 195 (in Gairdner 1896:265)

35 Maurer 2003:107

36 Paston Letter 226 (in Gairdner 1896:315)

37 Maurer 2003:119

38 Maurer 2003:121

39 Maurer 2003:151

40 Maurer 2003:165

41 Maurer 2003:180

42 Erlanger 1970:167

43 Hall's Chronicle (Johnson, et al, 1809:245)

44 Hall's Chronicle (Johnson, et al, 1809:249)

45 Hall's Chronicle (Johnson, et al, 1809:250)

46 Hall's Chronicle (Johnson, et al, 1809:251)

47 Maurer 2003:197

48 Maurer 2003:201

49 Paston letter 385 (in Gairdner 1896:5)

50 Erlanger 1970:196

51 Haswell 1975:160

52 Erlanger 1970:204

53 Dockray 2000:13

54 Bagley p199

55 Bagley p200

56 Hall's Chronicle (in Johnson, et al, 1809:386)

57 Paston Letter 668 (in Gairdner 1896:4)

58 Polydore Vergil (in Dockray 2000:14)

59 Hall's Chronicle (in Johnson, et al, 1809:300)

60 Hall's Chronicle (in Johnson, et al, 1809:301)

61 Paston Letter 687 (in Gairdner 1896:33)

62 Erlanger 1970:235

63 Erlanger 1970:246

Chapter 15: The Seductress

1 Baldwin 2002:1

2 Thomas Moore 2005:59

3 Baldwin 2002:5

4 Okerlund 2005:14

5 Baldwin 2002:8

6 Thomas Moore 2005:59

7 Dominic Mancini (in Armstrong 1984:61)

8 Thomas Moore 2005:59

9 Warkworth's Chronicle (in Halliwell 1990:3)

10 Warkworth's Chronicle (in Halliwell 1990:3)

11 Thomas Moore 2005:62

12 Dominic Mancini (in Armstrong 1984:61)

13 Dominic Mancini (in Armstrong 1984:63)

14 Laynesmith 2004:88

15 Baldwin 2002:17

16 Baldwin 2002:21

17 Laynesmith 2004:197

18 Baldwin 2002:25

19 Okerlund 2005:70

20 Baldwin 2002:38

21 Okerlund 2005:113

22 Baldwin 2002:42

23 Paston Letter 654 for 12 October 1470 (in Gairdner 1896:412)

24 Baldwin 2002:43

25 Baldwin 2002:45

26 Baldwin 2002:54

27 Crowland Continuations (in Pronay and Cox 1986:151)

28 Crowland Continuations (in Pronay and Cox 1986:153)

29 Crowland Continuations (in Pronay and Cox 1986:155)

30 Thomas Moore 2005:17

31 Crowland Continuations (in Pronay and Cox 1986:157)

32 Thomas Moore 2005:18

33 Thomas Moore 2005:18

34 Thomas Moore 2005:19

35 Dominic Mancini (in Armstrong 1984:79)

36 Thomas Moore 2005:20

37 Thomas Moore 2005:26

38 Thomas Moore 2005:39

39 Thomas Moore 2005:39

40 Thomas Moore 2005:66

41 Crowland Continuations (in Pronay and Cox 1986:163)

42 Thomas Moore 2005:43

43 Baldwin 2002:102

44 Baldwin 2002:106

45 Bacon's History of the Reign of Henry VII (in Lumby 1885:24)

46 Bacon's History of the Reign of Henry VII (in Lumby 1885:29)

47 Okerlund 2005:256

Chapter 16: Anne Boleyn

1 Ives 2005:3

2 Ives 2005:14

3 Ives 2005:19

4 Ives 2005:26

5 George Wyatt (in Loades 1968:143)

6 Ives 2005:40

7 Hall's Chronicle (Johnson, et al, 1809:631)

8 Cavendish's Life of Wolsey (Lockyer 1962:59)

9 Cavendish's Life of Wolsey (Lockyer 1962:59)

10 Cavendish's Life of Wolsey (Lockyer 1962:59)

11 Poem 97 (in Daalder 1975:15)

12 Poem 7 (in Daalder 1975:7)

13 Letters 1 and 2 (in Savage 1949:28-30)

14 Letter 4 (in Savage 1949:33)

15 Letter 5 (in Savage 1949:35-6)

16 Ives 2005:97

17 Cavendish's Life of Wolsey (in Lockyer 1962:66)

18 Cavendish's Life of Wolsey (in Lockyer 1962:132)

19 Ives 2005:131

20 Ives 2005:127

21 Hall's Chronicle (Johnson, et al, 1809:790)

22 Hall's Chronicle (Johnson, et al, 1809:790)

23 Ives 2005:132

24 William Latymer (in Dowling 1990:48)

25 William Latymer (in Dowling 1990:56)

26 William Latymer (in Dowling 1990:61)

27 Ives 2005:163

28 Ives 2005:163

29 Hall's Chronicle (in Johnson, et al, 1809:795)

30 Wriothesley's Chronicle (in Hamilton 1875:18)

31 Ives 2005:141

32 Ives 2005:143

33 Hall's Chronicle (in Johnson, et al, 1809:803)

34 Ives 2005:184

35 Ives 2005:256

36 William Latymer (in Dowling 1990:63)

37 Ives 2005:192

38 Ives 2005:145

39 Ives 2005:194

40 Lisle Letter 127, Thomas Broke to Lady Lisle 18 December 1534 (in St Claire Byrne 1983:201)

41 Ives 2005:291

42 Hall's Chronicle (in Johnson, et al, 1809:818)

43 Wriothesley's Chronicle (in Hamilton 1875:33)

44 Wriothesley's Chronicle (in Hamilton 1875:33)

45 Ives 2005:316

46 Hall's Chronicle (in Johnson, et al, 1809:819)

47 Wriothesley's Chronicle (in Hamilton 1875:35)

48 Wriothesley's Chronicle (in Hamilton 1875:36)

49 Lisle Letter 141: John Husee to Lord Lisle, 19 May 1536 (in St Clair Byrne 1983:217)

50 Wriothesley's Chronicle (in Hamilton 1875:39)

51 Wriothesley's Chronicle (in Hamilton 1875:41)

52 Hall's Chronicle (Johnson, et al, 1809:819)

53 Dixon 1873:339

54 Hall's Chronicle (Johnson, et al, 1809:819)

Chapter 17: Treachery & Misjudgement

1 Denny 2005:8

2 Baldwin Smith 1961:39

3 Letter 49: Lord Edmund Howard to Lady Lisle (in St Clare Byrne 1983:107)

4 Baldwin Smith 1961:36

5 Examination of Henry Manox, 5 November 1541 (Paper 1321) (in Gairdner and Brodie 1898:608)

6 Examination of Henry Manox, 5 November 1541 (Paper 1321) (in Gairdner and Brodie 1898:608)

7 The Council to Paget, Ambassador in France, 12 November 1541 (Paper 1334) (in Gairdner and Brodie 1898:616)

8 Baldwin Smith 1961:50

9 Baldwin Smith 1961:52

10 Examination of Henry Manox, 5 November 1541 (Paper 1321) (in Gairdner and Brodie 1898:609)

11 The Council to Paget, Ambassador in France, 12 November 1541 (Paper 1334) (in Gairdner and Brodie 1898:616)

12 Baldwin Smith 1961:54

13 Chapuys to Charles V, 3 December 1541 (Paper 1401) (in Gairdner and Brodie 1898:652)

14 Baldwin Smith 1961:57

15 Examination of Henry Manox, 5 November 1541 (Paper 1321) (in Gairdner and Brodie 1898:609)

16 Katherine Tylney, 30 November 1541 (Paper 1385) (in Gairdner and Brodie 1898:633)

17 Baldwin Smith 1961:58

18 Marillac to Francis I, 21 July 1540 (Paper 901) (in Gairdner and Brodie 1896:446)

19 Marillac to Montmorency, 3 September 1540 (Paper 12) (in Gairdner and Brodie 1898:5)

20 Denny 2005:153

21 Marillac to Montmorency, 3 September 1540 (Paper 12) (in Gairdner and Brodie 1898:5)

22 Baldwin Smith 1961:136

23 Chapuys to Charles V, 27 March 1541 (Paper 662) (in Gairdner and Brodie 1898:319)

24 Baldwin Smith 1961:135

25 Chapuys to the Queen of Hungary, 26 May 1541 (Papers 864) (in Gairdner and Brodie 1898:410)

26 Marillac to Francis I, 18 July 1541 (Paper 1011) (in Gairdner and Brodie 1898:482)

27 Report of Henry VIII's visit to Lincoln, 12 August 1541 (Paper 1088) (in Gairdner and Brodie 1898:518)

28 Baldwin Smith 1961:163

29 Confession of Margyt Morton to Sir Anthony Browne (Paper 1338) (in Gairdner and Brodie 1898:617)

30 Baldwin Smith 1961:155

31 Baldwin Smith 1961:130

32 Crawford 2002:210

33 Baldwin Smith 1961:143

34 Hall's Chronicle (Johnson, et al, 1809:842)

35 Denny 2005:198

36 Denny 2005:206

37 The Council to Paget, Ambassador in France, 12 November 1541 (Paper 1334) (in Gairdner and Brodie 1898:615)

38 Baldwin Smith 1961:168

39 Marillac to Francis I, 11 November 1541 (Paper 1332) (in Gairdner and Brodie 1898:614)

40 Baldwin Smith 1961:167

41 Baldwin Smith 1961:169

42 Cranmer to Henry VIII, November 1541 (Paper 1325) (in Gairdner and Brodie 1898:610)

43 Baldwin Smith 1961:171

44 The Privy Council to Cranmer and Others, 11 November 1541 (Paper 1331) (in Gairdner and Brodie 1898:613)

45 The Privy Council to Cranmer and Others, 11 November 1541 (Paper 1331) (in Gairdner and Brodie 1898:613)

46 Fraser 1992:350

47 Baldwin Smith 1961:174

48 Chapuys to Charles V, 3 December 1541 (Paper 1401) (in Gairdner and Brodie 1898:652)

49 Chapuys to Charles V, 3 December 1541 (Paper 1401) (in Gairdner and Brodie 1898:652)

50 Chapuys to Charles V, 11 December 1541 (Paper 1441) (in Gairdner and Brodie 1898:672)

51 Fraser 1992:349

52 Chapuys to Charles V, 11 December 1541 (Paper 1441) (in Gairdner and Brodie 1898:672)

53 Giovanni Stanchini, Secretary of Mons. Capo di Ferro, to Cardinal Farnese, 11 January 1542 (Paper 19) (in Gairdner and Brodie 1900:10)

54 Hall's Chronicle (Johnson, et al, 1809:843)

55 Wriothesley's Chronicle (Hamilton 1875:133)

56 Baldwin Smith 1961:188

57 Marillac to Francis I, 13 February 1542 (Paper 100) (in Gairdner and Brodie 1900:44)

58 Chapuys to Charles V, 25 February 1542 (Paper 124) (in Gairdner and Brodie 1900:50)

59 Chapuys to Charles V, 25 February 1542 (Paper 124) (in Gairdner and Brodie 1900:50)

60 Marillac to Francis I, 13 February 1542 (Paper 100) (in Gairdner and Brodie 1900:44)

Chapter 18: Aspiring to the Crown

1 Taylor 2004:7
2 Chapman 1962:29
3 Chapman 1962:29
4 Taylor 2004:8
5 Plowden 1986:54
6 Plowden 2003:45
7 Chapman 1962:39
8 Plowden 2003:58
9 Davey 1910:115
10 Plowden 1986:77
11 Plowden 1986:82
12 Plowden 2003:79
13 Plowden 2003:101
14 Letter from Northumberland to Suffolk (in Taylor 2004:17)
15 Vita Mariae Angliae Reginae (in MacCulloch 1984:245)
16 Plowden 1986:85
17 Plowden 1986:87
18 Vita Mariae Angliae Reginae (in MacCulloch 1984:245)
19 Plowden 1986:91
20 Plowden 1986:91
21 The Chronicle of Queen Jane and Two Years of Queen Mary (in Nichols 1996:1)
22 Plowden 2003:107
23 Peter Heyling's 1661 History of the Reformation of the Church of England (in Taylor 2004:54)
24 Lady Jane Grey to Mary I (early August 1553) (in Taylor 2004:95)
25 The Chronicle of Queen Jane and Two Years of Queen Mary (in Nichols 1996:3)
26 Plowden 2003:vii
27 A letter from Lady Jane Grey to Queen Mary, early August 1553 (in Taylor 2004:95)
28 Taylor 2004:95
29 The Chronicle of Queen Jane and Two Years of Queen Mary (in Nichols 1996:5)
30 The Chronicle of Queen Jane and Two Years of Queen Mary (in Nichols 1996:8)
31 The Chronicle of Queen Jane and Two Years of Queen Mary (in Nichols 1996:8)
32 The Chronicle of Queen Jane and Two Years of Queen Mary (in Nichols 1996:9)
33 Plowden 2003:123
34 The Chronicle of Queen Jane and Two Years of Queen Mary (in Nichols 1996:9)
35 Plowden 2003:124
36 The Chronicle of Queen Jane and Two Years of Queen Mary (in Nichols 1996:12)
37 Plowden 2003:124
38 Vita Mariae Angliae Reginae (in MacCulloch 1984:271)
39 The Chronicle of Queen Jane and Two Years of Queen Mary (in Nichols 1996:19)
40 The Chronicle of Queen Jane and Two Years of Queen Mary (in Nichols 1996:25)

41 The Chronicle of Queen Jane and Two Years of Queen Mary (in Nichols 1996:32)
42 The Chronicle of Queen Jane and Two Years of Queen Mary (in Nichols 1996:37)
43 Plowden 1986:119
44 Plowden 1986:121
45 Letter from Lady Jane Grey to the Duke of Suffolk, late January or early February 1554 (in Taylor 2004:123)
46 The Chronicle of Queen Jane and Two Years of Queen Mary (in Nichols 1996:56)
47 Plowden 2003:156
48 The Chronicle of Queen Jane and Two Years of Queen Mary (in Nichols 1996:56)
49 The Chronicle of Queen Jane and Two Years of Queen Mary (in Nichols 1996:59)

Chapter 19: Bloody Mary

1 Hall's Chronicle (Johnson, et al, 1809:584)
2 Mattingley 1944:145
3 Marillac to Francis I, 12 October 1541 (Paper 1253) (in Gairdner and Brodie 1898:586)
4 Loades 1989:32
5 Prescott 2003:35
6 Erickson 1978:61
7 Prescott 2003:46
8 Prescott 2003:67
9 Prescott 2003:67
10 Prescott 2003:82
11 Prescott 2003:95
12 Prescott 2003:100
13 Loades 1989:136
14 Loades 1989:136
15 Erickson 1978:216
16 Prescott 2003:122
17 Marillac to Francis I, 12 October 1541 (Paper 1253) (in Gairdner and Brodie 1898:586)
18 Robert Broke and Richard Goodrich to the Duke of Somerset, 15 August 1549 (Paper 339) (in Knighton 1992:130)
19 Prescott 2003:152
20 Prescott 2003:153
21 Prescott 2003:166
22 Prescott 2003:191
23 Vita Mariae Angliae Reginae (in MacCulloch 1984:251)
24 Vita Mariae Angliae Reginae (in MacCulloch 1984:253)
25 Vita Mariae Angliae Reginae (in MacCulloch 1984:265)
26 Vita Mariae Angliae Reginae (in MacCulloch 1984:265)

27 Vita Mariae Angliae Reginae (in MacCulloch 1984:269)

28 Statutes of the Realm, 4, i, 1 Mary (in Loades 2002:22)

29 Loades 1989:196

30 Vita Mariae Angliae Reginae (in MacCulloch 1984:273)

31 The Chronicle of Queen Jane and two years of Queen Mary (in Nichols 1996:28)

32 Erickson 1978:330

33 Erickson 1978:329

34 Vita Mariae Angliae Reginae (in MacCulloch 1984:279)

35 Vita Mariae Angliae Reginae (in MacCulloch 1984:281)

36 The Chronicle of Queen Jane and Two Years of Queen Mary (in Nichols 1996:70)

37 The Chronicle of Queen Jane and Two Years of Queen Mary (in Nichols 1996:76)

38 Erickson 1978:346

39 The Chronicle of Queen Jane and Two Years of Queen Mary (in Nichols 1996:77)

40 Loades 1989:224

41 Extract from a letter by John Elder (in Loades 2002:42-44)

42 Extract from a letter by John Elder (in Loades 2002:43)

43 Vita Mariae Angliae Reginae (in MacCulloch 1984:291)

44 Prescott 2003:258

45 Erickson 1978:385

46 Erickson 1978:411

47 John Foxe's Actes and Monuments (in Loades 2002:61)

48 Erickson 1989:415

49 Erickson 1989:422

50 Foxe (undated) p287

51 Foxe (undated) p374

52 Foxe (undated) p395

53 Erickson 1978:438

54 Erickson 1978:460

55 Foxe (undated) p394

56 Erickson 1978:470

57 Count of Feria's dispatch to Philip II of 14 November 1558 (in Rodriguez-Salgado and Adams 1984:328)

58 Count of Feria's dispatch to Philip II of 14 November 1558 (in Rodriguez-Salgado and Adams 1984:337)

59 Count of Feria's dispatch to Philip II of 14 November 1558 (in Rodriguez-Salgado and Adams 1984:336)

60 Erickson 1978:482

List of Illustrations

Bibliography

PRIMARY SOURCES: PRINTED BOOKS

Asser, 'Life of King Alfred', Asser's Life of King Alfred and Other Contemporary Sources, eds. Keyne, S. and Lapidge, M. (London, 2004)

Bacon, F., History of the Reign of King Henry VII, ed. Lumby, J.R. (Cambridge, 1885)

Barlow, F., ed., The Life of King Edward who Rests at Westminster (London:1962)

Bede, Ecclesiastical History of the English People (London, 1990)

Campbell, A., ed., The Chronicle of Aethelweard (London, 1962)

___, Encomium Emmae Reginae (Cambridge, 1998)

Camden, W., Britannia, ed. Piggott, S. (Newton Abbott, 1971)

Capgrave, J., The Chronicle of England, ed. Hingeston, F.C. (London, 1858)

Cavendish, G., Thomas Wolsey Late Cardinal, His Life and Death, ed. Lockyer, R. (London, 1962)

Crawford, A., Letters of the Queens of England (Stroud, 2002)

Dockray, K., ed., Henry VI, Margaret of Anjou and the Wars of the Roses: A Source Book (Stroud, 2000)

Douglas, D.C. and Greenaway, G.W., English Historical Documents, vol II: 1042–1189 (London, 1981)

Foxe, J., The Book of Martyrs (London, undated edition)

___, Acts and Monuments, vol 5 (New York, 1965)

Froissart, J., Chronicles of England, France, Spain and Adjoining Countries, ed. Johnes, T. (London, 1901)

Gaimar, G., Lestoire des Engles Solum la Translacion Maistre Geffrei Gaimar, ed., Hardy, T.D. and Martin, C.T. (London, 1888)

Gairdner, J., ed., The Paston Letters, 3 vols (Westminster, 1896)

Gairdner, J. and Brodie, R.H., eds., Letters and Papers of the Reign of Henry VIII, vol 15: 1540 (London, 1896)

___, Letters and Papers of the Reign of Henry VIII, vol 16: 1541 (London, 1898)

___, Letters and Papers of the Reign of Henry VIII, vol 17: 1542 (London, 1900)

Gray, T., The Complete Poems of Thomas Gray, eds. Starr, H.W. and Hendrickson, J.R. (Oxford, 1966)

Hall, E., Hall's Chronicle Containing the History of England, eds. Johnson, J., et al (London, 1809)

Halliwell, J.O., Warkworth's Chronicle of the First Thirteen Years of the Reign of King Edward the Fourth (Llanerch, 1990)

Hayward, J., The Life and Raigne of King Henrie IIII, ed. Manning, J.J. (London, 1991)

Henry of Huntingdon, The History of the English People 1000-1154 ed. Greenway, D. (Oxford, 2002)

John of Salisbury, The Historia Pontificalis of John of Salisbury, Chibnall, M. (Oxford, 1986)

John of Worcester, The Chronicle of John of Worcester, vol III: 1067-1140 ed. McGurk, P. (Oxford 1998)

Kelly, S.E., Charters of Shaftesbury Abbey (Oxford, 1996)

Knighton, C.S., Calendar of State Papers Domestic Series of the Reign of Edward VI (London 1992)

Latymer, W., Cronickille of Anne Bulleyne, ed. Dowling, M. (Camden Miscellany 30, 1990)

Loades, D., ed., Chronicles of the Tudor Queens (Stroud, 2002)

Mancini, D., The Usurpation of Richard III, ed. Armstrong, C.A.J. (Gloucester, 1984)

Maxwell, H., ed., The Chronicle of Lanercost (Glasgow, 1913)

Miller, S., ed., Charters of the New Minster, Winchester (Oxford, 2001)

Moore, T, The History of King Richard III (London, 2005)

Myers, A.R., English Historical Documents, vol IV: 1327-1485 (London, 1969)

Nichols, J.G., ed., The Chronicle of Queen Jane and of Two Years of Queen Mary and Especially of the Rebellion of Sir Thomas Wyat (Felinfach, 1996)

Odo of Deuil, De Profectione Ludovici VII in Orientem, ed. Berry, V.G. (New York, 1948)

Parsons, J.C., ed., The Court and Household of Eleanor of Castile in 1290 (Toronto, 1977)

Pierquin, H., Recueil General Des Chartes Angol-Saxonnes 604-1061 (Paris, 1912)

Potter, K.R., Gesta Stephani (Oxford, 1976)

Pronay, N. and Cox, J., The Crowland Chronicle Continuations: 1459-1486 (London, 1986)

Richard of Devizes, The Chronicle of Richard of Devizes of the Time of King Richard the First, ed. Appleby, J.T. (London, 1963)

Rodriguez-Salgado, M.J. and Adams, S., eds., The Count of Feria's Dispatch to Philip II of 14 November 1558 (Camden Miscellany 28, 1984)

Rothwell, H., English Historical Documents, vol III:1189-1327 (London 1975)

Savage, H., ed., The Love Letters of Henry VIII (London,1949)

Sawyer, P.H., Anglo-Saxon Charters (London, 1968)

Shakespeare, W., 'Henry VI Part 2', The Oxford Shakespeare: The Complete Works, eds. Wells, S. and Taylor, G. (Oxford, 1998)

Shirley, W.W., ed., Royal and Other Historical Letters Illustrative of the Reign of Henry III, Vol. 2 1236-1272 (London 1866)

St Clair Byrne, M., ed., The Lisle Letters (Harmondsworth, 1983)

Stevenson, J., The Church Historians of England, Vol II, Part I – Containing the Anglo-Saxon Chronicle and the Chronicle of Florence of Worcester (London, 1853)

___, (ed.), Simeon of Durham: A History of the Kings of England (Felinfach, 1987)

Stubbs, W., Chronicles of the Reigns of Edward I and Edward II, 2 vols (London, 1882)

Sturluson, S., Heimskringla: History of the Kings of Norway, ed. Hollander, L.M. (Austen, 2002)

Swanton, M., The Anglo-Saxon Chronicle (London, 2001)

Symons, D.T., ed., Regularis Concordia: The Monastic Agreement of Monks and Nuns of the English Nation (London, 1953)

Taylor, J.D., ed., The Documents of Lady Jane Grey (New York, 2004)

Vitalis, O., The Ecclesiastical History, ed. Chibnall, M. (Oxford, 1968)

Whitelock, D., English Historical Review, vol I: c.500-1042 (London, 1979)

William of Newburgh, The History of English Affairs, eds. Walsh, P.G. and Kennedy, M.J. (Warminster, 1988)

Wilkinson, B., Constitutional History of England in the Fifteenth Century (London, 1964)

William of Malmesbury, Gesta Regum Anglorum: The History of the English Kings, ed. Mynors, R.A.B. (Oxford, 1998)

__, Historia Novella, eds., King, E. and Potter, K.R. (Oxford, 1998)

__. The Deeds of the Bishops of England, ed. Preest, D. (Woodbridge, 2002)

Wingfield, R., The Vita Mariae Angliae Reginae, ed. MacCulloch, D. (Camden Miscellany 28, 1984)

Wriothesley, C., A Chronicle of England During the Reigns of the Tudors, 2 vols, ed. Hamilton, W.D. (Westminster, 1875-7)

Wyatt, G., The Papers of George Wyatt Esquire of Boxley Abbey in the County of Kent, ed. Loades, D.M. (London, 1968)

Wyatt, T., Collected Poems, ed. Daalder, J. (London, 1975)

SECONDARY SOURCES

Bagley, J.J., Margaret of Anjou: Queen of England (London, undated)

Baldwin, D., Elizabeth Woodville (Stroud, 2002)

Baldwin Smith, L., A Tudor Tragedy: The Life and Times of Catherine Howard (London, 1961)

Biles, M., 'The Indominable Belle: Eleanor of Provence, Queen of England', Seven Studies in Medieval English History and Other Historical Essays, ed. Bowers, R.H. (Jackson, 1983)

Bond, E.A., 'Notices of the Last Days of Isabella, Queen of Edward the Second, Drawn from an Account of the Expenses of her Household', Archaeologia 36:453-469 (1853)

Boyd, D., Eleanor: April Queen of Aquitaine (Stroud, 2004)

Campbell, M.W., 'Queen Emma and Aelfgifu of Northampton', Scandinavia 4:66-79 (1971)

Cazel, F.A. and Painter, S., 'The Marriage of Isabella of Angouleme', English Historical Review 63:83-89 (1948)

Chapman, H.W., Lady Jane Grey (London, 1985)

Chibnall, M., The Empress Matilda (Oxford, 1991)

Conway Davies, J., The Baronial Opposition to Edward II (London, 1967)

Davey, R., The Nine Days' Queens (London, 1910)

Denny, J., Katherine Howard (London, 2005)

Dixon, W.H., History of Two Queens, 4 Vols. (London, 1873)

Doherty, P., Isabella and the Strange Death of Edward II (London, 2003)

Erickson, C., Bloody Mary (New York, 1978)

Erlanger, P., Margaret of Anjou: Queen of England (London, 1970)

Fraser, A., The Six Wives of Henry VIII (London, 1992)

Fryde, N., The Tyranny and Fall of Edward II (Cambridge, 1979)

Griffiths, R.A., The Reign of King Henry VI (Stroud, 1998)

Haswell, J., The Ardent Queen (1975)

Hole, C., Witchcraft in England (London, 1990)

Howell, M., Eleanor of Provence (Oxford, 1998)

Howitt, M., ed., Biographical Sketches of the Queens of England (London, undated Victorian)

Huneycutt, L.L., 'Alianora Regina Anglorum: Eleanor of Aquitaine and her Anglo-Norman Predecessors as Queen of England', Eleanor of Aquitaine: Lord and Lady, eds. Wheeler, B. and Parsons, J.C. (Basingstoke, 2002)

__, Matilda of Scotland (Woodbridge, 2003)

Ives, E., The Life and Death of Anne Boleyn (Oxford, 2005)

Jones, M., Between France and England (Aldershot, 2000)

Kelly, A., Eleanor of Aquitaine and the Four Kings (Cambridge, 1950)

Kirby, D.P., The Earliest English Kings (London, 1991)

Kirby, J.L., Henry IV of England (London, 1970)

Laynesmith, J.L., The Last Medieval Queens (Oxford, 2004)

Loades, D., Mary Tudor (Oxford, 1989)

Martindale, J., 'Eleanor of Aquitaine: The Last Years', King John: New Interpretations, ed. Church, S.D. (Woodbridge 2003)

Mattingley, G., Catherine of Aragon (London, 1944)

Maurer, H.E., Margaret of Anjou (Woodbridge, 2003)

Meade, M., Eleanor of Aquitaine (London, 1977)

Menache, S., 'Isabelle of France, Queen of England – A Reconsideration', Journal of Medieval History 10:107-124 (1984)

Mitchell, M., Berengaria: Enigmatic Queen of England (Pooks Hill, 1986)

Mortimer, I., The Greatest Traitor (London, 2003)

Myers, A.R., Crown, Household and Parliament in Fifteenth Century England (London, 1985)

Nelson, J.L., Charles the Bald (London, 1992)

Okerlund, A., Elizabeth Wydeville: The Slandered Queen (Stroud, 2005)

Pain, N., Empress Matilda: Uncrowned Queen of England (London, 1978)

Parson, J.C., 'Eleanor of Castile: Legend and Reality Through Seven Centuries', Eleanor of Castile 1290-1990, ed. Parsons, D. (Stamford, 1991)

__, Eleanor of Castile (New York, 1998)

Plowden, A., Lady Jane Grey and the House of Suffolk (New York, 1986)

__, Lady Jane Grey (Stroud, 2003b)

Powrie, J., Eleanor of Castile (Studley, 1990)

Prestwich, M., Edward I (London, 1997)

Prescott, M., Mary Tudor, The Spanish Tudor (London, 2003)

Richardson, H.G., 'The Marriage and Coronation of Isabella of Angouleme', Historical Review 61:289-314 (1946)

Ridgeway, H.W., 'Foreign Favourites and Henry III's Problems of Patronage, 1247-1258', English Historical Review 104:590-610 (1989)

Snellgrove, H.S., The Lusignans in England (Albuquerque, 1950)

Stafford, P., 'Charles the Bald, Judith and England', Charles the Bald: Court and Kingdom, ed. Gibson, M.T. and Nelson, J.L. (Aldershot, 1990a)

___, 'The King's Wife in Wessex, 800-1066', New Readings on Women in Old English Literature, eds. Damico, H. and Hennessey Olsen, A. (Bloomington, 1990b)

___, Queen Emma and Queen Edith (Oxford, 2001)

___, Queens, Concubines and Dowagers (Leicester, 1983)(1998 too)

Stenton, F., Anglo-Saxon England (Oxford, 1971)

Strachan, I., Emma the Twice Crowned Queen (London, 2004)

Strickland, A., Lives of the Queens of England, 12 vols. (London, 1844)

Strohm, P., England's Empty Throne (New Haven, 1998)

Tanner, H.J., 'Queenship: Office, Custom, or Ad Hoc? The Case of Queen Matilda III of England', Eleanor of Aquitaine: Lord and Lady, eds. Wheeler, B. and Parsons, J.C. (Basingstoke, 2002)

Vincent, N., 'Isabella of Angouleme: John's Jezebel', King John: New Interpretations, ed. Church, S.D. (Woodbridge, 2003)

Warren, W.L., King John (London, 1997)

Weir, A., Eleanor of Aquitaine (London, 1999)

___, Isabella She-Wolf of France, Queen of England (London, 2005)

Wright, C.E., The Cultivation of Saga in Anglo-Saxon England (Edinburgh, 1939)

Yorke, B., 'Aethelwold and the Politics of the Tenth Century', in Yorke, B, (ed.), Bishop Aethelwold: His Career and Influence (Woodbridge, 1997)

Index